GW01090478

Mary was born in 1931 and brought up in the small market town of Ringwood, on the edge of the beautiful New Forest in Hampshire.

In spite of the war years, she had a happy childhood. When she was twenty, a young airman in Malaya was given her name and address by a chap who was billeted in the family home during the war.

They corresponded for a year and then met at his home in Bournemouth. She married Denys (the airman) in 1953. A daughter, three sons and two more daughters followed.

After twenty three years of service life, Mary and Denys became foster parents, caring from adoption babies to problem teenagers. In 1989 they decided to get out of the rat race and took to the road as 'Old Age Travellers' in a twenty foot motorhome.

JUST A DROP
IN THE OCEAN

Mary Fail

Just a Drop
in the Ocean

Vanguard Press

VANGUARD PAPERBACK

© Copyright 2002
Mary Fail

The right of Mary Fail to be identified as author of
this work has been asserted by her in accordance with the
Copyright, Designs and Patents Act 1988

All Rights Reserved

No reproduction, copy or transmission of this publication
may be made without written permission.
No paragraph of this publication may be reproduced,
copied or transmitted save with the written permission or in
accordance with the provisions
of the Copyright Act 1956 (as amended).

Any person who does any unauthorised act in relation to
this publication may be liable to criminal
prosecution and civil claims for damage.

A CIP catalogue record for this title is
available from the British Library
ISBN 1 903489 66 0

*Vanguard Press is an imprint of
Pegasus Elliot MacKenzie Publishers Ltd.*
www.pegasuspublishers.com

First Published in 2002

**Vanguard Press
Sheraton House Castle Park
Cambridge England**

Printed & Bound in Great Britain

Dedication

This book is dedicated to every lady who knitted a sweater for Bosnia, to every shopper giving a bag of sugar or a can of beans. To large companies passing on surplus goods.

To schools and churches collecting aid for refugees after listening to our talks on how the people are surviving in bombed towns and villages, or in refugee camps. People living in shipping containers, trains, deserted army camps and hostels in safe areas.

To everyone giving donations, large or small to help get the goods to the victims of a cruel war in the Balkans, without you we could not have helped a nation to survive.

To all our colleagues of many journeys, the friendship and camaraderie we experienced.

You may find you are mentioned within these pages.
Also to inform our children of how we spent their inheritance!

At the same time we would like to thank them all for the support they have given us in all our ventures.

Mary and Denys (Duke) Fail

TWO LITTLE PRAYERS

Written by school children of Spetisbury School in Dorset.

Dear Lord
We would like to help all the hungry people in the world
but we cannot
We are going to give some food to Bosnia and Croatia even
if they are not Christians
We have too much and they do not have any at all
We are trying to give some to the people who need it
We do not need it all
Thank you to Denys and Mary and all the people who help
We love our world but it has gone wrong somewhere
But if we work all the Bosnians and Croatians can have
food as well

Sarah

* * *

The story of the good samaritan teaches us that we should
help anyone who need it. Even our enemies and people we
don't know. That is why we are sending food to Bosnia
because there is a war in their country. We are sending food
in a lorry to a camp so people can have things that they
need.

David

FREE RANGERS

Having sold our big and outdated house in a suburb of Bournemouth, in 1989, we were travelling the country in a motor-home, free and able to visit places that we had only heard or read about. For the first three months we toured the Highlands of Scotland and enjoyed the wonderful scenery. On caravan sites and in country areas we met some wonderful and interesting characters and made friendships which have lasted over the years.

In the evenings we would have the radio on for the 'Jameson's', a husband and wife team hosting a programme of music and talk which we found relaxing and interesting. On Wednesdays they would have a 'phone in' spot. Listeners would phone the Radio Station with interesting points of view, topics including news items or to add their own thoughts to those already put forward.

One Wednesday in October 1992, while living in a field. On a caravan site at the Three Legged Cross, near Ringwood, something different caught our attention and imagination. A caller was asking for 'one hundred vehicles to join me on a mercy mission to save refugees in Croatia, before winter sets in'. It seemed that this caller had been a truck driver who visited the former Yugoslavia and had been taking supplies to victims in refugee camps. He was now out of work and intended to drive 1500 miles in early December, in his Volvo estate car towing a trailer loaded with goods to help the suffering refugees survive a harsh winter.

He was making an appeal for drivers with any type of vehicle to fill it with warm clothing to save lives. Denys, my husband of almost forty years and I looked at each other and we both said together "Let's go for it." A phone number was given, luckily we had a pen and a scrap of paper handy; in our camper nothing was more than an arm's reach away. I wrote down the number and could hardly wait for the morning to make the contact. At the time we hadn't really known where Croatia was. To us it was just the name of a place mentioned in the news where a civil war was going on.

The contact was made and we waited eagerly for instructions. Our youngest daughter collected our mail at her address while we roamed. Soon a bulky envelope arrived, postmarked Canterbury. It gave details of what to collect, how to pack boxes, how each box should be weighed, and the weight to be marked on each individual box then recorded onto a loading list. We would then have to raise about £500 to do the journey, this would cover fuel, border fees, customs' paperwork and ferry crossings.

We sent back the details of our vehicle and confirmed that we would be joining the 'Convoy of Hope'.

At first we guessed at how much our camper could carry, being a five-berth vehicle it did have a lot of storage space. Friends and family started to collect items of clothing, tinned and packet food, bedding and shoes, washing powders and toiletries, toys and medical dressings. We held raffles and collected donations from local folk interested in our proposed adventure.

Youngest son Tim showed a great interest and asked if he could come with us, then the local paper ran a story about Tracy a young midwife from Poole hospital. From the good-hearted people of her church, she had collected 73 boxes of goods for the refugees of Croatia and wanted someone to move them from her parents' home in Wimborne. Tim contacted her and said that we would take them directly to the needy people and refugees in Croatia.

We all went to meet Tracy, told her of our plans to make the journey and to everyone's surprise, including our own, we asked if she would like to come with us, to be able to hand over her collection to the people it was meant for. To use her own words 'I was gob-smacked' but she said she would love to come with us. When the news was passed on to her friends at the church, donations were given to help us make the journey.

Now with more than one hundred boxes of goods, and a

14

weight of 604 Kilograms meant that we had to hire a trailer. We had thought about taking our small caravan for the load and extra sleeping space, but the weight was too much for it. We were told that 'Ambrow Trailers' of Christchurch had the ideal type of trailer for the job. They were only too pleased to rent us a box trailer which could carry up to 2 tons. They were very interested in our planned journey.

Our instructions were to meet up with convoy members at a 'Happy Eater' restaurant on the Canterbury to Dover road on December 1st. At that time we had no idea how many vehicles would be making their way to the rendezvous. Monday, November 30th was a very wet day, Tracy's parents brought her to us at Tim's home in Verwood. A photographer from the 'Echo' arrived, keen to follow up Tracy's story, to take pictures of us leaving on the first leg of a journey none of us would ever forget.

On the road to Ringwood, Portsmouth and Chichester bypass, Brighton bypass, and on to Lewes, Polgate and Pevensey with a lunch stop at a McDonald's. Then on to Hastings and Winchelsea driving through wind and rain to New Romney and Hythe. We were forced to stop by an accident with a raging sea beside us until an ambulance arrived and we were able to set off again.

On reaching the 'Happy Eater' on the Canterbury to Dover road, we went in and asked if they were expecting a meeting of a convoy of vehicles en route to Croatia. The staff knew nothing about it. We ordered a meal, the staff were very friendly and sociable. They seemed glad of our company for a very wet evening. That night, with the kind permission of our new friends, we spent the night in the restaurant car park.

Our camper sleeps five adults quite comfortably, Tim in the Luton double berth, Tracy in the single divan and we were in the main double, which by day is the table and seating area. We settled down and spent the night with traffic thundering by, wind and rain shaking the camper as the storm raged.

The morning was bright and sunny. We had breakfast in the cafe, then Tracy and I killed time by finding spaces for our own stores and luggage. Tim and Denys did a bit of maintenance on the vehicle. We spent the day with coffees and chatting with the

15

staff hoping that (a) we had the right place and (b) that others would turn up soon. By late afternoon vehicles started arriving. The cafe was soon busy with people ordering meals.

We sat hugging our coffee cups and trying to guess which of the drivers arriving would be Tony Budell, the man behind the radio appeal. Suddenly a big built man loomed in the doorway, wearing a U.N. blue sweatshirt with the logo of a red heart; he was our man. He came to each group in turn and introduced himself and 'Uncle George' his right hand man. Asking our names and checking us off from his list, we were number 67 in the convoy and one of the few vehicles from outside the Canterbury area.

Next to arrive were the press and the TV cameras, they concentrated on Tony and the local drivers. We got talking to a couple of chaps travelling with a van towing a caravan. Each driver was given two large stickers with the red heart logo to put on their vehicles. Tony also had a box full of the blue sweatshirts like the one he was modelling, We bought four from him at £10 each, the uniform of the 'Convoy of Hope.'

Around 10pm we were all informed that we would be on the 5am ferry from Dover docks, some of us decided to get some sleep fully dressed.

At 2:30am we drove out into the night to Dover and on to the docks. The men went off to get our tickets, not knowing how much it would cost, they took £240 with them to get booked on the ferry. They were charged only £35 for the return fare. Drivers of smaller vehicles were charged £25 return fare. At 4am we had a cereal breakfast and the men put the stickers on the camper and trailer. At 5am we were all called to board.

Once we got under way a message came over the tannoy, asking all personnel of the Convoy of Hope to make their way to the Samba Bar. The sea was pretty rough and people were staggering about all over the place. When we were settled, Tony gave a talk, explaining the route we would be taking. It was more or less what we had read in the itinerary. Then he said with pride, "I asked for one hundred vehicles," a slight pause, "We stand at one hundred and five." The applause was long and loud.

The TV crew wandered around talking and filming with different groups. The lady interviewer came to ask us where we were from and seemed very interested in the fact that we lived in our camper and travelled. She asked if the camera crew could film us later on the trip.

At *Calais* we disembarked and drove out into the French dawn, it was raining. The plan was that we were to travel across Europe as individual groups, only meeting at two night stops, first at *Hockenheim* in Germany and again at *Graz* on the Austrian border with Slovenia. I had rewritten the entire route instructions so that it was in sections and clipped to a board, then it was easy for each navigator to keep an eye on that particular part of the journey. Tim and Denys shared the driving, with Tracy or me keeping a lookout for road signs and following the route. We snacked on sandwiches as we travelled needing only to stop for fuel. We had reached the Belgian border by 9am, as we motored on we were passed by or passed other vehicles sporting the red heart logo, it put me in mind of the 'Wacky Races' on the TV all different types of vehicles and drivers heading for the same destination.

The idea of travelling separately was to avoid putting filling stations under siege when all the vehicles needed fuel. Also some vehicles were slower than others so we all travelled at our own pace. Looking for the ring road around *Brussels*, somehow we missed it and found ourselves right in the middle of the city. In heavy traffic and long tunnels we thought we had lost the route. Then the van towing the caravan appeared beside us at a set of traffic lights, the driver shouted across to us, "Are we supposed to be here?" We weren't alone. Soon Tracy spotted a sign for *Liege* which is where we needed to be. We were back on route.

Crossing the Belgian/German border at *Auchen* there was no one to check us for our documents. We saw a couple of convoy vehicles parked outside a 'Resthaus', but we kept going, Later those vehicles passed us beeping their horns in salute, Tim gave them a blast on our 'Dixie Horns'. We pulled into a service station to refuel, where Tim was amused by being served by a German speaking Japanese attendant who spoke a few words of English.

On through driving rain and mile after mile of motorway, some local drivers passed us sounding their horns. Denys pulled in at one point to check the trailer lights, but nothing seemed amiss. To give our drivers a break we made a stop at a restaurant for supper. There we were told by a local trucker that lorry drivers were cursing our convoy because some of the vehicles were holding up the rush hour traffic. Hence the horns blowing at us.

Passing *Lugwigshaven* and *Speyer* we were to look out for Hockenheim Services. Tim was driving and found himself in the town, which was not where we were supposed to be. We were not the only ones to stray into this detour, but the town was quite a sight, all decorated with Christmas lights. Back on route 61 we found the service area, our halfway point and our stop for the night.

Parking among the vehicles already settled, the men went to stretch their legs while we girls put the kettle on. A couple of chaps came over to socialise. Peter and Paul were travelling in a car with a trailer, we had a 'getting to know you session.' They told us how they were going to sleep in the sitting position that night as their car was full of boxes. We settled down that night amid the noise and fumes of vehicles arriving, feeling very well off having comfortable beds.

We awoke feeling refreshed and ready for the off. Some convoy vehicles had already left when we joined the queue at the fuel pumps. The chap in front of us was English, but had a van with French number plates, he told us that he and his daughter were part of the convoy but had an accident when their car and trailer jack-knifed on the autobahn and they'd had to hire a van.

Out on the motorway following route 6 to *Nuremberg*, a much better day with bright skies and quite warm. We passed vineyards and villages on good roads. Travelling on and exchanging 'beeps' and 'Dixie' as we met up with our fellow travellers, we were enjoying our trip. Then we came into fog around nightfall as we crossed the border into Austria. The officials just waved us through, although we did have our passports and loading lists ready.

We felt that it was a great pity that we were driving through this part of the trip in the dark as we could just make out the shapes of the mountains and ski resorts. Denys found our route through a town called *Wells*, the first town we had driven through since we left *Calais*. We arrived at our first toll road, or 'peage.' Some negotiating had been done on our behalf. We, along with the Fireman's Aid lorry, the Romford Baptist Church truck and the van and caravan who had arrived at the same time as us, were allowed through free of charge, Tracy was given some stickers for our vehicle, as we noticed that one official in the office was wearing one of our convoy sweaters.

Travelling on through the night we passed through many tunnels cut into the mountains, one or two of them were 6 miles long. We needed to find Gralla Services, a few miles south of *Graz* and not far from the Slovenian border. No problem, the service station was well-advertised miles before we got to it. We refuelled before pulling in behind some of our vehicles to park for the night.

The men went off to look the place over, I put the kettle on for a welcome cuppa and plan our meal. A lady came to the door and asked if we could use a pan of hot pot, she told us that her crew had made too much and didn't want to waste it. Well we did our best but there was too much for the four of us, so we asked the occupants of the vehicle behind us if they would like to share the unexpected meal.

The three men and their lady companion jumped at the chance. When we explained how we came by the stew, the lady, 'Jackie' said that it sounds like the members of their team and that the stew would most likely have been their meal anyway. That night we met and socialised with a good many of our fellow travellers. Some told us how they would be sleeping under the stars in sleeping bags because their vehicles were full of aid for the refugees. In spite of it being December the weather was quite mild enough for camping.

On the morning of Friday 4th a meeting was held in the restaurant with the press present. They were to be travelling with us in a couple of vans. We were told that we were making history by being the largest private convoy ever known.

Tony then read out a letter from the Crown Princess of Yugoslavia thanking all of us for our help and humanitarianism to her country.

We were then told the sequence of events for the day, advised not to get into political arguments with 'angry young men' in bars etc. We were given a handful of forms to be signed at places where we dropped our supplies.

The convoy was supposed to move out at 9am. About that time Uncle George came to our door and asked if we could give a lift to a chap who had fallen out with his travelling companions, well, what could we do but say yes.

He arrived with loads of gear including a trombone, which he wanted to blow all the way into *Zagreb*. Tim soon had this problem sorted out, told him if he blew the instrument in the camper, it would end up somewhere where it would hurt. We did tell our hitchhiker that we would only take him as far as *Zagreb*, we had no room for a lodger. We could only hope that someone else would take him on board.

It was nearer 10:15 when we slowly moved out onto the Autobahn with a police escort, travelling south to the Slovenian border. The trombonist made himself quite comfortable with his feet up on our back seat. Most of the drivers had decorated their vehicles with balloons and streamers, we must have looked like a circus parade. We enjoyed the scenery and the attention of locals waving as we passed through pretty villages and open countryside. At points where there were bends in the road we could see the convoy as a whole, front and back of us, it was quite a sight, each vehicle showing dipped headlights.

From what we could gather only three vehicles had C.B. (Citizen's Band) radios, Tony at the head, us about half way and Uncle George bringing up the rear, messages from Tony to George and vice-versa were being relayed through us. From remarks made over the C.B. it seemed that the whole beautiful convoy was two miles long. Traffic from side roads were held back by the police to let us through as a whole unit.

A problem at the Slovenian/Croatian border, someone had to stay back to sort the paper work out for 105 vehicles. The officials wanted Tony to stay and the convoy to proceed to prevent the border being jammed up with vehicles. Tony wouldn't hear of it, he needed to be at the head of 'His Convoy'. The situation was resolved by Richard Friedrich, a representative of an organisation in *Vienna* and travelling with us to *Zagreb*, he offered to step in and deal with the red tape.

In *Zagreb* we were guided into a deserted fairground, we

parked and settled where we could. Everyone got out and greeted one another all wearing the blue shirts, our convoy uniform. The press photographers took group pictures. Dozens of cameras clicked away to record this unique occasion. In a large building food had been put out for us. On a long table the word 'Welcome' had been spelled out in bread sticks. Tony made a couple of speeches and thank you on behalf of all on the convoy. Music was played on guitars and tambourines, a lady with a triangle and a chap with finger cymbals kept time as they played very lively folk music.

They then surprised us by playing some English tunes. We found out later that some of these people were to be our guides to refugee establishments.

We felt a little guilty and uneasy about eating the bread, cheese and cooked meat put before us, in a country where we were supposed to be bringing much needed supplies. We were told that to turn down their hospitality would be an insult, so we joined in with the supper. We were given a choice, to unload into the huge storeroom, here in *Zagreb* or to travel the extra miles and deliver to the refugee camps. We had a mini conference and decided to go to where ever the supplies would do the most good. Tim went along to put our names on a list to go on to a camp.

With time to kill we went into town for a walk. Tim and Tracy were getting on quite well, We could see a good relationship building up between them. Tim had been divorced for about five years and as far as we knew Tracy had no one special in her life, they were often in deep conversation, getting to know each other. Back at the camper we were getting short of drinking water, the drivers of some of our lorries parked nearby asked if we would make them a cup of tea. On being told of our water shortage they fetched over a full 5 gallon container, tea all round for eight of them and four of us.

We settled down for the night while the lorry drivers sat outside talking about their journey into the war zone the next day. With no sign of the trombonist we had put his gear outside. Next morning we were all ready and waiting for instructions as to where we would go next. We did catch sight of the trombonist wandering around looking for a lift. A meeting was called and we were told that we would be split into smaller groups. The large trucks would go with Tony into *Slavonski Brod* where the war was ongoing and a dangerous area. Others were being taken to camps on the outskirts of *Zagreb*.

We were chosen to go with a group of twenty vehicles to the Adriatic coast where a great number of refugees were sheltered in former hotels and holiday accommodation.

There were hurried exchanges of addresses and phone numbers from those who had made new friends over the past week and were now going separate ways. Wishing each other "Good Luck" we sat with engines running, anxious to be away and do the job we came to do.

One vehicle from our mini-convoy wouldn't start, the chap struggling to get it going was soon surrounded by willing helpers, after a tow around the parking area, the engine started amid applause and cheers.

We moved out into rush hour traffic with help from the police and found ourselves on the motorway to *Rijeka* (Re-ayka), then we were on mountain roads. The weather had turned to wind and rain but the scenery was wonderful.

From *Zagreb* we had been able to see the distant mountains and now we were about to drive over them. In villages, we passed women hanging out washing or watching from balconies. Men in the fields working or on tractors, looked up as we passed by. Most of the houses were one-storey buildings and all had the neatest stacks of firewood I had ever seen. The road was very steep at times and we were constantly overtaken by local drivers. Sometimes the convoy would be split up by slow lumbering tankers, or heavy lorries negotiating steep hairpin bends on the narrow mountain road.

After about four hours of travelling, we were suddenly on a long steep decline, 20 miles of twisting and turning rough road which took us down four thousand feet to the Adriatic Highway. We were led into the parking area of the *Ad Turres Hotel*. A local lady came to each vehicle to inform us that a meal and accommodation had been arranged for us to stay the night, free of charge.

Inside, the hotel was quite beautiful, all wood panels and wood floors. Shown into the dining room we sat eight to a table.

Soup was served, quite thin with pasta ribbons, with it quite delicious local crusty bread. The main course was thinly sliced meat, which we guessed to be veal, in gravy with rice. After the meal our guide/interpreter told us that we would be unloading at two storage depots, one at this hotel and one about 600 metres down the road.

It was explained to us that the goods would be sorted and distributed to where they would be most needed, so that baby powder would go to where there were mothers and babies, walking sticks and overcoats would go to places needing supplies for the elderly. We would like to have given our parcels directly to needy families but were advised that this would be too difficult in this area.

We were told however, that we should keep a certain amount of toys and gifts for the children. We could give those personally the next day which was 6th December, St. Nicholas's day, when it was the tradition to give presents.

Ours was one of the vehicles to unload at a store a few yards down the road. Each vehicle was unloaded by a chain of willing hands.

Our load was a source of amazement. The locals kept coming to look inside the trailer to see "How much more?"

When the trailer was empty we still had two boxes of toys to give to the children from St. Nicholas. In socialising after unloading, Tracy had given her "Heart" shirt to a local lady called Zinka, who invited Tracy to come back to Croatia after the war to spend a holiday with her.

Back at the *Ad Turres* we took our washing kits and passports to claim the keys to our rooms. Small but basic, our room had a shower which was very welcome. A balcony was shuttered against the gale blowing outside. Refreshed we went down to join the others in the bar, some of us phoned to let the family know we were all O.K., another meal was laid on for us, beef-burger and chips.

Later while the four of us played cards and relaxed, a lady from Sheffield came to join us. She told us of her home which was an old Manor House built in the 1600's. She gave us her address and told us to visit her when we were next on our travels in the U.K. We turned in around 11pm. the twin beds were very hard but we were tired enough to sleep well.

December 6th was a Sunday, we surfaced around 8am local time. In the dining room breakfast was laid out for us, rolls and some kind of spread, marmalade, processed cheese and garlic flavoured sliced sausage, tea or coffee. A local lady, Vanda, came to be our guide for the day. She told us that our accommodation and food had been provided by the local council in appreciation for our help to their country.

Vanda told us all that we would be going to individual refugee hostels along this coast-line. One lady from our crowd was getting agitated about the delay, wanting to get on with the visiting. She was really getting up everybody's noses. We got separated into small groups, each leaving as they were selected to be taken to meet refugee families, until there were just the four of us to be dealt with. We were led out of the car park by a small car to a building just outside a seaside town, *Crikvenica* (pro: Sickvenitsa). Parking on the side of a busy road we walked down a steep slope down to a patio where we not sure what we would see.

We were surprised to find that we were in a small hotel, with chalets scattered about the back area. Vanda explained that this had been home to some thirty families since they had been driven from their homes by force from a town called *Vukovar*.

Two years before, the hotel had been a holiday retreat for the Serbian police. Since the war it had been commandeered by the Croatian government as a refuge for the homeless.

When we mentioned that we had toys for the children, Vanda passed on the message to to the curious groups who had come from various rooms to see the strangers from England. Denys and Tim fetched the boxes in and we left Tracy to play at 'Santa' while the rest of us recorded the scene on camera and video. Tracy had brought two large toy monkeys, they had come from her own collection of cuddly toys. They had soon found loving arms from two of the smallest tots. We were told that some of the children were attending the local church so we left one box intact for them.

When the excitement had died down we were served coffee, Turkish style with a glass of water. In the dining room Vanda introduced us to a very tired looking young woman, her name was Nada, which we learned meant Hope. She was in charge of the group and was a refugee herself. She and Vanda did their best to answer all our questions and give us first hand information on what was happening in their world. They sat with us at a table and told us how their beautiful town of *Vukovar* fell to the Serb forces in 1991.

With most of the public and historic buildings destroyed and many people killed, *Vukovar* was now held as a symbol of this horrific war and the suffering of old and young alike. Women and children had been forced onto buses and trucks and taken to places such as *Crikvenica*, they had arrived with just what they were wearing at the time of invasion. Although they now live in comparative comfort, food and clothing was in short supply.

Each family lived in one small room with a shower, no hotel staff to cater for their needs. The women had learned to cook communal meals for the families, they ate together in the dining room. *Vukovar* had been a wealthy area, most of the families had lived in lovely homes close to the River Danube. Many of the folk living in the building had Serbian relations including Vanda. A real civil war.

Vanda told us that looking back over the years, the Croatians should have been able to see the situation coming. The Serbs had built the motorways and got into all the government departments but as she told us, "We thought that if we ignored it, it would all go away." Nada was the 'director' or social worker/housemother of the group.

In her thirties, she had two teenagers, Boris who was 16 and Ivana who was 17, both still at school. The three of them lived and slept in the one room, no bigger than the one we slept in at the *Ad Turres*. Nada really showed signs of suffering and strain with dark sunken eyes and drawn face.

We accepted offers to visit some of the families in their own rooms, where we were treated like visiting royalty. One young lady of 16 drew a picture for us, very dramatic and symbolising their hometown. The name *Vukovar* entwined with razor wire and drops of blood dripping onto stone crosses and an ancient relic of a dove of peace. All of this incorporating a young girl's face. We still treasure this unique work of art.

25

Over more coffee, Vanda told us that many of the elderly residents were still in a state of shock, not able to take in the fact that they were not likely to see their homes again. Nada's parents were in the same state, they were living in one of the chalets out the back, her mother was quite ill.

We were given statistics such as, the Adriatic resort of *Crikvenica* normally had a population of 6,000 and 4,000 holiday tourists at the height of the season. In 1992 the number of refugees numbered around 8,000 and no one took holidays there now. A few tourists did come to satisfy their curiosity about the plight of the unfortunate Vukovarians. Every one was suffering from a recession imposed by so many extra mouths to feed, with a lack of employment and very little money.

The four of us agreed that we would come back again and that we would like to adopt '*Odmaraliste*' which means a refuge, and its inhabitants. We already knew that a convoy had been planned for March 1993, we started a list of items that would be most useful. Most needed was food, toiletries and kitchen rolls, sewing needles and cottons, material and scissors, knitting wool and needles to give the older ladies something to do and to make them feel useful. Soap powder and baby items, one expectant mum would be having twins in February. School items for the children, pens, pencils, books and pads, jigsaws, colouring books and crayons.

As we had already unloaded our trailer we took as many canned and dried goods that we could spare from our own camper stores and handed it over to the kitchen staff to help swell their supplies a little. Our packs of playing cards were given to a group of elderly men along with a bag of woolly hats that had been stored in the camper. Tracy gave Ivana a matching set of writing paper and envelopes.

While we were preparing to leave Denys had a strange experience, an elderly lady slipped an envelope into his pocket and by signs made him understand not to open it until later. Time to leave and warm goodbyes all round, moist eyes and hugs, promises to come back. Outside some of the youngsters had written "VUKOVAR" in the grime on the back of the camper in case we should forget.

Back at the *Ad Turres*, Denys opened the mystery letter,

hand written and in Croatian. In the hotel we asked if someone could translate it for us, a young man said that he would try. It was from and elderly couple living at the refuge, asking for help and our prayers for their family living in *Slavonski Brod* on the front line of the war. We felt helpless at the plea for aid.

It said:- "To our friends who help us from a foreign country. This is a cry of despair of a poor family who need help in order to survive. I am writing this letter on behalf of my family and friends of ours. Our income is very low, my husband and some of our friends are ill. We have 40 marks monthly pension (about £100) and haven't the money to buy fuel for heating or for food.

They say aid will come to our town but by the time we get there it has already been distributed to others. I am writing you this letter from *Slavonski Brod* where we lived in an air-raid shelter, we now live on the front line. Our house has been destroyed and with winter approaching I am begging you to help us because we hardly survive. Our town and our home have been devastated. Please send us money or goods urgently, our children are 17, 14, 4 and 2 years old. Please send us warm clothing, some money as well so that we can survive. Hear the cry of the poor and God bless you all.

From Banovac. Matija and Stjetan

Franjekuhaos 20, Slavonski Brod 5500. Hrvatska.

The full translation was made for us by a Croatian lady living in England, when we arrived home. It was too late to help this family.

In the hotel car park a group of young boys asked for the balloons that were still attached to the vehicle. They were a bit deflated and muddy but the lads were pleased with the trophies. We still had unopened packs of streamers which with some Red Arrows stickers and crisps added to their treasures from England.

We then met up with Sandy and others from our mini convoy. They were very depressed at what they had seen. In the hotel they had visited there were 15 people to a room, no hot water or heating and one tap for everyone's use. Sandy and friends had given some of their own clothing to help until the supplies were distributed.

27

We talked about our reservations as to whether the people we met would get the aid that we brought. One thing for sure, any supplies we brought in future would be given to the people we met this time.

We set out and got under way to cross the mountains and head back to *Zagreb*. We hadn't been travelling long when the first snowflakes hit our windscreen. The snow got thicker as we climbed into the mountains and the scenery was beautiful. Soft and fine, the snow covered every twig, every branch on every tree. A scene fit for a Christmas card.

Near *Zagreb* some of our group decided to stay overnight, we planned to press on after a short rest. Tim and Denys were outside talking to Sandy while I put the kettle on to make tea. Seeing the group outside I made an extra brew and put a 'T' sign in the window. Instead of the nine cups I had expected to pour, there were twenty nine. The cuppas were greatly appreciated as we all started out on the long journey home.

OUR FAMILY BACKGROUND

We arrived back in the U.K. just in time to get organised for Christmas with our family all around us. Our family was a large and happy brood, three daughters and three sons, married and with families, giving us 16 grandchildren.

Chris the eldest, with her husband Steve are parents of two daughters. Eldest son Steve had one son, and two stepsons from his second wife Judy. Second son Mike and wife Sharon, were in a troubled marriage, their family are two girls and three boys. Tim was divorced but had two lovely daughters. Kate was next, she and her husband have a boy and a girl. Last but not least came Marion with husband Bernie, they also have a boy and a girl. Not surprising because Marion and Kate always did the same when they were little girls together.

I met Denys in 1952, after we had become pen pals while he was in the R.A.F. serving in the Malayan jungle. A mutual friend gave this young Bournemouth serviceman the address of this young lady in Ringwood. We married in 1953, and started life as a service family. Our first home was a caravan in the wilds of Somerset and our daughter Christine was born in Taunton. Stephen and Michael were born in Bransgore, Hampshire, where we lived in married quarters of R.A.F. Sopley.

Tim was born in Ringwood when his dad was on a posting in Cyprus during trouble times.

Six weeks after Tim's birth we travelled to Cyprus to be a family again. That was just after the troubles on the island, E.O.K.A., Grievas and Makarios times, when British children were taken to school on buses with armed guards. Col. George Grivas had threatened to kidnap children of forces families. On public holidays we were advised to stay at home behind locked gates.

Arriving home in 1961, we were moved to R.A.F. Benson in Oxfordshire. Kathryn was born in Wallingford, Berkshire, in 1962, and Marion decided to arrive in a hurry in July 1963. I was taken to the Radcliffe Hospital in Oxford for her birth. Only days after her arrival, an R.A.F. chap came to visit me and asked if I would consider looking after his two young children after school until he finished work at 5:30.

His wife was dying of brain cancer, she was at home because the doctors could do no more for her. It would only be a matter of time and he didn't want the youngsters to be on their own with her for the two hours after school. So I became a foster mother. We did actually keep the kids overnight now and again to give dad a bit of a break. Denys had a posting to Singapore in 1965, I and the family followed a few months later. We spent a wonderful three years in a hot and sunny climate. The children lived in swimsuits, or less in the case of our two toddlers. We became foster parents for S.S.A.F.A. Forces families had a problem when mothers of young children had to go into hospital. With foster families to look after the youngsters, fathers could still do their jobs.

We came home to normal life and posted to R.A.F. Bicester, living in married quarters there. All our children then were of school age and we took on fostering adoption babies for Social Services. Those tiny mites would come to us at five days old and at six weeks their prospective new parents would come to look them over. People often accused me of being hard-hearted because I could hand these babies over quite easily. I am sure it was because I was quite happy with my own large family. I could feel for the new parents who often had to wait a couple of years to adopt a tiny portion of what I had six times over.

The years rolled by, Denys retired from the R.A.F. and we settled, first at Ringwood then into Denys's old family home in Winton, a suburb of Bournemouth. The children grew up. Two of the boys took after dad and joined the R.A.F. We tried our hand at running a pub, first in Portland then one back in the Bournemouth area. That was an education on human nature.

Being so tied to the job, we had little time for family so after three years we gave it all up and went back to the old homestead.

At that time an appeal was going out for foster families to take on problem teenagers. Well I thought, we've had a couple of those in our time I will give it a try. A year of meetings, and a taste of problems we might come across, drugs etc., The family was scrutinised, our backgrounds checked, medicals to see if we were fit enough for the trials, tribulations and heart attacks to come. We were accepted.

The first lad chosen to come and live with us ran away rather than be put in our care! In all we had eight teenagers go through our home in five years. One of the girls aged 16, had a two year old son. Those young people had so many built in problems that all we could hope to do was to keep them from breaking the law while they lived with us.

We were about coming to retirement age when we decided to sell the old house. We needed something smaller and easier to maintain. One day as the sale of the house was underway, Denys saw a wonderful motorhome for sale and he suggested that we postpone buying another property and tour for a year.

What a brilliant idea!! That was in 1989. Then as we were really enjoying our freedom, we just happened to listen to the radio on that night.

INTO THE WAR ZONE

With Christmas and New Year over, we started concentrating on the March Convoy of Hope. Tim and Tracy were all fired up and working towards our second mercy mission to the former Yugoslavia. An application to the Poole council gave us permission to make street collections for our funds. With generous help and support from a dozen different sources, we raised enough money and goods – medical, food, clothing, recreation toys and games to fill the trailer towed by our camper and a transit van, the hire of the transit, fuel for both vehicles and the ferry crossing.

Second son, Mike, decided to come along to help with the driving so it was becoming a family concern. We had hoped to return to our friends in *Crikvenica* on the Adriatic coast. Everything on our load was geared up for their needs. When March arrived we heard that deep snow over the mountains and a Serbian 'Killing Zone' around *Karlovac* meant that the area was a 'No Go' for us. We were advised to stay with the main convoy.

Setting out from Dorset on the 12th March 1993, Tim's birthday, we arrived at Ramsgate to make the thirteenth vehicle for this trip. Tony B. had a brand new transit van with matching trailer, donated to him by Canterbury Round Table. The van was well decorated and equipped with a 'glory board' and flashing lights making it easier for us to follow him on unfamiliar roads and Autobahns. On this second trip into the unknown, the drivers had been advised that a C.B. radio would be an invaluable asset to them in cases of emergency or getting lost in strange territory.

Sally Ferries were giving vehicles taking aid to Croatia and Bosnia, a 50 percent discount on their Channel crossings. We were a pretty mixed bunch for this convoy. Dave and Russ in a four wheel drive affair with trailer. Chuck and Iris from Dover in a small camper van, they were with us in December. Gillian and Carolyn, sisters, driving an old BT van, this was soon nick named 'The Yellow Peril' by the rest of us. Sandy, who had been with us in December with co-driver Phil in a Chevrolet Estate which had been towing a caravan from Yorkshire to Ramsgate. The caravan gave up the ghost on the docks where it had to be unloaded. Its contents, hundreds of Zimmer frames and medical aid were distributed among the other vehicles before going on to the ferry.

With Sandy was an articulated lorry, the drivers were Alan and his boss. A truck from Romford Baptist Church, Marie and Robert with a transit. Frank on his own in a car towing a caravan, Patsy and Dillon from North Wales in a Lada car, (a lot of jokes about 'Ladas'). Ray and Peter from Huddersfield, in a transit. Tim and Tracy in a hired transit, and Mike with us in the motor-home. Ambrow Trailers had let us have the trailer on loan, free of charge.

We arrived in *Dunkirk* at 7.30am. This time the convoy stayed together, more or less. With an easy to follow itinerary we arrived in *Peppenhoven*, Germany at 2.30pm. on the 14th March. Sunday was spent crossing Germany and Austria, the third time we had been through that lovely mountainous country and each time in the dark, such a disappointment.

The four drivers in the family took a couple of hours sleep on a shift system on the made up bed in the camper. Quick meals on the wing and our main meal in *Wells*, Austria, when I made a pot stew using various cans of meat and vegetables. We catered for ourselves as much as possible while others ate in service restaurants when they could, or cooked on Calor Gas rings in the back of trucks or on the roadside.

There was plenty of ice and snow as we continued on mountain roads. As we approached a 'peage' or toll road, we took passports and loading lists into the office to check out if we would have to pay. At the first toll we were allowed to go through without charge, but at the second, the chap decided that as we had a camper, we must be on holiday and we had to pay 19 marks about £8. We arrived at Gralla Services on the Austrian border around 2am. ready to fall into bed after a hot drink.

After a very cold night, a lovely sunny day as we left at 9am. to drive the short distance to the Austrian\Slovenian border. Tony dealt with the paper work while the rest of us socialised, took group photographs and watched the coming and going of lorries and coaches until the signal that we were on the move.

30 miles through the countryside of Slovenia, and on to the Croatian border for another wait and dealing with papers. Then seven hours of travelling on old roads, a couple of 'comfort stops' and grab what we could to eat. We were lucky in the fact that I could sit in the back of the camper and make up sandwiches as we travelled.

A lunch pack was sent across to the Verwood van for Tim and Tracy at one of the "loo" stops. As dusk fell Tony's voice over the C. B. told us that we were now entering the area where we could start seeing shelled, bombed and deserted homes. We soon saw the evidence for ourselves. Everyone fell silent as we passed what had once been lovely homes on country roads. Some buildings had been completely flattened, just heaps of bricks and timber, others were with walls open to the sky. Although we had been prepared for that kind of scene, it still shocked us.

On a country road the convoy was brought to a halt by a U.N. checkpoint, we were near the Serb front line. Tanks in a row on standby only yards from our vehicles. After checking us out they allowed us to go on. The roads were rough, pitted by the star shaped mortar shell craters. On one side a steep drop made the manoeuvring tricky, our drivers were really having their work cut out dodging the holes.

We entered *Pakrac* (pro:Packrats) with a U.N. guide, our drop was to be at a large hospital on the outskirts of town. As we approached we could see that the huge building was in darkness. Dave had been there and dropped aid in December and was mystified by its desertion. The building which then had been used as a storeroom was damaged and now stood empty.

The entire convoy used the hospital car park to turn around, we and the artic needed plenty of turning space.

Our drivers parked whereever they could in the main street among the ruins of the fair sized town. Although the buildings

34

were battle damaged, people were still living in them, lights were showing behind shutters.

We found a building being used as an emergency hospital, inside we were met by a very warm and friendly staff, Doctors and Directors. A pan of tea was brought in and the liquid ladled into various cups and glasses, but what tea!! It was laced with the local "cockle warmer". Then it was schnapps and biscuits all round. Lovely people showing their appreciation at our coming.

We were told that the Serbs had taken the six-year-old hospital in January and destroyed all they could. Some of them were encamped in buildings only yards from where we had driven in and turned around. We heard of how *Pakrac* was now a divided town, with a U.N. checkpoint at a crossroad not far from us. Our people were advised not to stray away from the area of the main street.

Mike and I went back to the camper to get a meal ready. Drivers started shunting the vehicles around to box in the trailers, just in case!! We ate and there was no sign of the others. Mike got his bed sorted and was soon asleep. Tim and Tracy arrived "Home", Denys not long after. He had bought a beer in the bar, changing a 100 mark note and ended up with a mountain of local dinar. Then we settled down among blitzed buildings, with U.N. soldiers on guard in the street outside our door. It didn't seem real. We slept fully dressed.

We were up early next morning wanting to see as much as we could. Children were going to school at 6.30am. life going on as usual. We started giving soft toys to some of the small children passing by with their mums, that started an avalanche. Even elderly ladies and old men were jostling each other to get a teddy or a doll. One chap with twinkling eyes stuck a teddy in the basket of his bike and went off as proud as punch.

Peter and Ray parked in front of us, opened the doors of their transit and gave a couple of women some toilet rolls. Within a few minutes the van was under siege. You would have thought those toilet rolls were worth their weight in gold.

Chuck had a video camera and the batteries needed re-charging. Denys started our petrol generator to do this for him, which meant that we had to stay put for an hour or so. The rest of the family went off to see what our next move was to be, leaving me alone to catch up with my diary.

While taking photos earlier, we had waved to a lady looking out from what we had taken to be a damaged block of flats across the road. While I was writing, two ladies came to the camper door asking me to 'Come, Cafe' taking my hand and pulling me to go with them. Not knowing what it might lead to, I locked the camper and followed them into the large building. Up three flights of stairs and much to my surprise came into a very modern office. I was gently put into a chair and given a cup of coffee.

I wondered what Denys would think when he found me not at home. More ladies came into the room, each one saying her name. One was Georgia and one Freda, they tried to talk to me with signs and words that I could not understand. I was getting a little worried that no one knew where I was, then I heard Tracy's voice the men were just behind her. They had been 'collected' like me. They crowded into the small office with coffee and biscuits all round, everyone wanting to shake our hands.

Discovering that Freda, Georgia and one of their co-workers each had two children, Tim and Mike fetched up some teddies and we took group photos. As we got back to the street we found the convoy about to move, going back to the main hospital to unload into one of the outbuildings. Tim and Tracy in the Verwood van went with them. The camera batteries were still not charged and as we were not carrying medical aid, we decided to stay put.

A large group of school children under the watchful eyes of two teachers came past the camper. We gave each child a 'Red Arrows' pen and pencil, small gifts donated by one of our special friends. A little later a lovely man came over to talk with us. He spoke just a little English, and wanted to show us around his town. The first stop was at a bar, we refused a schnapps saying more by signs than words that we would be driving on to *Slavonski Brod* later. Our new friend Anton, laughed and told us "There is no law here." We settled for coffee and heard that the bar tender had been in the local police force.

We toured the north end of *Pakrac*, the part still in Croatian hands. Anton took us to see the Town Hall, the Catholic Church and the Priest's house, all badly damaged. He then took us down a back street to show us his own house just about destroyed, he opened the door of what had been a workshop, Anton had been the local shoe-mender. The roof had collapsed with machines still in the rubble, his home and livelihood had all gone. The backyard to the house and the garden were still under a couple inches of snow and ice.

Across the road from Anton's house, were tall gates peppered with bullet holes. Anton went into the house asking us to wait, after a few minutes he came to beckon us in. His friends made us very welcome with coffee and schnapps, this time Denys and Mike didn't refuse. We were shown into the next room where a shell had entered the house and exploded. The room had been decorated around the damaged wall.

Explaining as best we could, we made Anton understand that we should get back to our vehicle, he walked back through the main street with us and wished us luck. Shaking hands with us he walked away with tears in his eyes. With no sight or sound on the C.B. from our colleagues, we lunched on cheese and local bread

All the while U.N. trucks and tanks rumbled through the streets, Denys chatted to one soldier who was from Ontario. While we were drinking coffee a Range Rover pulled up sharply in front of us creating a cloud of dust. The driver shouted "Hey mate! Do you come from Christchurch?" He had spotted our trailer with 'Ambrow Trailers Christchurch' on it. A driver for the United Nations Commissioner for Refugees, Russ wanted to know what we were doing in this neck of the woods. He couldn't stop long but he knew our son-in-law, a builder in Christchurch. We shook hands, he wished us luck and was off in a cloud of dust.

Hearing voices on the C.B. Mike called for 'Timo', Tim answered and told us that they had finished at the hospital and one of the drivers would be coming to lead us to the main convoy. Chuck and Iris arrived in their camper to take us through the main street and about 500 yards to the hospital. The convoy was in line ready to leave, Denys drove us across the grass area to join up with the convoy. I had a few minutes to get a photo of the vehicles with the blitzed hospital in the background. A voice over the C.B. warned me not to walk on the grass as it could be mined.

On the road again, retracing our way to *Daruvar* and *Virovitica*, heading towards *Osijek*, just before the town we turned off to *Slavonski Brod*. Tony informed us that we had about 10 miles of rough track to cover, which would save us about 30 miles in distance. Before we reached the turn off however, a U.N. checkpoint diverted us onto unfamiliar ground. Country roads took us through villages where people waved or stared as we passed through. There were plenty of tractors on the narrow roads, the locals used their tractors as cars. Chickens and ducks scratched for their living alongside the cottages and farms.

Drivers and their passengers whiled away the miles by cracking silly jokes or making funny or rude remarks about local traffic passing or overtaking us.

According to convoy members, a horse and cart was a 'Croatian Juggernaut', local cars hopping in between the convoy vehicles were 'Kamakaze locals'.

The motorway into *Slavonski Brod* was held by the Serbs. At times we travelled alongside or over the motorway with only wooden fences between THEM and US. At one point a very strong and acrid smell permeated into our vehicles. Mike, who had been a serviceman said he was sure that it was C.S. gas, he would know that smell anywhere. We all hoped that he was wrong.

After one stop for fuel and a couple for comfort and driver changes, we reached our destination in darkness after a spectacular sunset. The large town didn't look too badly damaged as we pulled into the car park of the hospital. We all got in, even the artic lorry. A chap came out of the hospital to greet us.

I had noticed that Tim had been very quiet all day. We had missed his voice in the chat over the C.B. radio, he was usually the joker in the family. When we got together for a hot meal in the hospital dining room, he didn't look well. We queued at a servery for chicken and rice. One of the doctors brought a couple of bottles of slivovic, we relaxed and chatted.

An hotel was offered to those needing a good night's sleep, at 30 marks per person. Tim and Tracy decided to use the hotel, hoping that after an undisturbed night he would feel better. We sat talking until a guide came to lead the hotel guests to their accommodation, only a matter of yards. The rest of us retired to our vehicles to spend the night in the car park, gates locked and with an armed security guard wandering around and chatting to our drivers. He came to our door interested in our 'mobile home', he showed off his Russian machine gun and .32 calibre automatic pistol and was impressed by photos of Denys in Western gear with his Colt 45. Feeling secure, the three of us settled down for an early night.

On closing the world outside, we did hear a couple of bumps, Denys said it was Concorde. Then we heard a few rattles of machine gun fire at a distance. We had just about got cosy, when there was a knock on the door. Tim and Tracy were back, the hotel wasn't quite up to standard. It was minus windows and no hot water, with bullet holes in the walls. The beds were mattresses on boards and they were told not to put the lights on because the Serbs were only a few yards away. Tim had a high temperature, it looked like flu.

Next morning he felt better. The convoy crew took the opportunity to use the hospital showers. From time to time the rattle of machine gun fire could be heard while we were waiting to find out our next move. There was a meeting to inform us that we had to wait for the customs officials to arrive before we could unload the hospital equipment, medicines and dressings.

A very well dressed couple came to talk to Tony. They handed him two bottles of brandy and two pairs of hand crafted dolls in national costume. Tony thanked the couple for their gifts and decided there and then to put registration numbers of each vehicle in a hat and draw out four to receive the gifts. The first number out was ours, Denys chose the brandy.

Someone said there was an open market just down the road, just about everyone took a wander down to have a look. Only 7am. but the market was pretty busy. Denys still had a fair amount of local currency so we did our best to spend it for him. With 10,000 dinar to the pound, we felt like millionaires.

A doctor from the hospital came to let us know that the Customs Officers had arrived. We all dashed back to start the unloading. The hospital car park soon looked like a car boot sale. We had two boxes for the hospital, one containing a nebuliser and one with dressings etc. The nebuliser had travelled inside the camper but we could not find the box of dressings, it must have been put into the transit.

Hospital staff were loading all the aid onto trolleys as it was checked off the lists. Zimmer frames, a bedpan, which had been decorated with a large bow of red ribbon, this had been christened "The Po with the Bow." A box of therapeutic Teddies, hand knitted teddy bears each with a label round its neck saying "To be given to a child in hospital."

Piled up were boxes of drugs, some 2,000,000 Paracetamols, sterile dressings, catheters, surgical gloves and draw sheets, bedding, pillows, vitamins and baby milk. While all this was going on the constant rattle of machine gun fire could be heard. Denys recorded the scene on video. British aid workers relaxed and chatting, with boxes all around us and the Serbian forces doing their best to wipe out the Croat population not so far away, it just did not seem real.

When the job was done, the convoy moved out with customs officials leading. We were to drive to the *Caritas Centre* on the outskirts of town, where the rest of our loads were to be left in charge of Catholic Priest, Father David.

We parked in a very narrow lane, while the artic was being unloaded. Alan's truck was carrying sacks of potatoes, beds and mattresses, large boxes of food and clothing. As soon as the goods were off the truck the two drivers would be on their way to Italy to pick up a load for the U.K.

While the truck was being unloaded, the smaller vehicles were being off loaded by a chain of willing volunteers. The goods were being stacked up in the hallway of Father David's Church, a pack of children were running around clamouring for handouts, sweets and lollipops. A lady brought a bottle of some local brew and this was passed from hand to hand.

With plenty of help carrying the boxes into the hall, I had time to wander around and take some photographs, not just for our albums but to show folks back home that their particular parcel or package did get to the needy. We had tins of baby food and milk under the seat in the camper so I dragged them out for our turn to unload. Tim came to join me, he was still a bit under the weather. I made coffee for him with a couple of painkillers and he dozed off amid all the bustle.

A young lad came to the window and asked very politely in English if he could have a toy for his little sister. We had a show of cuddly toys on the dashboard, I gave him a pink rabbit for his sister and a set of draughts for himself. A short while afterwards he was back with a friend who had a small brother. He went away happily with a teddy and a chess set.

Our camper and the transit were last to unload. The church hall was choc-a-bloc by then so our load was man handled on to an ex brewery truck, driven by Father David. He was backing up to our trailer when there was a loud crunching noise and a shout of 'STOP'! He had hit the mudguard of our trailer. The lorry took the load round to a door at the back of the church. Denys and Chuck videoed the event. One of the customs officers explained to us that the refugees in this area were billeted with local families. She said that the families were poor, without employment on low incomes, and having extra mouths to feed. She told us that the enemy were burning houses and leaving empty land. Until things were sorted, Father David was in charge of doling out the food and essentials on a ration card system.

At 3pm. we drove back to the hospital where a meal had been prepared for us. Most of us were totally embarrassed by the fact that the people we hoped to help were feeling duty-bound to feed us, but how could we refuse?

Each convoy member was given a tray containing a small bowl of soup, a saucer of sauerkraut, a plate with a thin slice of meat with carrots and gravy and a bowl of pear pieces.

Tony told us that he had friends at a convent in town and invited us to join him on a visit there. In December he had noticed that the Sisters had been using cut up newspapers in the toilets. On this trip he had brought a supply of toilet rolls and soap for them. We pulled in beside a group of buildings close to a wide river. On the far side of that river was the Serb army. We were right on the front line. Tony introduced us to the Sisters and we were given a tour of the buildings. In the rooms facing the river the windows were shuttered, the glass had been shattered by gun shots so many times that they had given up replacing it. The Serbs used the convent for target practice. We were shown marks on the courtyard walls from exploding mortar shells. One had actually gone through a window and into the church. The shell had exploded against the wall, and peppered it with shrapnel but a large crucifix against the wall was unmarked.

Our gifts were greatly appreciated as the nuns were not able to ask for necessities for themselves. They bustled about bringing bottles of homemade wine and cordial, glasses were fetched from one of the sitting rooms. After a short rest we were shown into a room which contained a monstrous piece of furniture. An ornately carved chest which was used to store vestments, holy books and relics of the church. A priest entered and was about to put on his robes so we left.

Returning to the vehicles we drove a short distance along the riverbank. A bridge nearby had been blown up by the Croats to stop the Serbs from coming across into Croatia. The centre part of the structure disappeared beneath the water. We could see and hear the soldiers shouting across the river. We all took good care not to get too close to the water's edge by keeping trees between us and any stray bullets. Black bordered posters nailed on the tree trunks told of the danger, with names and dates of victims.

Facing the river were a group of badly damaged buildings, one had been *Slavonski Brod's* main library. We drove back to the main hospital car park for our last night in the town. Crusty bread and cheese had been put out for us with fizzy drinks. Tim didn't eat, he was still not feeling well. We were asked how many would be staying the night, as the Baptist Church van, Frank with the caravan, Sandy and the artic had decided to leave right after they had eaten.

We opted to stay on, to give Tim another night's rest. He was asleep in no time. The rest of our crew played cards and relaxed with a nightcap before turning in. We were all up at 6.30am. on a warm and sunny day. Tim was feeling better, well enough to go for a shower. Before breakfast we all took a walk down to the open market, determined to spend the rest of Denys's Croatian money. We bought decorated candles for Tim's girls and Mike's children. Croatian crest stickers for the vehicles, some of the local bread and bottles of homemade slivovic, or rakia. We spent 'thousands'. The remnants of the convoy were ready to move, we were just waiting for Patsy, Dillon and Ann who had stayed at 'THAT HOTEL'. (Ann was Tony's passenger and they hadn't got along very well).

At last the team was complete and ready to go, heading out to *Nasice* and *Virovitica*, we came to the dirt road where we had been diverted on our way out. What we had missed!! No more than a mountain track with steep hills and sharp bends. Muddy in places where we were having to squeeze past lorries and tractors hurtling along in the opposite direction. At one of the hairpin bends, some of our passengers got out to take photos of the convoy, the vehicles were bouncing and sliding in the mud. Mike took my camera and jumped out of the cab. Then at another exciting point he grabbed the video camera and climbed onto our roof to film the trucks and vans.

10 miles of that track and a very rough ride. Then thankfully we were back on made up roads through villages where people waved and blew kisses as we passed into the town of *Virovitica*. At a crossroads Tony pulled in and said that he would like to treat us all to lunch. We were close to a fair size hotel. In the large dining room which had been empty when we arrived, we all played safe and ordered mixed grill or chicken, the only two items on the menu in English.

Of the 17 convoy members to be fed, our five were the last to be served, our meal arrived just one hour after ordering. We played 'I spy' while waiting. The meal was worth waiting for, on a large oval platter were onions, liver, pork chops and kebabs with chips, pepper sauce and a side salad. With Coca-cola the bill came to less than £2.50 a head. We travelled on all voicing our appreciation over the C.B. to our convoy leader, for our meal and our experiences over the past week. By the time we got into Austria, Tracy was feeling unwell.

Among our home comforts in the camper we carried a portable TV and a video recorder. At our night stop Denys gave a showing of Chuck's film of the trip to a full house. With standing room only he played the tape while recording it to put with our own.

The next morning Tracy was feeling ill, she had slept in the transit and had got very cold. We were at last travelling through Austria in the daylight and enjoyed the snow covered mountains and villages. Our colleagues had gone off at different stages. It was nice to be independent although we missed the chat over the C.B.

Tracy slept wrapped up in a blanket as we travelled, crossing the border into Germany. Somewhere near *Nuremberg* we missed a turning and ended up in the city, running alongside trams as they trundled through the cobbled streets among very interesting buildings. We had to find our way back onto the motorway, Mike driving with me helping to look for signs, Denys in the back with the map tracing roads and shouting directions. Tim in the van behind us giving advice over the C.B. we soon got back on track.

Minutes later we heard familiar voices over the airwaves, we had caught up with some of our convoy. It was nice to hear the mad chat. Travelling towards home, Mike became ill as we neared *Dunkirk*. On boarding the ferry we found it teeming with daytrippers bringing mountains of bargains from France. Our three young people slept on most of the homeward stretch. We had quite a shock when we saw the price of fuel in England. We had missed the budget!! Denys and I held out against the mystery illness, until we were safely back in our field with no lodgers. As we recovered we were planning our next trip to Croatia.

OUR THIRD MERCY MISSION

The word had spread about our successful mission into the devastated areas of Croatia. Goods came to us from caring folk, one chap, Tony P. contacted Tim and offered him a space in a warehouse for the sorting and packing of goods which were pouring in from all directions. Only one problem, access to the room was up a steep narrow staircase.

An article in the local paper told how an organisation calling themselves 'The Bosnian Crisis Appeal', wanted someone with a refrigerated van to take some vaccines out to the former Yugoslavia. Their address was on an industrial estate at Somerford. So we took it upon ourselves to go and see the man in charge, maybe we could take the vaccines in our camper fridge.

Peter H. was interested in the fact that we were making these jaunts into the areas for which he and his colleagues were collecting goods. They were sending loads by lorry and it was costing them a lot of money.

As it turned out, the vaccines were rather a large amount and too much to take in our camper fridge. It was then suggested that we might join up with the Bosnian Crisis Appeal and work with them.

We went to one of their monthly meetings and it was agreed that we should join forces. The B.C.A. offered to fund our next trip which was planned for June. Circumstances however meant that the unit they were using to store the aid was sold, a new place had to be found. A large building once used as an aircraft hangar by the De Havilland Company at Somerford and recently vacated by Pickfords removal firm was available. The B.C.A. were given permission to use this gigantic space until such time that it was sold for demolition.

By advertising and word of mouth, people brought carloads

of clothing, tinned and dried goods, they were able to drive right in through the massive roller doors to unload the goods. Sorting and packing the clothes had become a full time occupation, for us and the members of the B.C.A. We gave up living in a field and drove the camper into the hangar to stay inside, thus giving some security of the goods stored there. The doors were open from 9am. until dusk, from time to time the local bobby would ride in on his bike for a chat and to see how we were making out.

A security firm van also dropped by some evenings to check out the building. There had been fears that a 'rave' or unofficial pop concert was being organised in the area. The hangar would have accommodated a very large number of young revellers. The only sounds that had caused concern while we were in residence, were loud bangs on the roof. On going outside to see what was happening we discovered that young seagulls hatched from nests in gullies on the roof were taking flying lessons, some of them just couldn't get the landing technique right.

Tony P. was keen to help our cause and took over a large disused store. He turned it into a charity shop with room to store and pack goods for the refugees in the back area. Selling bric-a-brac, books and odd articles not suitable for taking to ease the plight of the starving and homeless on our next convoy planned for June. He offered to fill and fund a seven and a half ton lorry for son Tim to drive on that trip. One of his schemes was to get permission from a well known supermarket to let us hand leaflets to customers as they entered the store. Asking each one to buy one extra item with their groceries to donate to Bosnia, then have a group of volunteers at the exit to collect the items.

Twenty-eight shopping trolley loads of goods were collected in this way. Some folks gave money instead of, or as well as rice, pasta, cooking oil, flour, sugar, dried milk and baby goods. Some of the shelves in the store were just about emptied. We were kept busy packing the goods as they were collected. Tim and Tracy were to be driving the hired truck with one of Tim's mates, Adrian, going along as second driver.

We collected the trailer from Ambrow's, by now it was known as 'our trailer', on the agreement it said F.O.C. (free of charge). It was a very hot day as we loaded up in the hangar. B.C.A. members, Peter, his wife Jean, Jill and husband Tony, Denys's cousins Rosemary and Derek with Roy and Mary visiting from Canada, waved us off from Somerford as we set out for Ferndown to meet up with Tim and his crew.

They were hard at work loading bottled spring water which had been donated by *Somerley Estate* near Ringwood, adding crates of it to the load already in the large white truck. Son Mike was not joining us this time, he was there to video us leaving. While we took a short break at Fleet services, a driver from one of the lorries parked nearby came over to the camper with a large cardboard box, it was full of little kiddies' shopping baskets. He asked if we would take them as a donation from his firm.

On our way then, keeping in touch with C.B. radio, we were doing fine until we reached the M2 motorway. I could hear a strange rattling coming from the back end of the camper. Denys pulled in to investigate just at the time a wheel came off the trailer. We drove alongside the wheel as it trundled down the hard shoulder. We let Tim and company know what was happening over the C.B., they were travelling in front of us at that point. The truck stopped and backed up to us just as the wheel came to a standstill. It seemed that the wheel nuts had been loose and worked themselves off. The breakdown service was called out and 'a very nice man' arrived, he removed one nut from each of the good wheels for a temporary repair then led us in convoy to a trailer hire firm in Sittingbourne. It was 9.30pm. and there was no hope of a repair until morning.

We decided to stay put outside the trailer firm and hoped that they could fix us up first thing in the morning. The young'uns went off in the truck to find fish and chips for our supper. Denys phoned Tony B. to let him know that we had a problem. Tony told him that if we didn't make it in time for the ferry that had our booking, we could get the next boat out. Tony knew Trident trailers well and was sure they would do all they could to get us on the road.

We all slept well considering the noise of the traffic and a very hot night. At 7am. we were up and waiting to see signs of activity in the yard next to us. Our men had tools out on the

47

pavement ready to tackle the job when the gates opened at eight. A chap weighed up the problem and got down to sorting it. Finished by 9 and the bill was £35.

On to Ramsgate with a fuel stop at Manston, we arrived at the docks amid cheers and applause, we were last to check in. Tim and the truck had to travel as freight, the truck weighed nine tons. Our fare was £145. On board we met up with old friends and some new faces, coffees and chat as we whiled away the crossing. At *Dunkirk* we met up with Chuck and Iris in the lorry park. They had made the crossing by Hovercraft.

An uneventful journey across the continent, with our usual stopover at *Hockenheim*, then on again. Tim, Tracy, and Adrian took shifts at driving the truck. Denys was sole driver of the camper. As a non-driver my main duty was to make tea and to feed anyone travelling with us. At times I travelled in the truck with Tracy driving, a good way to get to know each other as she and Tim were now more than just good friends. At the Austrian border, Tim and Adrian took the truck through the freight lanes, with long queues of trucks already waiting we arranged to meet up at a picnic area further on.

While we waited, I cooked up a pot stew from canned meat and vegetables, it was cooking nicely when the lorry pulled in behind us. We ate outside at one of the picnic tables, a family nearby were enjoying their lunch. The man of the group raised a bottle in salute to us then walked over to chat, he was impressed that we were travelling so far to help Croatia. I joined Tracy in the truck again, I thought she handled the laden vehicle very well. She told me that the largest vehicle she had driven before was the transit on the March trip.

On through the mountains, until in one village where the road was being widened the tarmac had been removed. As we bumped over the rough surface, we heard someone calling "Duke" on the C.B. Peter and Ray in a car and towing a trailer, had a problem, a wheel had come off their trailer. We had been there!! As the rest of the convoy had gone through they had thought that they were on their own. Our two vehicles pulled into the car park of a restaurant.

The men decided that the trailer would travel well enough on two wheels (on one axle) if they lightened the load.

The heaviest of the packages were transferred to the already overloaded truck, while I did what I do best, made tea for the workers. On our way again and already a long way behind the main convoy. At the toll road the truck was allowed through free of charge while we and the car had to pay. 2am. when we pulled into *Gralla Services*.

Through the borders next morning and the usual wait for documentation. After a very hot and dusty day's travelling we arrived in *Pakrac* at 5pm. We had been shocked the first time we entered this friendly town but it looked far worse on a summer afternoon. Not one building had been left undamaged in the mindless conflict to gain territory.

After checking at the emergency hospital in town, we found that we had been expected at the derelict main hospital. In an outbuilding at the back of the main complex was a working kitchen where the townsfolk could go for a hot meal each day on the lines of a soup kitchen, for those in need. There a meal was waiting for us, chicken stew, one thing there seemed to be plenty of in this country was chicken. Three vegetarians among us were given fried eggs with delicious crusty bread. Jugs of coffee, or juice for those preferring cold drinks.

We started the unloading into what had been the hospital mortuary. Each driver left what he thought would be most useful there. Not only medical supplies but food and clothing for the locals. When we had been there in March we had spent the night in the main street, this time we were advised that we would be safer if we spent the night in the hospital grounds. Serbian soldiers and local Militia roamed the town at night and could cause problems for us.

It was just about dusk when the last van had finished unloading, the word was passed around that the priest travelling with Peter and Ray had a few words to say to everyone. We congregated to where he had set himself up in a corner under a lamp. A table was set out with sacraments for Holy Communion. Good in its own way but some of the younger members felt that they had been conned, as once they had gathered with rest of the group they could not very well back out without looking disrespectful. They told us that they would have liked a choice.

The insect population had a field day on unprotected legs

and arms, as under the light we were easy targets. 'Back home' for a good old cup of English tea with an invitation for some of the others to join us. Beds were available in the hospital for those needing a good night's sleep. Eagerly taken up by drivers and passengers trying to sleep in loaded vehicles.

Adrian decided to take up the offer as our spare bed was not really long enough for his lanky legs.

Denys and Tony stood outside on the warm June evening and chatted to a couple of U.N. soldiers who had a base at the ruined hospital, they were Canadians. They told of how they had watched our convoy coming into *Pakrac* from the hills above the town, we wondered then who else had been watching! Some of our crowd had been on the local brew and were having a rather noisy party until the rain started and sent them scattering. As I drifted off to sleep I thought about the two giant teddy bears who had travelled all the way attached to the roof rack. They had gaily waved their paws to the vehicles behind us, now they would be getting wet.

Breakfast was being set out in the dining room, a boiled egg served on a saucer to each person, mounds of fresh bread, which needed no butter or spreads. Pots of meat-paste were available. Those of us who had made friends with local people in *Pakrac* the last time we were here were keen to go and visit them.

Anton the local shoemaker who had shown us around his town, also his blitzed home, had touched our hearts. We found the road and pulled up outside his friend's house, he was there visiting. Anton, and Margaret, lady of the house, came out to greet us. Across the road, the shell of our new friend's home was being cleared of rubble. With sign language and the odd word we could understand, they told us that the first floor was to be removed, leaving a one storey building.

They were so pleased that we had come back to visit their stricken town, more friends were called to come and meet "My friends from England." We fetched out the made up family parcels we were carrying for occasions like this, along with a box of toilet rolls. Time was creeping on and we had to go, promising that we would come back again.

The next visit was to the office block in the main street, taking some of the food boxes and a half dozen jars of Nescafe.

The ladies had apologised for having only the local brand when we came before. Georgia, Freda, Maria and a couple of ladies we hadn't met before fussed around us getting chairs from other offices. One of the new ladies was introduced to us as the director, she spoke a little more English than the others. We asked her if there was anything specific that they needed.

The director took Denys away for a few minutes, he came back to say that there was a shop attached to the offices.

They were trying to get tools for people to repair and rebuild their homes, they would be glad of any such tools and building materials for locals like Anton. We made a promise that we would do what we could, to put out an appeal when we return to the U.K. We were sure that there must be many sheds or garages with tools just rusting away in corners that could be of use out here.

After goodbyes and hugs all round we returned to the vehicles to hear the convoy moving out from the hospital. Familiar voices called to tell us they would meet us in town. They drove through the main street leaving a space between the vans for us to slot into. We refuelled at *Nasice*, almost opposite the filling station was a row of small houses. Tony called us to a halt and he disappeared into one of the houses, before we knew it we were all invited in for a drink.

Taking a couple of food parcels we joined a group on the patio at the back of the house. Over a choice of beer or fruit juice, Tony explained that he had made friends here in December with people who were refugees from *Vukovar*. Some of our crew had brought soft toys for the children of the family and of neighbours who came to see what all the fuss was about. After the pleasant break we were on the road heading for *Slavonski Brod*.

On reaching the town, we merged with the local traffic and made our way to the hospital car park. Some manoeuvring got all the vehicles in, everyone more than ready to stretch their legs. We had been expected, messages had been sent from one hospital to the other and a meal was being prepared for us. Tracy and I went into the hospital to see if we could have a peep at the children but were unable to find the children's wards. We did catch a glimpse of two tiny mites in a side cubicle, one of them

51

in an incubator.

In the hospital dining room we were served with some kind of stew with what at first glance looked like mashed potato, on tasting it we discovered that it was semolina served as a vegetable. Lots of socialising with our colleagues.

With customs officers in attendance the vehicles started the unloading process. The piles of boxes and bags grew and were loaded onto some hospital beds which had been brought on one of the lorries, then ferried into the hospital store room. The weather was so hot, most of the men worked shirtless and in shorts. We had been given a small package of expensive drugs by an English doctor, these were put into the hands of the doctor in charge. It did not take long to do this job as there were plenty of strong men and willing hands.

Our next port of call was to a large complex of flats, where refugees from across the River Sava had been re-housed. These were Bosnians who had escaped across the now destroyed bridge as the Serb forces moved in to claim the area known as *Bosanski Brod*. The Croatian government housed the refugees but would not provide an allowance to help them to survive.

"Caritas", which is like our Salvation Army, had an office in the main building. The vehicles were backed up to this building and unloaded one by one. A large part of our load was 500 cans of quiche filling, given by friends in Buckinghamshire. While the men and young people did the work I gave out soft toys to youngsters looking on expectantly. The mums of young babies were given packs of Pampers as they were found among the piles of goods on the trucks and vans. Tim, Tracy and Adrian were completely emptying the lorry here as they intended to make for England later that day. Most of the bottled water had gone to *Pakrac* hospital because the mains water supply was on for five days and off for five days.

Some of our drivers had been given shell cases and spent bullets for souvenirs by refugee teenagers. While we were lunching in the hospital later that day, Tony asked how many of the men had souvenirs to take home. Then he said that Timo, my son, had been given a live hand grenade. I was horrified and could see that Tracy was not at all happy about it. Then Tim explained that as he was about to drive away after unloading the lorry, a young man had put an object under his driver's seat. As he drove away from the flats, he fished under the seat to find the object, luckily complete with pin!! The men crowded around to inspect the plastic, American manufactured grenade, then there followed a discussion on what to do with it. Tracy didn't want to travel with it, Denys said that it would be safe enough if it wasn't tampered with. The best idea was to hand it over to the U.N. as soon as possible.

We were to make a call at the convent next, we sat in our vehicles as Tony had an interview on local radio. While we waited in the hot sunshine, some boys came to our window asking for 'caps'. Baseball caps were well sought after by the kids, especially if they had a slogan or brand name on them. I shook my head but found some balloons and crisps for them. That started the ball rolling, more lads came and more balloons given out. We still waited, one or two of the crew wishing that they had gone to the market for souvenirs.

Suddenly a face appeared at my side window, one of the first lads to have the crisps. He was offering two cans of cold drinks and a packet of local cigarettes.

I was most concerned to see a livid red scar across his neck, it looked as though someone had tried to cut his throat. I did not realise it then but since, I know that it could have been the truth. Some of the men were getting restless at the waiting and went for a beer at a nearby bistro.

At last we were moving down to the river bank and the convent. Some roads in the area had tank traps so we needed to take a roundabout route. Parking close to the bullet scarred walls of the ancient buildings, we each took some suitable goods in for the Sisters living so close to the enemy. First we were served coffee then invited to take a look inside their church. It was so beautiful with bowls of fresh lilies on every available surface filling the air with their scent. So peaceful and quiet as we wandered and wondered at the statues of saints and lovely wood carvings among the mortar shell traces across the ceiling and one wall.

We had the freedom of the buildings and in the courtyard, very thin and scruffy cats were sunning themselves around the gardens. I wandered outside and came across an elderly lady sitting on a bench overlooking the river. She said *"Dobar Dan,"* the formal greeting, and I answered, *"Dobar Dan,"* then she started talking to me in her own language. I explained that I was *Engleska*, (English), and pointed to the vehicles nearby.

Then she did her best by signs and facial expressions to tell me she came from *Sarejevo*. She cried as she spoke putting her hands together as if in prayer. I suddenly thought of a teddy bear we had been carrying in the camper. His eyes closed and his hands held together with velcro. I fetched the toy along with a jar of coffee to give this lovely old lady who had probably lost everything she had ever owned.

She was so pleased with the small offering and kissed my hands as she thanked me with '*Huala*'. She didn't mind me taking her photograph, by then other convoy members had joined us. She was so sweet and friendly, I would have liked to have brought her home, to show everyone the kind of people that the Serbs were trying to exterminate. We returned to the vehicles and as we left the convent grounds, a young man rode past on a bike with his small son on the crossbar. They were given some soft toys from each van, the poor chap soon had his hands full. As we passed him I held out a carrier bag for his collection.

With the convoy heading towards *Maribor* we would be splitting up en route. Tony and Dave were going on to Switzerland, where a British lady was gathering goods and money from her friends and acquaintances for the refugees.

Tim, Tracy and Adrian were joining the main group going on to *Graz* and making for home. We, with Chuck and Iris, John and June had goods for refugee families that we had met on the December trip and who had made us very welcome.

Just before the parting of the ways, the chap in the van behind us told Denys over the C.B. that we had a problem with one of our trailer tyres. At the first convenient pull-in we all stopped. We had one wheel with a puncture and another one with a bulge. All hands got to work, the puncture was fixed and the tyre with the bulge changed for the one from the spare wheel, the wheel itself was of no use since the M2 incident.

In 20 minutes the job was done, but this left us without a spare. At *Nasice*, the convoy broke away, with good luck wishes following over the airwaves. Chuck and Iris had a problem with their C.B. As we headed for the *Zagreb* motorway, they pulled into a layby, we followed. Chuck then came to tell us that he has decided not to go on with us to *Crikvenica*. His brakes were giving cause for concern and he would not like to trust them on the steep mountain roads.

He would make for *Gralla Services* and if he had a real problem he would wait for us, as we would be only twenty four hours behind him. With just John and June following in their transit with no C.B. we found the motorway pretty deserted. We travelled until 11.30pm. then pulled in to what had been a service station for the night. All the filling stations and services on the motorway had been destroyed, just shells of buildings and twisted metal, but there was plenty of parking space. As we settled down a nightingale was singing not far away.

Sunday morning, we travelled on only passing the occasional car. From *Zagreb* Airport we followed signs to *Karlovac*, which was often under fire, it was very quiet this time. On roads winding up and over the mountains, the weather was much cooler. The war hadn't reached this part of Yugoslavia. The locals were still earning a living. We passed bistros and roadside barbeques with whole lambs or pigs roasting on spits.

Every four hours or so we made a "loo" stop, allowing June the privacy of our facilities. As we were about to made one of these stops just outside of a mountain village, a large truck loomed up behind us. We thought the truck would overtake and carry on ahead. We were quite surprised when it pulled up in front of us. The driver leapt out of his cab, took a good look and shouted "Well, it could only be you guys out here in the wilds." Paul from Barnsley had been with us on the first convoy.

Two ladies followed from the cab, Jackie his wife and their friend, Jenny. They were on their way to Bosnia, taking medical aid to a hospital near *Sarajevo*, well within the conflict area. Jackie told us how they had tried to get some Gluten-free liquid diet for a child desperately ill in the hospital where they were heading. John quietly mentioned that on his van there were five cases of this medicine and he hadn't known the best place to leave it. The cases were soon transferred from the van to the truck.

They told of some of the horrific cases they had come

55

across. One lady had her legs beaten to a pulp, because she tried to save her grand daughter from having her throat cut. They showed us photos of this lady, and others who were badly treated, lying in the hospital. They used the pictures as evidence for their publicity campaigns to get aid and funds to enable them to make frequent trips to Sarajevo. It seemed a small world, meeting them on that mountain road on a different mission. They gave a wave goodbye and were gone.

Arriving at the *Ad Turres Hotel* car park, we separated to find the refugee families we had taken to our hearts in December. Then Chuck and Iris, John and June were taken to one building down a side road very close to the sea. Where as *'Odmaraliste'*, our hostel was on the far side of town and on the main coast road. The refugees from both buildings were from *Vukovar*.

This was only the second visit and we received some very puzzled looks as we walked into the reception area. Then one chap recognised us and sent for Nada, the lady in charge and who had talked with us last December. Dressed in shirt and shorts she looked a lot less haggard than before. She was so pleased to see us and others came to welcome us. There was great excitement when we told them that we had food and goods for them.

All hands were called for to help with unloading, we took great care to take photos of specially donated boxes given by scouts and schools. Nada told us that they had not seen sugar or milk for more than a year. We had plenty of both, powdered milk for normal use and baby milk. We asked if they had received any of the goods that were brought on the December convoy, the answer was 'No'. All they'd had were the toys we had brought on St. Nicholas' Day. We felt very let down but determined that we would bring more aid to these families in future.

Coffee and juice were brought out to us on the patio, some of the younger people, including Nada's teenagers, spoke good English.

We had brought the photos taken on our previous visit and showed them over and again as more residents came to join us. Nada wanted to put on a meal for us, once again the guilty

56

feeling that they really could not afford to feed us. We tried to make the excuse that we had eaten just before coming to *Crikvenica*.

Nada's son Boris, took us for a walk to the beach. One hundred steps leading down from the patio to the promenade, passing small chalets on our way, a very pleasant walk. There was not so much beach as there were rocks and pebbles. We passed other hotels which Boris told us were filled with refugees. The name of *Vukovar* was written everywhere, on walls, paving stones and rocks. Their home town now just about flattened and in the hands of their enemy. On our first visit here, the children had written *Vukovar* in the grime on the rear of our camper. It could still be seen even after many washes.

It was lovely strolling in the warm sun, with a blue sea and mountains as a backdrop. But as Boris put it, nice for a holiday but it is not home. His sister Ivana came to tell us that our meal was ready, we must come to eat. They are both very good looking young people and interested in learning how we live.

A table was set out for us on the patio. We were served soup, then some kind of rissole with mash and peas, apple fritters for sweet. Nada and her friend Leo sat with us, we found out later that Leo had been a TV chef in happier times. He had brought a bottle of wine to celebrate our returning. This is what had pleased them most, that we had kept our promise to return.

Nada was keen to have us give out the chocolate we had brought for the children, after their main meal. I explained that we had arranged to meet with our friends at 8pm. We would come back afterwards. We reached the rendezvous point half an hour late, John and June arrived after us, saying goodbyes was a very long process. Leading John's transit to 'our peoples refuge' we all went in to a great welcome from the children. Nada made a great ceremony of us handing the chocolate, sweets and a small teddy in one of the little baskets, to each child. One little boy called Josep, had such a wistful look with big eyes, we remembered him especially from December. Also remembered was Vladimira a 6 year old who had followed us as we made the rounds of the accommodation, then.

We had brought sewing materials for the older ladies along with knitting wool, needles and crochet hooks. Nada had explained to us that the younger women had the day to day running of the hostel and their families to keep them busy. The older ladies had nothing to do except dwell on what had happened to them, with homes and a lifetime of personal belongings gone. These ladies would be happier knowing that they could help by knitting warm clothing for the children.

A box of dental care items had been sent by one of our local scout groups. A brightly coloured poster had been stuck on the outside of the parcel by the boys. Some of the older refugee children carefully removed it and wrote their names on the back for us to give to the scouts on our return home.

On being asked what was most needed if we were able to return before winter, Nada asked for marmalade, margarine, cooking oil, and shoes for the children. One of us mentioned that we would like to get a Croatian flag. Leo went out in his car and a little later returned with a flag for us, blue and white with the chequered crest. Nada gave us a tourist brochure about the hotel as it was in its holiday mode.

They wanted us to stay the night in one of the chalets, a nice gesture but we explained that we needed to stay with our vehicles. There were many souvenir hunters abroad, our stickers and British number plates would have been a great temptation. We still had a fair amount of Croatian currency, which would be no use to us on our journey home, so we pressed it into Nada's hand as we left. After giving her our address in England in case they should be moved, we said farewells.

On the long trek over the mountains, it was difficult to take in the fact that amid such beautiful scenery there could be such suffering and misery.

At *Gralla Services* there was no sign of Chuck's van, he must have managed to get home. We had one more flat tyre on our trailer. The problem was solved by using a cylinder of repair gunge which one of the lorry drivers had given us on leaving. It did the trick and we travelled on to Austria, such delightful countryside, houses with balconies ablaze with flowers, perched on the mountainsides.

On the Autobahns in Germany, John decided to go on ahead as his van was faster than our camper. We plodded on but on approaching *Aachen* took a wrong road and ended up in

Holland. It was no big deal and quite late at night so we tucked up and slept in just one more continental country.

As we arrived on *Dunkirk* docks, we were pleased to see the 'Fireman's Relief' lorry and the Romford Baptist Church truck, two of our one hundred and five vehicles on the original Convoy of Hope, December 1992. From that massive get-together some like us, had gone on to keeping the relief convoys rolling into places of dire need. The drivers told us that they had been down the Adriatic coast to *Split*. We told them we had been as far as *Crikvenica*, then they asked how we had got through *Karlovac* because it had been under attack at the time they were coming back. We must have just been lucky.

During our two weeks away, the Bosnian Crisis Appeal had been working hard on our behalf. The publicity and evidence by photographs, video and newsletters, that the goods given to our appeal had reached the people needing help and it had also helped to bring the desperate plight of many thousands of displaced persons to the public eye. The staff of the B.C.A. worked full time to sort and pack all good quality clothing.

A firm had donated a huge quantity of flat packed cardboard boxes. Many of those a good size to make up family parcels, with a dozen or so canned foods, packets of rice and pasta, dried milk, salt and sugar. Filling the spaces with tooth paste, matches, chocolate and sweets, it was quite an art to fill the boxes just right. If they were not full, the weight of more on top would make them collapse, if over full they wouldn't sit right on top of one another when stacked.

We had a little thief in the warehouse. We noticed that some packed boxes had been nibbled at the corners, then realised on repacking them that only boxes containing chocolate had been attacked. Fearing at first that we might have rats, we called in a pest control chap who laid poison around the area. Then one day we saw the culprit, a squirrel, from then on all the food parcels were locked in a small secure room which had been an office.

St. Leonard's Hospital near Ringwood had offered us a large amount of artificial limbs. While we all struggled to fit these articles into suitable boxes, the local paper sent a reporter to up date our progress on our fourth mission to helping the helpless. A rep trying to sell us a converter gadget which was supposed to save on fuel, asked us to test one on our 3,000 mile trip. He was explaining to Denys how there were different models at different prices.

Some were not so expensive, then he took one out of its box held it up and said, "Now this one would cost you an arm and a leg." My husband, ever the joker, said, "It's funny you should say that, right now I could afford it."

Donations of money were coming in, along with our street collections we raised enough funding to make another mission in September. With the amount of aid pouring into our warehouse, Tony B. came down from Canterbury to fill his van and trailer from the selection of goods we had available.

SEPTEMBER 1993

The first vehicle we met on the docks at Ramsgate on September 7th was a white Land Rover. The driver was a Scot and seemed to us to be very full of his own importance. The Rover had a collection of cardboard boxes on the roof rack, squashed together and tied on with string.

Jock went into great detail to tell us how he had been 'turned over' by customs and asked if we would carry a flak jacket in our camper until we arrived in France. Too surprised to refuse we did just that, realising afterwards that it was not a wise thing to do on our part. The equipment must have weighed a good few kilograms and took two of us to lift it. He boasted about how he would be making trips into the 'danger zones' once we arrived in Croatia.

Next to arrive was Tony B. he said that a couple of lads from a Kent newspaper were to join us on this convoy. Scott, a photographer, was to travel in a transit with Terry and his co-driver. Tim the reporter, was to get a lift with our new friend Jock in his Land Rover.

Our house guest for this trip was Irene, her connections with Christchurch hospital had brought in some very useful supplies, which we hoped to get to *Split*. Irene, a friend of our daughter, Chris, wanted to come with us after hearing tales of our former missions into refugee camps.

Eight vehicles made up our convoy. Terry in a transit, Robin and his wife Lut in their Land Rover Discovery, Gordon, Peter, Alf and Kevin in a transit, Derek and Jill in a transit, Hugh on his own in a car loaded until he could hardly see out, Jock in his Land Rover, Tony and us.

On the 11.30am. ferry, we arrived in *Dunkirk* at 2pm. While we travelled across Belgium and Germany, Jock became a bit of a pain. At filling stations he would go missing then turn up

61

driving like a madman, explaining that he had been catching up on sleep lost over the previous week. Tim the reporter was not happy with Jock's driving and at one stop, over coffee, we said more joking than serious, that we had room for another lodger if he wanted a change.

Later that evening, Tony called a conference. He told us that in spite of warnings about his erratic behaviour, Jock was still being a nuisance and a liability to the convoy. Tony wanted to send the man packing but that would leave the problem of what to do about Tim. Denys said then, that we had more or less told Tim that he could travel with us, we had room in the 'guest flat', the Luton over the cab. Tim fetched his gear from the Land Rover while Jock was persuaded to hand back the C.B. borrowed from one of our drivers, his route itinerary and heart stickers.

We could not afford to have anyone causing problems at borders from Austria onwards. It would not take much for the border police to send us all back, if even one vehicle in our company did not conform to their rules.

We found Tim a very interesting young man. From the Whitstable Times, he and Scott were covering our journey into the former Yugoslavia. I told him of some of our earlier experiences and he made notes as we travelled.

Ours was the slowest vehicle in the convoy, most of the time we were a few kilometres behind the rest. A burst tyre on the trailer cost us an hour but with my own kitchen to prepare snacks and sandwiches with coffee from a flask we had the edge on those who ate in service stations. Then we would catch up and overtake the parked vehicles, giving a blast of the Dixie horns as we passed by.

On crossing the Austrian border in late afternoon, Tim and I took shifts in the navigator's seat, Irene seemed quite happy to sit in the back. We enjoyed the wonderful scenery until darkness fell, then came the tunnels and tolls. There again we were able to forge on ahead. Vehicles like ours and cars, having windows at the back had to pay. Vans, trucks and commercial vehicles carrying aid, could get through free but they must take their papers into an office to get a special ticket. That took time, while we paid the required marks and went on. At *Gralla Services* we arrived at least an hour ahead of the others.

The night was very humid, we slept well enough and were on the road after breakfast making for the border. In Slovenia we burst a second tyre on the trailer. A chap in a garage gave us directions to a Vulcanizer (tyre fitter). No tyres of the right size there but the helpful mechanic drew us a map of where to find a place that might be able to help. The second Vulcanizer was down a series of back streets, the whole convoy were with us as we parked in the narrow road.

The owner looked at our shredded tyres and shook his head, he told us that we would not find a tyre of that size in Slovenia. He offered to fetch some from Austria if we were prepared to wait for the three hours that it would take. We really had no choice. The other members of the team opted to stay with us and have an early break.

I made tea for everyone then sat in the shade with my knitting. Some of the crew went walk-about to shops not far away. Irene had made friends with a couple of the ladies, one of them Sue, Tony's passenger on this trip. They sat on the grass chatting until they discovered that ants were sharing the shaded patch with them. Just on the three hours later the tyres were in, the job was done. The charge was £36 for the two tyres fitted.

On then into Croatia and we made for *Zagreb* where we were to pick up a lady interpreter. Kella was to be our guide taking us into the camp of *Rangi Nekova*, where 35 families from Bosnia lived in army huts. In this camp Tony B. had a goddaughter. One year before he had met with Sylvana, 22 years old, pregnant and her husband was dead. Some months later Tony had come back bringing a cot, a pram, nappies and baby clothes. Sylvana was overjoyed that he had not forgotten her that she asked him to be godfather to her baby daughter.

The camp was close to a busy railway track, as we drove in all the kids came out to meet us. As some drivers unloaded, others gave out sweets and toys. Loads of photos were taken, Scott posed some of us in groups and Tim was getting facts and figures from Kella for their story. As each van left food and clothing, blankets and bedding, shoes and toiletries, our ladies spent time admiring the babies and giving away toys and teddies. We were anxious to meet Tony's goddaughter but she was in hospital suffering with a chesty cough.

Most of the families had no hope of returning home, we were told that family groups included Grandparents, Uncles and Aunts, Mums and Dads and the children living in small rooms in the huts. Just one more desperate situation.

Most of our drivers had been without a main meal for a couple of days, Tony suggested that we stop at the Holiday Inn on the road to *Zagreb*. Scott and Tim had told us that all they had brought with them were a couple of packs of sandwiches. They had been told that they could eat at restaurants on the trip. That was all well and good while on civilised motorways and main roads, not always possible when we are in the back of beyond, a good thing our meals were usually elastic.

After parking we all trooped into the dining room of the Inn, we found the menu a bit pricey. A couple of our team had a word with a waiter, he looked around at our group and showed us into a Taverna, much more within our price range. Tim, Denys, Irene and I shared a table, we ordered kebabs and chips which arrived with loads of fresh bread. As we paid the bill, Tim slipped me some marks to pay for his accommodation.

Set up then for another long drive, we pulled out to take the mountain road for the coast. As we approached *Karlovac*, Tony warned us that the town had been under fire for the past four days, we decided to go for it and to see what happened. If it were to be too dangerous the U.N. would have set up a checkpoint at the crossroads, to turn us back. Each vehicle edged a little closer to the one in front and we travelled slowly expecting to be stopped. No checkpoint, no problems.

Karlovac behind us and into the mountains, darkness and a pity that we couldn't see the views, or perhaps a blessing as far as Irene was concerned. She was a little nervous on the bends with the long drop to the sea and rocks below. As we climbed a fog came down on us, or rather we went up into it. We almost missed a turning at the top of one climb, Tony's flashing lights on his van were there to warn us of the turn. On the steep descent to the coast road, we could feel the weight of the still laden trailer behind us. The fog cleared in time to give us a view of *Rijeka* and the oil refinery flame below. We parked in our usual rest area in front of the *Ad Turres Hotel*. We all decided to give ourselves the luxury of an hotel room. For us the luxury was going to be the hot shower.

At 2am. we booked into the hotel, very dirty and dusty from our visit to *Rangi Nekova*. I was first in the shower but the water was cold. I just cannot bear water that is colder than my body, but I had plunged in regardless gritting my teeth to have a very cold wash. I emerged complaining but I was wasting my breath, Denys was already asleep.

Our room and breakfast cost us around £10. Breakfast consisting of fresh bread with jam, cheese and ham slices. The war had not touched this lovely part of Croatia but there were very few visitors using the hotels on the coast. A lot of them were being used as refugee hostels. We used the phone in the reception to call our family to let them know we were O.K.

We were to hit the road south at 9am. but it was nearer 10 when we set out and pulled into a filling station only yards from the *Ad Turres*. Someone had found out that the owner of the garage and adjoining bar had once been a world champion speedway star. Back in the 1950's he had been riding in the U.K. All his medals, trophies and photos were on display in the bar. We all went in to admire the collection and to meet *Mika*.

On the road again, as we passed our refugee hostel, one of the elderly ladies was on the patio. Denys sounded the Dixie horns so that they would know we were back in the area. Following the coast with spectacular views and passing quaint little fishing villages we turned off the main road at *Prizna*. The bridge at *Meslenica* had been destroyed making our route along the coast impassable. We were to catch a local ferry across to *Pag Island*, a causeway on the far end of the island would take us back on track. On a steep slope down to the ferry, we joined a jostling mass of local vehicles all determined to get on board first. We became very un-British, Robin in his Discovery blocked the local traffic and we all got on board, except Robin!! Over the C.B. it was arranged that we would wait for him on the other side if he hadn't been lynched!

The crossing took only twenty minutes. The ferry was being protected by a gun emplacement and U.N. soldiers. They waved and whistled as we drove out. We all carried Union Jack pennants on our vans, proudly declaring our nationality. Robin and his Belgian wife, Lut soon joined us, then we were driving over a barren and desolate landscape. It would have made a good location for a science fiction film set of the moon.

The bare sandy coloured rock gradually gave way to scrubland with very scraggy looking sheep. trying to find enough to graze on within stone walled enclosures. As we travelled on, the land become greener. Clumps of bamboo grass were growing alongside the road. Suddenly we came to a halt. The police had stopped us at a bridge which had a weight limit of two tons. Most of our vehicles were well over that. As there was no other way the police officer let us cross one at a time. I think we all held our breath as each vehicle drove across the bridge, it was high above a chasm, we all made it safely across. At the far end of the island was the town of *Pag*, and the causeway to the mainland.

From there on the roads were badly pitted by mortar shells, they made a shallow star-shaped crater in the road surface. We arrived in *Zadar,* ancient capital of the Adriatic coast. It had been arranged that we should meet with customs officials in town. Our journey had taken longer than expected and no one was in the building.

The *Kalovare* hotel allowed us to use the car park, the hotel was used by the U.N. Government officials and aid convoys like ours. Two floors of the huge building had been turned over to house refugees. Tim, Scott and a few of our crowd booked in to stay the night. I started to cook our meal when our Calor gas ran out. No problem as we carried a spare cylinder. We enjoyed the meal and while the family were out socialising, I sat with my knitting, listening to taped music over headphones.

Irene rushed into the camper to say that the children who had been playing in the car park, had disappeared at the first bangs. Puzzled I asked her, "What bangs?" The music had completely drowned out the sound of mortar shells falling only yards away from our vehicles. Police came to advise us to go inside the hotel for safety, what a way to get customers into the bar. We sat around chatting over a drink or two, I am sure that none of us felt that we were really in danger.

Our tame pressmen wandered around with cameras at the ready, some of our drivers sat out on the hotel steps watching for more 'fireworks'. We watched locals coming and going, not looking very concerned but I suppose that this was just part of life for them. The bar closed at 11pm., all was quiet outside as we returned to our vehicles parked in a neat row in front of the hotel. Someone jokingly called them the 'Magnificent Seven'. Three U.N. Land Rovers arrived to park nearby as we settled in.

At 9am. we drove to the customs building in town, where we were advised to unload at a *Caritas* warehouse. We were told then that the refugee camps were the main targets at that time and it would not have been wise to visit them. None of us were happy to do this, the building was already full of sacks of flour, pallets of baby food. Piles of bedding and clothing were thrown in a heap in one corner, not even folded or stacked. Tim made the most of having an interpreter, Anna gave him information about what it was like living in this situation.

We just left a token amount of food parcels to lighten our loads for the journey to *Split*. After every one had added a few parcels to the stocks in the warehouse, Anna offered to take us to a village called *Dracevac*. A narrow track led us up hill to a completely devastated hamlet. Where the village green might have been, the centrepiece was a burned out Croatian tank, it had been defending the village and its people from the Serb forces. The tank had received a direct hit in the fuel tank, all the crew inside had perished.

The little church was just a shell with only the bell tower intact. At the entrance of the church a cross had been painted in human blood, to show contempt for the villagers' religion. Graves in the churchyard had been desecrated, corpses had been dug out and mutilated. We were soon surrounded by the few surviving locals; the villagers who lived among the ruins. One old man told us in broken English that he and his wife had been living in *Trieste*, on retirement they had moved to *Dracevac* to be near their two sons and their families. He was the only one left.

Anna told us that the school had gone with a direct hit. The Serbs took *Dracevac* then used the village as a vantage point to bombard *Zadar*. Scott called us all together for a photo call grouped around the tank. To some people it might seem ghoulish to take photos of such scenes but when we got home the 'horror pictures' were what motivated the public into giving more. People are not impressed by pictures of smiling children who had been given bon-bons, they want to see the misery. That's human nature.

Back to the *Kalovare* and a snack lunch. We were to move out at 2pm. Some of our lads had taken on the local boys in a football match in the large car park, At 2 most of us were all ready to go, the game was at a draw. Extra time was asked for to make one side or the other the winners. The next thing we knew was that Kevin hobbled over to ask if we had a plaster, as he had cut his toe. There was no sight of blood at that moment but by the time we had the first aid box opened it was obvious that more than a plaster was needed. Blood was pouring from a wound in his big toe. Irene took charge with padding and bandages applied.

A decision was made to get Kevin to a hospital, A young lad told Denys that he would show him the way to the hospital as his mum worked there. We got Kevin inside the camper, on the floor with Irene holding his leg up as far as she could manage. Denys drove with our young guide in the passenger seat. Although the hospital was not far walking distance, it was quite a way by road.

With a very narrow entrance to the casualty department we managed to get the patient to the door. Soon Kevin was rushed away on a hospital trolley. We were told to return in an hour to check on him. Then we drove back to report to the waiting team. A discussion then as to whether we should go on to *Split* after so many delays.

Terry in his blue transit went back to the hospital after the given hour. While we waited some one reported that a white Land Rover had been seen in the area. Probably not Jock as the U.N. Land Rovers were white. Just after the hour Terry was back with the patient, he'd been x-rayed, injected, stitched and well bandaged. He declared that he was fit enough to travel.

The story was, that Kevin, for some unknown reason had been playing football with bare feet. He had cheated by moving the oppositions goal post, (pile of stones) in a couple of feet, hoping his team would get the winning goal. As he kicked the ball his foot caught the goal post, containing a piece of slate, which sliced into his toe.

5pm. when we moved out, it was decided that we should go on to *Split*. Beautiful scenery, very blue sea, distant mountains, and vineyards, with grapes hanging in great purple clusters in just about every garden. As we left *Zadar* the country side was undamaged, the war and devastation seemed miles away. The Croatian drivers must be among the world's worst. Convoy hopping seemed to be a favourite sport and we saw many a near miss. On rounding one of the bends we saw a truck on its side lying across someone's garden.

A few miles from *Split* the skies darkened then opened up with thunder and lightning. Such a storm, our windscreen wipers could not cope with the lashing rain. We were trying to find a pull-in but as quickly as it had started the rain slackened off. We could see the sun shining on a town way over to our left. It was *Split*, all we had to do then was to find the hospital.

After directions from a local couple, we saw the sign '*Bolnica*' (hospital). Even the countries as far away as Croatia still use the 'H' sign for Hospital. The men went into the building to find out where we were to unload. But it seemed that we had taken them by surprise, no one knew we were coming. For some reason the message hadn't got through.

At last we were directed to an outbuilding behind the hospital complex and were called to a halt. A couple of transits backed up to the doors ready to unload. A chap in a long white coat came and invited us to follow him up a flight of steps and into a boardroom. Two young ladies brought us orange juice, then a gentleman came to greet us introducing himself as the chief eye surgeon at the hospital.

He asked how we had come to bring aid to this particular hospital. Tony explained that he had met with a doctor in Switzerland some months earlier. This doctor had told Tony how *Split* hospital was desperately short of drugs and equipment. The eye surgeon asked to see our load sheets, these were examined and talked over by the surgeon and a head nurse. After a discussion in their own language, some of it clearly an argument, the surgeon told us apologetically that they were unable to take what we had to offer because the paperwork did not name their hospital.

Tony told them that the paperwork was from his own office and that the heading could be altered. It still would not do. Although the hospital desperately needed what we had brought, they could not accept it. The only way around the problem was to take the load to the '*Caritas*' centre in town, the hospital could request it from there. RED TAPE at work.

Coffee was brought in while Zelko our friendly surgeon was happy to tell us about the situation in his country. His wages before the war had been £1000 per month. now he gets less than £200 a month. He told us that his wife was also a surgeon working mainly with children. He apologised for our long journey to bring help and for the fact he could not take it.

We were a little concerned about where we would be staying that night. The hospital car park was not large enough for the seven vehicles. One of the hospital staff suggested that we try the Hotel Split, which was not far from the hospital. As the convoy moved into spaces available at the hotel, we could see that 30foot length of our camper and trailer was too long to get in. We found a convenient spot on a lay-by opposite the hotel.

The few that had gone in to find the price of a room in the hotel, soon came out again. 260 marks per night (more than £100) and that didn't include breakfast. A couple of locals passing by told of more reasonable lodgings just outside town. We opted to settle where we were, not too much traffic on the road as it was late and there was a kind of curfew. Only vehicles on military or official business risked being on the road at night.

I made up one of our famous convoy stews, out of cans from our store cupboard, packet soups for flavour and thickening. Plenty for the four of us, then Tony arrived at the door. The rain was still pouring and to save muddying our carpet, he left his shoes outside. We got talking and invited him to join us for dinner. A couple of hours later as our guest was leaving, he stepped into his shoes to find they were full of water.

Waking to a lovely sunny morning, we waited for our colleagues to return from across town. We took 'holiday snaps' of each other outside the *Hotel Split*. In the hotel car park was an armoured Land Rover. A local chap told us that it was used by Kate Adie, the news reporter. Soon we heard the voices of our

70

missing members trying to find their way back to us. We moved out taking the main route out of town, meeting up with the others on the way.

We needed to find the *Caritas* warehouse, the only instructions we had been given, was that it was near a sports stadium. Problem, there were two in *Split* and we found the wrong one first. At every street corner one of our drivers would stop to ask for directions. Eventually we arrived in a narrow back street with tall blocks of flats. The *Caritas* office and storeroom were on the ground floor of one of these blocks. Being a Sunday, the place was closed but someone walking by knew the key holder.

A short wait until the man with a key arrived, then we were able to offload the goods. Irene and Sue sat in the sun with a big bag of toys and teddies, they didn't have to wait long before the children started to arrive, coming to see what we were about.

Part of our load and Tony's were the huge boxes of artificial limbs. We stressed to the man in charge that the limbs, medical equipment and drugs etc. were to be held for the hospital only. A list of all those items was made out, one copy for them and one for us, the hospital already had a list from the night before. We warned the staff that if the hospital did not receive the goods we would hear of it.

As usual I took photos to prove to folks back home that their good hearted gifts had made it to the people in need. I was clicking away and suddenly discovered that I was out of film. I asked Scot if he had a spare film that I could borrow. He did but it was black and white.

Job done we made our way out of town then on to the coast road for the return journey to *Zadar*. The news hounds were spending the night in the hotel to get first hand stories from local victims living under the daily shelling. The rest of us just had a short break before leaving, all was quiet but it seems that *Zadar* was under fire the night before.

At the far end of *Pag Island* our convoy had the ferry to ourselves. While Denys was buying the tickets I brought a huge bunch of grapes for the equivalent of 60p. We stopped for lunch on a layby, a beautiful spot by the sea, soon the smell of frying eggs and bacon filled the air. Some of the crew were wandering around munching on egg and bacon sandwiches. Some were having a conversation with a lady hanging out her washing in a nearby garden.

We spent the night at *Crikvenica* and made phone calls home to say that we were on the last leg of our journey. Then said goodbye to those who were going to make for home. The next stop for us was at the refugee hostel '*Odmaraliste*', to hand over food and toiletries we had brought for our friends. They were all surprised and pleased to see us, hugs all round while Irene was introduced. Nada was cross when she heard that we had arrived the night before, she asked why we hadn't come to see her then. We were almost ordered to stay for lunch, coffee and pancakes were brought to make sure we did not starve until then.

With plenty of help we unloaded the food, including marmalade requested from our last time there. Knitting wool for the ladies, books and games for the children. A large box of home made cakes given to us by a lady as we left Ramsgate, was added to the goodies. The boxes brought from our trailer were lined up along the kitchen wall, it looked rather like a car boot sale as the ladies rummaged to see what we had brought.

I had made up some toilet bags, for men and for women and handed them out as far as they would go. One lady asked how had we known what they needed most, we told her that we had a shopping list made on our previous visit.

Lunch was served in the dining room, chicken soup with dumplings, then more pancakes with chocolate sauce. We ate amid curious glances from some of the residents. Later we walked along the sea shore, it was nice to relax and stretch our legs. The sun was warm, the water crystal clear, war and mortar shells a long way off. Irene had fallen in love with the place and imagined what it would be like to live in one of the pretty little houses on the promenade. She collected a few pebbles to take home as there were no sea shells. Back up the 100 steps to the hotel patio, Nada and some of the children were sitting outside.

We were about to join them when we heard some one call out " Duke", (Denys' C.B. name.) Tim, Scott and the boys who had stayed over in *Zadar* had seen our camper and had come looking for us. Introductions all round, Nada was quite used to us bringing our travelling companions and organised fruit juice served by Ivana, her daughter. There were a few shy glances between Ivana and good looking Tim.

Tim jotted down all he could find out about the little community, while Scott took some group photos of the children, they loved being posed and looked their sweetest. The boys told us that they had collected some good material for their paper in *Zadar* but they were disappointed that nothing spectacular had happened while they were there.

They had to leave us then and said that they would be in touch when we were all back home and promised to send us copies of their paper. Denys and I went out on the road to see them off, we returned to find Irene and one of the young ladies teaching the children some English words. On this trip I had been knitting a school sweater for Carl, one of our grandsons, I picked it up to knit a few more rows while sitting in the shade. An elderly lady who had been sitting nearby came over to examine the almost finished sweater. I had noticed that the Croatian ladies knitted in a different style to our way, the left needle was held under the arm somehow.

Her interest had broken the ice, a second lady then invited me to her room, where she showed me some of her handiwork. She made cushions from odd scraps of material hand sewn together. That made me start thinking that a sewing machine and cottons would be useful the next time we came. Irene made a list of things needed and wanted. Ivana asked for paper and files for her school work, Boris asked for honey. Underwear was needed for children and adults, I was asked by one lady, "Have you ever tried to make a bra?"

There was no doubt in our minds that we would come again. The children had made a card for us, in English it said, "Have a good trip home." As we left to spend the night parked up on the side of the main road, we were invited to come for breakfast in the morning before leaving, We asked for a '*malo*' (small) meal. Some time in the night I awoke to hear voices, but soon got back to my dreams.

At 8am. breakfast was set out for us, fresh bread and meat paste. The children had already gone to school. The schools worked on a shift system, with so many refugee kids as well as

73

the local children, the schools would be swamped.

Some classes started at 6am. and we had often seen children going home as late as 8pm.

The goodbyes were long and tearful, so many hugs and good wishes for a safe journey and our returning. As we left Nada gave Denys a video film of the arrival of this group at '*Odmaraliste*' in 1991, after the destruction of *Vukovar*. As he checked over the camper before our long journey home, Denys discovered that our Heart stickers had been removed, most likely when I had heard the voices in the night.

As we were now empty of goods and classed as tourists, we could use any of the border crossings on leaving the country. With the maps Denys had discovered a more straight forward route. Through *Ljubjana, Salzburg* and *Stuttgart*. Then to *Heilbrohn* and onto our original route. As we came to *Aachen*, a young German lad came to ask us for a lift. We did not often pick up hitch hikers but made an exception this time. On chatting as we travelled we mentioned that we came from Bournemouth. Would you believe that he had attended school in Christchurch when he was eight years old? His parents were living there for some years. He asked to be dropped at the Germany/Belgium border as he was on his way to *Paris*.

We made it to the docks at *Dunkirk* just in time to see a ferry leaving, no big deal, I put the kettle on for a good old cuppa. We talked the time away until the next boat at midnight. On board we treated ourselves to a coffee then tried to rest, but the boat rolled and I was not the best of sailors. We arrived at Ramsgate in the early hours and spent the night in a lorry park. We had arranged to visit a friend who lived in *Beltinge* near Herne Bay, on our return from the trip. Mike had been an old R.A.F. mate of Denys's from way back in the 1950's. Now a civilian driver at R.A.F. Manston he had been collecting clothing and goods for our charity from folk in his area.

We called in at Manston where Mike was just finishing his night duty. He invited us to his home for tea and toast breakfast. His wife Anne was involved with scouts and guides, their garage was choc-a-bloc with boxes and bin liners of goods for our next trip. We got it all packed into the trailer to take back to the warehouse where it would be sorted and packed for the next mercy mission.

An hour later while we were heading for the M2 motorway, road works forced us to make a detour, then we spotted Tony B's, transit travelling behind us. On the C.B, he told us that he was going to a transport cafe for his breakfast and invited us to join him. Denys tucked the camper and trailer in among the heavy lorries and we followed Tony into the busy cafe.

He ordered four cooked breakfasts with all the trimmings and mugs of steaming tea.

We told him of our trip from the Adriatic coast and he told us of what had happened after our parting of the ways. He was planning another trip out to the camps in October. Tony settled the bill and we pulled out of the parking area. As we left, Denys called Echo One, Tony's C.B. handle, to thank him for our meal and that we would be in touch. There was no reply and no sign of his vehicle !

There was quite a welcoming committee at the warehouse when we arrived back. Friends and family all relieved that we were okay. Before leaving on this latest trip we had come across a chap in Highcliffe who had been collecting goods and money for Bosnia. He had hoped that the British army would take this aid for refugees. By opening a collection centre in an empty shop, he had amassed a good load of packed and ready to go supplies. The army had not been able to help.

On reading about our exploits in the local paper while we had been away, he had got in touch with our friends in the B.C.A. and offered his collection to our cause. The very day we arrived back, this chap Vic, had organised a fashion show in one of Highcliffe's hotels to raise funds for the transportation of his goods to the needy. He had requested the pleasure of our company at this event, with instructions to, " Come as you are, tired, dirty and straight from the war zone." Which we did.

We had a wonderful reception, a selection of high class outfits from one of the local stores were modelled by ladies of all ages and cute little tots. After the show an auction of a pair of *Bet Lynch's* earrings, (from Coronation Street) raised more cash. A couple of weeks later, Vic had organised a concert in the sports hall at one of the local schools, again we were to be guests of honour.

That evening we set out to find this school, not easy as we were not familiar with the area. We arrived late, Vic was on the stage apologising for the delay when we walked in. To our embarrassment he announced, "These people could find their way 3,000 miles across the continent but couldn't find our school." The show was very good, four local singers gave us songs from pop to opera and musical shows.

A donation of over £600 was made over to the B.C.A. from the two events. Our next convoy trip was funded.

The video which Nada had given us turned out to be quite a shocker. Although some of it was of a show of music and comedy put on at the hostel, the rest was of scenes of the people we knew and had befriended, as they were herded onto lorries and buses by Serbian soldiers There were propaganda scenes of Serb soldiers giving their victims cigarettes and one old man obviously frightened was seen being questioned as to the whereabouts of his son, shaking with fear he says he does not know. There are terrible pictures of the way many people were murdered, goods and bedding, bodies and debris left behind in a *Vukovar Barracks*. It told how Serbs tried to keep some local people in the town to be used as hostages.

Efforts were made by the Red Cross to evacuate the worst of the wounded from the battered *Vukovar* hospital. Shown in the film is an encounter between a commander of a Serb Army unit and a representative of the International Red Cross, who insists on keeping to the Geneva Convention. He says that permission must be given to evacuate the wounded. The Serb Commander tells the Red Cross Representative that he is in command and will make the decisions and that there is a war going on. If he does not like the way the Serbs are conducting the evacuation he can 'go away'. The film tells that this confrontation was seen on British TV News. Martin Bell with his crew recorded it.

Women and children were seen waiting to be taken away from their home town. Many of them not knowing what had become of their men folk. Among them we could recognise the friends we had made in the *'Hotel Odmaraliste'* There were scenes inside a temporary hospital, with nuns caring for orphaned babies, the sick and the wounded. A Red Cross representative complaining that the Red Cross were used to more co-operation than they were receiving from the Serb forces. He avoids eye contact to appear submissive and to take the heat out of the situation.

OCTOBER 1993

October 13th saw us once again on Ramsgate docks waiting to board a ferry. We were in the company of old friends from previous convoys, Chuck and Iris from Dover, Tony B. from Canterbury, Peter Bishop, Nigel Monk and their local priest, Father David from Manchester, a trio named by our crew, The Holy Brothers. Marie and her son from Sheffield, first timers with us were Tony P. with co-driver Kelly from Bournemouth. Chris from Portisham near Weymouth, Tim M. an ex-headmaster from Wimborne with his daughter Susie. A young lady driving a Skoda and towing a large trailer had asked to join our convoy as far as the Adriatic coast. She then hoped to go on to *Mostar* where she intended to work in a hospital.

With son Tim and his now fiance, Tracy, once again our house guests, we travelled across Europe without problems, until nearing *Hockenheim*, Tony P. had trouble with his van's gearbox. He limped into the services long after we had settled in for the night. Without a C.B. radio he had not been able to warn us that he had a problem. At 6.30am. he knocked on our door, asking if Tim could sort out the trouble. Tim came back with the opinion that Tony's van would not make the long journey. Breakdown was called and the recovery vehicle arrived with a German driver who could not speak or understand English. The only person among our crew who had any knowledge of German was Tim M. who acted as interpreter. Tony with his transit and trailer were to be taken back to the U.K., a sad ending to his first convoy experience We all set to unloading as much of the load from Tony's as we could get into the other vehicles. Kelly was invited to have a lift in the Skoda with Christina.

Not long after leaving the services, Tony B. developed the first puncture. The wheel was soon changed and we bowled along with banter and chat over the C.B. radio. It was quite some time before we heard Christina's voice, when we did my instincts told me that it was male. Later at one of the stops for coffee and comfort we discussed this with other members who had noticed strange things about our new friend. Big hands, a bit over the top with masses of gold jewellery and a near empty trailer, which seemed to be only carrying a generator.

There was speculation as to which gender Christina belonged until someone noticed 'she' sported an 'Adams apple'. Kelly who had been travelling in the Skoda, helped to prove what we had suspected by taking a quick look at her driver's passport. The first name was Leonard. From then on the Skoda outfit was nicknamed 'Transvestite and trailer'.

We arrived at *Gralla Services* earlier than usual, Tony B. offered to buy everyone a drink at the bar. Later Tracy and I went back to the camper to catch up with our diaries. Tim came back next all happy and giggly, rambling on about how some of the girls were sleeping in the services restaurant. Denys home, and all secure we turned in around midnight.

As we drove down into Slovenia there were three vehicles needing replacement tyres. We used the Vulcanizer we had found on the last trip. We entered Croatia around lunch time, having time for a picnic while documents were processed. Our first dropping zone was to be *Pakrac*. The route to this town took us up some very steep hills. The Skoda was in trouble, the tow-bar was coming adrift from where it was welded to the engine mounting.

Not much could be done except lash it together with binder twine, (it was surprising what some of the vehicles were carrying).

As we approached the town, there were remarks about the lightning ahead, then it was noticed that the sky was clear. Soon we discovered that the 'Lightning Flashes' was artillery fire, as the Serbs were bombarding *Pakrac*. In the town we parked in the main street, noticing that there were street lights, an improvement since our last visit.

A doctor came to tell us that staff were waiting at the main hospital. We drove to the open area and parked up behind the huge hulk of the hospital, on the Croatian side out of view of the Serb snipers. The building had been attacked early that year. All

79

we knew was that mentally ill patients had been taken out and shot, no one in the town really wanted to talk to us about what had happened there. The top part of the building was being used as a look-out post by the Croat police and the Militia. They kept watch on the Serb forces (Chetniks) only 100 yards away.

In the soup kitchen we were given soup and local bread. Then we had a get-together with hospital staff in their newly decorated hall. With U.N. keeping the Serbs at bay, work was being done to open up some of the least damaged parts of the hospital to be used as clinics. Although we were all advised not to go into town after dark, a few of our younger members went to renew friendships made over the last few months. A curfew was in force from 8pm. but the bar was calling.

Next day the medical supplies were unloaded into the secure building which had been the hospital mortuary. We ourselves only carried a small amount of cough medicine and diphtheria vaccines. After handing these over we drove into town and parked beside the large office block where we had met the lady asking if we could bring tools which could be used in rebuilding and repairing damaged homes.

We had managed to fulfil their request. Local schools in our area had offered us their Harvest Festival collections. When they had heard that our friends in a bombed town needed tools, the headmaster of a village school had asked parents to send these items instead of the usual fruit, vegetables, bread and canned goods. There were saws, planes, screwdrivers, chisels, nails and hammers, paint brushes and even electric drills, many items that would be useful in the rebuilding of a town which was 95 percent damaged.

We were taken into a small office for cakes, coffee, and local brandy,

We could not speak each other's language but we had a great party. Just as we were about to leave, a chap came in with papers in his hand and asked for the name of our organisation. On being told 'The Convoy of Hope' he wrote this on the top page and presented it to Denys. It was a complete inventory in Croatian, of all the tools that we had brought. They were a little shy in asking for things that we could bring on our next visit. With prompting we found that they needed typewriters, calculators, and printing paper. It seemed that they produced a local newspaper and they gave us a copy of their latest issue.

Outside the building a chap greeted us, he spoke a little English. We asked him about the school that Anneka had come out to rebuild on one of her challenges, he told us it was only five hundred metres away. At the school we found that the rest of the convoy had arrived there before us, everyone anxious to see what Anneka Rice had achieved. What a shock. In the huge school complex work had been done but nothing finished. New windows were stacked around the walls waiting to be put in and new radiators stood in the middle of classrooms. A grand piano was covered with dust sheets in the empty hall. A brass plaque on the wall proclaimed that the school had been reopened by Anneka Rice.

Our local friend told us that the hall had been decorated for the T V cameras, children had been brought in by bus for the film. The rest of the school was a shambles and unusable. Being overlooked by enemy forces it would be a very long time before it rang to the sound of children's voices. We all took photographs of the school, someone tinkled on the keys of the brand new grand piano. Outside in the playing area a new slide and a swing stood unused. Houses opposite had huge holes blown through the walls, with furniture still recognisable, wardrobes open and clothing spilling out. We gave food parcels to some of the local families near by.

While we had been sightseeing, U.N. lads at the hospital had welded and strengthened the Skoda's tow-bar. Its driver kept out of contact with the rest of the crew. Kelly, not happy with the situation accepted a lift on one of the other vans. We went on then, to *Slavonski Brod*, our load to be taken to the complex of flats which housed hundreds of Bosnian refugees. Surrounded by dozens of excited children, the supplies were moved into a storeroom by human chain. While we were waiting for our turn to unload, Denys asked one of the ladies if there was an accessible tap where we could refill our fresh water tank.

On being shown to a tap inside the building he found that the hose wouldn't reach. Then a helpful lady said that she knew of a tap not far away behind the block of flats, Denys followed her to a long low building with a tap just inside the door. There was plenty of parking space as he drove the camper close to the door. Then he found out that the building was a centre trying to care for refugees who had settled in the area. This was called the *Antun Mihanovic Centre.*

Denys noticed that the hall was empty except for a few sacks of powdered milk and flour. It seemed that the centre was completely unknown to aid convoys and they had received nothing. Denys came back to the main convoy to tell what he had found. Two vehicles which had not yet unloaded volunteered like us to unload at *Antun Mihanovic.* Our loading forms were stamped by a lady in the small office, as a receipt.

The next call was to the building by the river which was known to us as the 'Convent'. We were enlightened on this trip by being told that it was a Franciscan Monastery. The confusion had arisen from the way we had been entertained by nuns on our visits. It seemed that the nuns and some of the priests were refugees from across the river in Bosnia. Tim and Tracy were interested in a huge map of the former Yugoslavia, with areas coloured pink, grey and black. The map showed even before the war the population was dwindling, There were more old people dying than there were babies being born. One of the sisters rolled up the map and gave it to Tim as a souvenir.

The next morning saw us heading for the Adriatic coast, a full day's journey. Most of the bistros and restaurants were cooking spit roast hogs and lambs outside the buildings, tempting travellers to come in and eat. The convoy pulled into one of these eating places for a hot meal. Some of the younger members did not fancy eating something that still had its head and eyes attached. They ate from the supplies from their vehicles. We enjoyed the succulent pork or lamb with salad and fresh baked bread.

On again, taking the steep bends and turns of the mountain road we overtook the Skoda, Denys called out as we drove by and asked if everything was O.K. He got a nod in reply. Arriving in *Crikvenica* we parked in the hotel car-park and joined some of the other drivers. The Skoda arrived minus its trailer. We were told that the car had lost power on the hills and would not pull the trailer. It had been left about 12 miles back. Tim got behind the wheel of the Skoda to try it out, his verdict was that it was

O.K. (for a Skoda).

While we were talking over the plan for the next day, the Skoda took off. It was back within half an hour with the trailer. The driver told us that a U.N. chap had told him of a short-cut!! We were to part company with the odd creature who was to take the Adriatic Highway to *Mostar*. We were to make a quick visit to our refugee friends from *Vukovar*. They were living in safety after the horror of seeing their homes and city fall to the enemy.

Tony B. was to spend the night with friends near the port of *Rijeka*. After our social call at *Odmaraliste* with sweets and goodies for the children, we spent a quiet night. We had arranged to meet up with Tony the next morning on the outskirts of *Rijeka*. As we met up we saw that he had a passenger, a lady named Zinka. She was a pharmacist working at a clinic in *Rijeka*, Tony and Zinka belong to *the 'Sathai Sai'* organisation. She worked at a clinic for the very poor, some of Tony's load was destined for this clinic.

We went along for the experience, taking a road out of *Rijeka* and into the hills. We helped to unload Pampers and baby milk, incontinence pads and bed socks for the elderly. The clinic contained a dental care surgery and anti-natal unit. After the unloading we were refreshed with fruit juice and entertained by the doctors, all ladies.

On our way home Tony B. phoned his wife, to check if Tony P. had made it back safely. He came to tell us that our friend had made it back, also that the police had been to Tony's home in Canterbury, It seems that Christina was on the wanted list. The Skoda had been 'borrowed' from a neighbour without permission. The trailer had been hired for one day and had been paid for by a cheque that had bounced. Before boarding the ferry we collected Kelly to see her safely home. I'm sure she wouldn't forget her experience for some long time.

Back home the warehouse was very busy, more voluntary staff had been taken on. We now had a warehouse manager, Jack a retired Yorkshire man who had settled in our area. He was quite a dour character but took pride in working for our cause. He was so interested in our journeys that we invited him to join us on the next one.

Around that time, Oxfam had made an appeal over the local

radio, for warm winter clothing for Bosnia. We heard this appeal at the time that we had become a little concerned about the mountain of packed boxes of clothing. They were sorted into:- babies 0-5years, 6- teens. ladies' and men's. The appeal had come at the right time, Denys phoned the number given and arranged for the Oxfam rep. to come and see what we had.

The offer was accepted and a team was sent into our warehouse complete with mobile gas heaters to sort through the already packed boxes. We were about to set off for yet another trip into Croatia on the 1st November.

Our wedding anniversary is on the 31st October, 1993 year was to be our 40th, the Ruby Wedding. Daughter Chris had invited us out to lunch on that day. Arriving at the Elm Tree Inn at Ringwood, we were very surprised to find all our family there to welcome us.

An even greater surprise came as a convoy of vehicles pulled into the car park. Tony B., Chuck and Iris, Chris from Weymouth and Rob and Lut, who, coincidently celebrate their wedding anniversary on the same day as ours. We didn't realise just how busy our daughter had been. After the gifts and cards from family and friends, there was a presentation by Jean of the B.C.A. She had got together with our daughters to nominate us for Esther Rantzen's *Hearts of Gold*. A letter told that there were more than the usual amount of nominations for that year. For those not featured in the T V programme a plaque had been sent along with the letter from Esther and Mike Smith the presenters. Our convoy colleagues presented us with a large framed photograph of our group standing with the burned out tank in the village of *Dracevac*.

On November 1st a late departure from Bournemouth owing to an invitation for drinks and a buffet in the Mayor's Parlour as members of Bournemouth Regatta and Carnival Committee. We then drove to Somerford to pick up our house guest for the trip.

Jack had accepted our offer so that he could see the end result of all his hard work in the warehouse. While we were away the work would continue. Tony with his wife Jill, Peter, and Jean, founder members of the B.C.A. would be there to deal with the Oxfam team.

NOVEMBER 1993

At Ramsgate we found Chris from Weymouth had already arrived. We sat and chatted in our warm and cosy little home, tea and anniversary cake for supper and then turned in. When setting out from our base in Dorset we never knew how many vehicles would be travelling with us until arriving at the docks. Tony B. always made the bookings on the ferry as he was local and had the contacts. Each of the drivers wanting to join any particular convoy would phone in vehicle registration number, how many were travelling, their passport numbers, weight of the load carried and length of vehicle. Our camper plus trailer was 10 metres.

This time just four vehicles boarded the *Sally Ferry*. Ours, Tony B., Chris with his small camper towing a horse box, and Tony no: 2 with his mate Don driving a seven and a half ton lorry. The last two were without C.B. radio.

In France we drove into thick fog, losing the lorry soon after leaving the docks. They caught up with us at the Belgian border with the aid of their itinerary and maps. On into Germany and our night stop at *Hockenheim*. 595 driving miles from Bournemouth. The next day on through fog and cold weather. We did our usual trick and burst a tyre on the trailer, a quick wheel change and reached the Austrian/Slovenian border by 10.30pm. 1,055 miles from home at our overnight stop at *Graz*.

Day three we were passing through Slovenia, with a stop at our friendly Vulcanizer. A new tyre cost us 10 marks, about four pounds. I think he must have stocked up on our size of tyres. Refuelled at a filling station near *Maribor*, diesel at £1.50 a gallon. Into Croatia by mid morning, at the border we were pleasantly surprised when the paperwork was processed quicker than usual. Heading for *Slavonski Brod* we burst another tyre. Luckily we had the spare and set off again.

On nearing the town we did it again, it was late at night and nowhere to get a replacement. Some of our load was transferred to the truck, the offending wheel was removed and we travelled on three. It was very late and in foul weather we pulled in beside the flats which housed hundreds of refugees from *Bosanski Brod* across the river. We parked door to door with Tony B's van and I made a pot stew for the eight of us, all squeezed into our camper for the meal. We settled down for the night with the sound of the wind, the rain and a machine in a nearby gravel pit.

In the morning, in better weather we strolled around to the *Antun Mihanovic Centre*, Two or three of the ladies were there and greeted us warmly. The boss was called on the phone and soon arrived in his little old car. He shook hands with all of us but we did have trouble in that we could not speak or understand each other's language. The vehicles were backed up to the doors and unloaded in turn. Willing hands seemed to materialise from nowhere.

We had all brought a good assortment of aid, such as canned food, rice, flour and sugar. Warm clothing and shoes, soap and shampoo, tooth brushes and toothpaste, toys, puzzles, games and sweets for the children. In our home town a well known maker of rock always donated some sticks of their sweet product for the children. After the work, we were given coffee in the office, with the ladies fussing around us.

We had become used to the hospitality of these people but Jack seemed a little overwhelmed. A female reporter turned up on the scene and asked questions about us and our convoy friends. Her questions were answered by Tomi, son of the head of the organisation, whom we believed to be *Antun Mihanovic*.

We each received a certificate of thanks, a rose vase and a tie pin with the *Slavonski Brod* crest. A lady called Nada, which means 'Hope' in Croatian, gave me a medallion of the Virgin Mary. She was learning English and asked me to write to her when we returned home. On leaving we mentioned that we were next heading for *Pakrac*. On hearing the route that we would be taking, Tomi told us of a much shorter way.

Then back to the vehicles for a tour of the river area and a sight of the blown up bridge for the benefit of our newer members. The river was the front line between the Serbs and the

Croats. Denys had his video camera with him as we walked in the damaged part of the town. We were stopped by police who warned "No photos." We could have been arrested for spying as the Serbs were only yards away on the other side of the river.

Slavonski Brod and *Pakrac* were only about fifty miles apart. The Serbs held the territory in between the two. Usually we drove north from *Slavonski Brod* to *Nasice*, then west to *Virovitica* before turning south to *Daruvar* and *Pakrac*. On old roads this meant about a four hour journey. Tomi had advised a shorter route by travelling west then turning north. As we followed his directions it was noticed that we seemed to be the only vehicles on that road. On coming up to a U.N. checkpoint we were informed that we should not have been on that road without an escort. We were in Serbian held territory.

By this time we were feeling a little tense about the situation we were in. Next came a police checkpoint, the chaps there just let us go on when Tony in the lead told them that we were making for *Pakrac*. We noticed a soldier standing watching as we drove on, he was wearing a blue-grey uniform which we hadn't seen before. To relieve the tension, Denys waved, to our relief the soldier waved back. A mile further on we passed a group of soldiers with machine guns; they were standing behind sand bags among the ruins of what had been a village.

This time we all waved, they looked a little surprised but they did wave back. Soon without any further encounters of the wrong kind, we arrived in *Pakrac*.

Until then only Tony and we knew what had been happening, as the two vehicles between us had no C.B. contact and had not heard the exchanges as we realised where we were.

In *Pakrac* town square, we parked next to the shell of a building which had been a supermarket and restaurant. We made for the office block which had requested typewriters and telephones on our last visit. We had arrived late on a Friday afternoon, and the place was closed for the week end. The owners of the bistro next door offered to take the office equipment and would make sure that it got to the right people.

While the rest of the team went to look around the town, Jack went with us to pay a visit to Anton our shoemaker friend. At his friends' house, Margaret and Stephan made us coffee,

87

when we asked about Anton, all we got was a shrug of the shoulders. We left them and their neighbours a couple of food parcels and some cooking oil.

Back in town we met up again with our group at the bistro, they were chatting to a young American woman and a young man who was Dutch. The boy was wearing shoes with the soles hanging off, Tony gave him a pair of his own size 10s. The young people told us that they were part of an organisation of volunteers working in war torn areas like *Pakrac*. Twenty of them, all different nationalities, were living in a house nearby. Jan, the American girl asked us back to the house to meet her colleagues.

As it was only walking distance we left the vehicles in the main street. Jan led us down a back street to a house, damaged like many others in the road. We met Lynette, another American, who told us about her work in schools with the local children. Others in the group were English, French, Polish and Danish. They were involved with helping to repair homes in the town. One of the American girls made us tea, telling us that she had been trained to make it the English way. During the chat we discovered that Jan was wanting to get to *Karlovac* to visit friends. As we would be going that way the next day, we offered her a lift which she accepted.

On returning to our vehicles we found that all the pennants and stickers had been removed, probably by souvenir hunters. Tony was very upset and blamed it on the local kids. We drove down to the blitzed hospital for our overnight stop. After a nightcap we settled in. It had started raining which was a relief, the war stopped in wet weather. I was still awake as the rain eased, then stopped. Then the bumps in the night started, double explosions, which Denys had at first kidded me on that it was only Concorde. He and Jack were sound asleep and I did feel rather alone.

A little later it all went quiet and I slept.

In the morning Jack and a couple of our crew who had not been there before went into the devastated hospital to see and take photographs of the damage by mortar, grenades, and machine gun fire. They found it shocking to see the operating theatre with the machines smashed, patients records and X-ray plates scattered around. From the hospital we made a stop at the Anneka school, some work was being carried out there. Both Tonys played tunes on the grand piano which had been brought from England for the *Challenge Anneka Program*. The floor of one of the classrooms which was seen being laid on the T V was a mess, the wood blocks were in heaps, ruined by damp.

We returned to town where some of the ladies from the office block were waiting at the bistro to see us. We helped to carry the equipment into the offices, and were soon drinking coffee with Veshna, the director. She thanked us for everything we had brought to help their town. A man came in and started talking quite urgently to her. With the aid of pen and paper he drew pictures and it took some time to get our men to understand the need, but finally the message got through, they needed a hammer drill. Denys just happened to have one in the toolbox of the camper. He fetched it out and donated it to *Pakrac*.

The sound of Tony's horns told us it was time to go. As we left the town centre, Anton and his friends were there on the corner to see us off. Jan was travelling with Tony and Glenda, our next call was to *Rangi Nekova* camp near *Zagreb*. It was a very wet day which had created a lot of mud around the camp area. As the men unloaded the supplies of clothing, shoes, food, baby food and Pampers, I stayed in the van handing out sweets to the kids milling around the vehicles. With no storeroom at this camp the aid had to be stacked outdoors whatever the weather. I gave a teddy to one little girl called Nicolina and took photos of the scene.

Jack had found a couple of dogs or rather they found him. He fed them with a packet of biscuits from our stores. We were able to admire Tony's goddaughter this time, she was brought out in her mother's arms to meet us. The last time we were there she was in hospital with whooping cough.

An hour later we were on our way to *Karlovac*, where Tony dropped Jan off at the railway station. No problems as we drove through the town and we made our way once again over the mountains in dense fog. As darkness fell the fog worsened but on the downward run to the coast the skies cleared.

Tony B. was to spend the night with his friends in *Rijeka*. Tony, Don, Glenda and Chris booked themselves in the *Ad*

Turres, while the three of us made ourselves comfortable in the car park.

The staff of the hotel were always very helpful to us, with discounts for convoy members staying overnight, allowing others like us to use the hotel toilets while sleeping in our vehicles. They even turned a blind eye to the 'campers' in the car park using the showers of paying guests.

The lorry still had some food parcels on board, they had decided to come and meet our friends from *Vukovar* and leave the goods for them. Nada welcomed all of us and had coffee ready, then all our goods were carried into the storeroom, leaving only the medical items for the clinic at *Rijeka*. We had brought some personal gifts for Nada and her family. A camera with film and photo albums, pet food for the little dog that they had adopted the last time we were there.

There was wool for the old lady who spent all her time knitting socks for the children, perfumed soaps for Ivana and a couple of cans of English beer for Boris. We enjoyed a walk along the shore, wonderful to stretch our legs after so much travelling. As we returned to the hostel we met up with a young English lady. She was asking for help for some refugees from *Karlovac*, who had not long been sent to a building just across the road. She had noticed a box of spectacles among the aid we had just unloaded and asked if we could bring some for her friends on our next visit. She also asked if we would post letters for her when we returned to the U.K.

Glenda had accepted a lift back home with Tony and Don, they and Chris were leaving right away. We, with Jack fancied a ride into *Crikvenica* town, which once had been a seaside holiday resort for tourists. We walked by the sea and admired the boats, each owner boasted what good value their trips were. We met the Captain of a Polish ship, he was very interested in what we were doing in the area.

Back in the camper we relaxed over a cup of tea and we all fell asleep in the warm sunshine. As darkness fell we made our way back to the hotel, had a meal, played cards and settled in for the night. Next morning we went along to say goodbyes to our friends. Boris shyly asked Denys if we could possibly get him an old bike, even one which needed attention would do. Jack overheard his request and mentioned that he had a bike in his shed at home which he no longer needed.

The ladies in the kitchen asked if we could get them a heavy duty can opener. The one they were using was just about worn out. We promised that we would do our best and that we hoped to be back in December. We left then, to meet with Tony B. He took us to a warehouse in *Rijeka*, a distribution point for medical centres in the area. It was being run by three lovely ladies under the *Sathai Sai Organisation*. In one corner of the building a small shrine had been set up in honour of *Sai Baba*, an Indian Holy man.

Natasha, the daughter of one of the team, was suffering from cerebral palsy and was joining in the banter and laughter from her wheel chair. She was delighted with some air show stickers which Denys put on her chair. A large amount of Pampers and blankets were left there to be sent to hospitals.

One more call to make to a clinic for unregistered refugees, most of these were people who had fled from their burning homes. Without having time to take documents such as birth certificates they had no way to prove their identity or nationality. They did not get help from the Government or other official sources. The baby milk, cough mixture, disinfectant and dressings would help just a little. We were invited to meet some of the medical staff in an upstairs room for coffee and we each were given a very nice letter of thanks for our help.

Then we started the long journey home.

After each trip we came home and more or less hibernated for a couple of days, resting and recharging our batteries. While we had been away, Oxfam had removed seven tons of winter clothing from our stocks in the warehouse. Good, because we would never have been able to get it all to where it was needed ourselves.

Our fame as a charity was spreading, we even had lorry loads of donated goods arrive from as far afield as Birmingham. A firm in Southampton got in touch and offered a load of canned and packet foods, all on pallets and cling film wrapped. We stopped asking for clothing, we had so much. The unsuitable or unusable textiles were bagged and sold for rags, giving us the much needed money to fund our missions.

One question we were often asked was, why didn't we hire huge trucks to take larger quantities of goods? First and foremost lorries cost a great deal of money to hire and fund. Fuel and ferry for one truck would cost more than two or three smaller vehicles. The camps in the former Yugoslavia are usually inaccessible to large vehicles.

We felt that by taking the goods to the people in the camps, part of what we take is ourselves, showing a despairing community that the world cares about their plight.

We pride ourselves that we have made a mark, by giving 'hand to hand and heart to heart'. We laughed with them and cried with them. We cannot change the brutality of a civil war but we might ease the suffering a little. We ourselves were lucky in the fact that we had the time, the strength, the motivation and the support of the B.C.A. and the public. This enabled us to go on supporting groups of human beings struggling against the odds to survive.

DECEMBER 1993

Our seventh mission with the Convoy of Hope was eventful and successful in spite of snow and icy conditions. Our first destination in Croatia was to a row of small houses opposite an army base in *Nasice*. Refugees living there were from the devastated town of *Vukovar*. As food parcels were handed over, toys and sweets were given to the children, refreshments were on hand to any one willing to accept the offer by very warm hearted and hospitable people. They had very few personal possessions of their own. Soon every child in sight was loaded with toys, gifts and chocolate; each household was given goods from our loads. Photographs were taken with many cameras, but there was a problem as we started to leave. Armed soldiers barred our path with machine guns at the ready. Young women from our vehicles had taken snaps of the military establishment and soldiers on guard duty.

The convoy was not allowed to move until the rolls of film were handed over. This served as a reminder for those regarding it as a holiday trip, that we were in a war zone. With us on this trip, was a lady who worked hard in our warehouse packing and sorting goods given for our appeal. Jean mentioned that she would like to join us on one of our treks to the camps. She was a friend of Jack's who was our houseguest on the November convoy. When we asked her to come with us this month, she thought at first that it was one of Dukes' leg-pulls.

On then to the *Antun Mihanovic* centre. We had plenty of food parcels and toiletries for the families resettled in the area. Toys and shoe box gifts were left for St. Nicholas to distribute and there were refreshments in the hall with the group of lovely lively ladies, they had great fun trying on Duke's (Denys's) Stetson.

Giving them chance to laugh is as morale boosting as the

aid we carried. Photos taken this time would be shown on our next visit. After a night stop in the parking area of a social club, we drove on to the battle-scarred town of *Pakrac*, the journey took most of one day. Wintery conditions and rough country roads slowed our drivers considerably. We arrived well after dark and parked behind the friendly shelter of the hospital.

A meeting was held the next morning, in one of the repaired and redecorated rooms of the hospital. The plan for unloading was discussed and on returning to our vehicles, I slipped on an icy path. As a couple of colleagues rushed to help me up, we all realised that my left arm had been dislocated at the elbow. A doctor in town tried to give me a pain killing injection, I was wearing so many layers of clothing that he needed help in finding some flesh in which to plunge the needle.

The nearest hospital with X-ray was at *Kutina* about twelve miles away. A young lady from the Farron (Pharoah) Bistro came with me and Denys in a small ambulance to be our interpreter. At the hospital I received V.I.P. treatment, bones set in place and no charge. The surgeon gave us a letter to present to our doctor on returning home. I was a little worried about how our doctor would understand Croatian, then realised that medical language is universal.

On returning to *Pakrac*, Jean was missing. With the urgency of getting me to hospital, Denys had locked the camper. Jean, left out in the cold had gone into town in one of the other vehicles. We followed suit feeling very guilty about leaving her in the lurch. The month before, we had met with a group of young volunteers who were working in conjunction with the U.N. assisting the local population to survive. Our team was so impressed by the work they were doing and their friendliness to us, we asked if we could bring them anything to make life a little easier.

They had two requests, soft toilet rolls and an old washing machine. The first had been easy, the second, well, we had a brand new twin tub machine in our trailer. At home we talked to many people about our experiences and of things needed. A very generous and sweet lady from Christchurch had been inspired by our story of the youngsters working by choice in such conditions. Also of the fact that not all young people are vandals or selfish. This lady took me shopping and asked to see a twin tub machine. As she paid for her purchase she told me it was her Christmas present to God.

We also left a large box of toiletries for the guys and gals.

We felt so privileged to be middlemen, taking the generosity of folks at home and enjoying the gratitude of the folks receiving it.

Setting out from *Pakrac* that evening was extremely hazardous, the day had been sunny and warm melting the snow slightly. Darkness had brought on a big freeze, turning the road into a skating rink. Our twenty-vehicle convoy slipped and slid along for about four miles and two of the vans had a slight collision on one of the steep hills. Denys suggested to Tony that it might be better to go back to *Pakrac* and get a better start in daylight the next day. Everyone agreed and we turned all the vehicles round using part of a driveway to extend the width of the road. Vans with trailers were able to turn around in one go. We then returned to the shelter of the bombed out hospital in *Pakrac*. Empty and devastated as the building was, someone had taken the trouble to put up a small Christmas tree with lights at the main entrance.

While talking over the day's events, Denys realised that the route we had taken in the ambulance that morning, would have taken us onto the road we used to *Zagreb*. On looking at the map it was agreed that we would go that way. Although it was along the front line with Serbs on our left about 1000 yards away for a few miles, there were no hills. It also saved us quite a few miles cutting out the wide berth we were giving the Serb occupied areas. We were soon entering *Kutina*, We had only taken about 45 minutes to get to the town which normally would have taken a couple of hours.

Two refugee camps on the outskirts of *Zagreb* were now home to people from *Vukovar*. We split the convoy there to visit both camps. The one to take delivery of our goods, was for 35 families living in squalor. Each vehicle unloading in turn, food, soap, candles and matches, disposable nappies, toilet rolls, sanitary towels, and family medicines. We also carried shoeboxes, all marked for a boy or girl, the contents of each chosen for the sex and age group written on the label.

Our boxes came from Spetisbury School and patients and staff at Christchurch hospital. Each one was lovingly wrapped and decorated. After the work the crews were entertained by families in their living quarters, the curtained sections of the huts were quite cosy with blankets on the floor for warmth. The hospitality was warm, many of the new convoy people vowed to come back and help their new friends to survive.

Late afternoon when we started down the narrow lane from the camp to the motorway. Tony B. leading the way got his van stuck in the deep snow and ice. He made a few attempts at getting free but without success. One of the vans returning from the other camp had heard over the C.B. what was happening. He put snow chains on his van, came in and towed Tony out of trouble.

While we waited during this operation, it gave our heavy vehicle time to settle in the deep frozen ruts left by our vehicles going in earlier. Behind us were Bill and Gillian in a four-wheel drive *Frontera*, which could have towed us out easily if it could have passed us. Bill and Gillian borrowed shovels from a lady who had seen what was happening and was standing by. The couple dug us out foot by foot. This was fine until we started sliding towards a telegraph pole, which loomed up on my side of the cab.

By that time Tony had dropped his trailer, put his snow chains on and came to pull us out the last few yards. From *Zagreb* the convoy was splitting up, some drivers with hired vehicles had to get back to the U.K. The rest of us planned to take the road south to the coast.

The snow gradually disappeared, those of us who had been wearing thermals were feeling slightly overdressed. While travelling in the mountains my damaged arm started to swell, I had to get Denys to cut the plaster from the shoulder down to just above the elbow to ease the tightness. On through rain and fog arriving at the *Ad Turres* at 1am. One of the transits was having mechanical problems, a decision was made to take it into a garage in the morning. Some of the crew including Jean, booked into the hotel for the night.

We paid a visit to Nada and friends in the morning. On our previous trip Boris had asked for a bike. Jack had overheard and had sent his own trusty steed out for the lad. He told us that it had been lying unused in his shed for some time. The bike had travelled all the way from England on our roof rack in all weathers and was not looking its best. Sixteen year old Boris was delighted with it. Another special gift was a sewing machine which we had brought for Evitsa, the lady who spent her time hand sewing pieces of material together for cushions and bedspreads. We had managed to get a heavy-duty can opener for the kitchen, a gift from one of our top hotels in Bournemouth.

Most of our goods were for this refuge and we had kept about 50 gift boxes for the children. They were handed over to Nada, to be put away until the traditional Christmas Day, December 25th as the families here were not Moslems. Some of our travelling companions still had sweets and goodies which they fetched from their vans for the kids. Nada insisted that we all stayed for lunch, this was where it became embarrassing for most of us.

To turn down their hospitality did offend these wonderful people. Soon sausages and chips for twelve of us were set out in the dining room.

We could never hope to remember the names of all the lovely characters met in that hostel, but now and again a smiling face would peep around the door and wave hello. We spent some time thanking everyone for the hospitality. Then returned to the rendezvous to discuss plans. As a result of an injury to one of our members on the September trip to *Zadar*, a pledge had been made to take medical supplies to the hospital involved as a thank you gesture. The van that was in for repair, was to have been used by one of the team hoping to make the journey down the coast. To overcome the problem, Denys offered to take the parcels of dressings and medical equipment onto our trailer. With the crew in the camper we could set out at 6am. the next morning.

As the sun arose we enjoyed the spectacular scenery. At *Prizna* we took the ferry to *Pag Island* the fare 250,000 dinar, about £25 return. A 20 minute crossing and one hour drive across the island. *Pag* was a 'safe area', protected by the U.N. with anti-aircraft gun emplacements. Families from *Zadar* sent their children to the island at times when their city was under attack.

Driving across the causeway and past the harbour with its yachts and small craft, we parked at the *Kalovare Hotel* as before. Children had been playing in the parking area, as soon as our engines were stopped they crowded around the vehicles. Sad faced tots and cheeky older lads looking for sweets and chocolate. Some of them remembered Denys with his Stetson and came looking for the 'cowboy'. We had nothing much left in the way of goodies, only a couple of dozen pens, some one else had some lollipops. Jean handed these out trying to get the kids to queue up English style, to make sure that they all got a share. Our crew members got in line to show how it was done, the kids thought it great fun to get a lolly and a pen then run round to the end of the queue to get more.

I was still feeling sorry for myself, nursing a well-plastered arm and a bruised ego but I could still take photos of the scene. The trailer was offloaded and the girls were taken off for a tour of the hospital, they came back to us looking very upset. Around the corridors of the hospital they had seen photographs of women and children, lying in the streets, where they had been slaughtered by the Serbs.

A nurse from the hospital invited us to her parents' home, not far from the hospital for refreshments. Outside the house stood a huge truck. It belonged to our new friend's father, he was employed by a local building firm but now there was no work. He told us that he washed and cleaned his lorry every day to be ready when the time came. They survived on £5 a week government grant.

The family consisted of Majda the nurse, her parents, her brother and sister and her small daughter Anne-Marie, nicknamed 'Tinka'. She was four years old and had recently come home from *Pag* because things had been quiet during the past three weeks. One of the girls had given Tinka a teddy bear and she kept us amused while we sat and drank the thick black coffee.

Late afternoon as we left the house and couldn't help noticing that next door but one had been demolished by shells, a realisation that we were within range of Serbian guns. We boarded the ferry before dark and found the boat almost empty. For some reason the fare had gone up to 300,000 dinar, £30!!

Not speaking the language we couldn't argue.

Back at *Crikvenica* we popped in on our friends to say goodbye. Boris had been working hard on the bike, it shone like new. They wished us a safe journey. One more drop at the Primary Health Care clinic in *Rijeka*. A nebuliser, Pampers, disinfectants, medicines and a large box of dental care products given by a dentist in Christchurch.

While we took coffee in the director's office, a letter of thanks for the supplies we had brought was typed out along with a request for more technical items than we could hope to obtain. The director gave us an interesting short history of events leading up to the civil war, as he saw it. Then presented us with a souvenir plaque from the port of *Rijeka*.

We were ready then for the long trek home, from the warmth of the Adriatic back to the cold harsh winter of Austria and Germany. There we ran into snow and blizzards. Near *Stuttgart* the traffic was almost at a standstill, the snow was so thick. Then as we drove across a viaduct a blanket of snow came up over the cab and windscreen. At a crawl Denys got us safely into a motorway service area. We spent the night huddled among the huge trucks and hoped that we wouldn't wake up snowed in.

In the morning, what a surprise. The snow had gone and it was raining. Driving towards *Heilbrohn* we made a slight detour to visit a nephew who lived near *Darmstadt*. After an hour with Paul and his family we made for *Ostende*, the ferry was just about ready to leave. On showing our return ticket we were rushed on board and we reached home at 8pm. on December 13th.

I had my arm checked out at Bournemouth hospital. When it was found that I could not move my thumb I was sent for X-ray. It was found that I had a fracture in the wrist, it was replastered and I was told to return in six weeks. After the experiences of ice and snow on the continent, the English winter months did not seem so harsh. We were soon making plans for another convoy in the New Year. If our family thought that we were mad, they were kind enough to their aged parents not to say so. We had wonderful get-togethers over the Christmas period.

JANUARY 1994

Son Mike was working at Bournemouth Airport, one of his workmates Dave, was keen to join our next mission. We often had young men offering to join us as a second driver, mostly they were looking for an easy ride, or a holiday to foreign parts. We would tell them to fill a van, raise some funds and really take part in an aid convoy. Dave did this with a friend Paul, who was a student at college. They hired a transit from Verwood Van Hire and filled it with goods from our stocks in the warehouse. With their load, ours and one other van from the convoy four tons of goods were on their way from Dorset to *Mostar*.

Mike came along with us, and we left on the 11th January. Eight vehicles left for the continent and at the Slovenian border we found that the rules had been changed. As from the 1st January we were to have an escort. As we drove the 30 miles across their country, it was a good thing that we didn't have need for a tyre this time. The escort vehicle was a small car following our convoy of four transits, one Range Rover, two lorries one of them on loan from the Body Shop, and our motor home. At the Croatian border more problems, the fact that we intended going into Bosnia complicated matters somewhat. An hour later and all the questions answered to the satisfaction of the officials on duty, we were on our way heading for *Zagreb*.

From the city, which was not touched by the war so far, we took the motorway to *Karlovac* which was regularly shelled by Serbian forces. All quiet as we drove through in close convoy. From *Karlovac* over the mountain roads to the coast. The change in temperature as we travelled was amazing. Taking the descent to *Rijeka* after dark, a new moon was shining over the port and its oil refinery flame could be seen way below.

Some of our crew had been sleeping in vehicles loaded to the doors, so a night in the *Ad Turres* hotel was a luxury. A modest charge for a room with shower, and breakfast. During the evening we made a visit to our refugee friends, our daughter Chris had donated a knitting machine to the community. Nada, the house mother-cum-social worker of the group was the same age as Chris.

We were told on this visit that Nada had been ill of late, stress of the job and living for two and a half years in an hotel with no hope for a future was taking its toll. We handed over the knitting machine and a good stock of wool. The young people at the *Odmaraliste* learn English in school so there was no problem (nama problem) with communication. We mentioned that we were going to *Mostar* and they seemed very concerned for our safety.

The morning was warm and sunny, hard to believe that we had been travelling in winter conditions over the previous two days. We headed out for *Zadar*, travelling along the wonderful Adriatic coast. With lovely weather, gorgeous scenery and good company over the C.B. we all felt in a holiday mood. Our previous route had been by way of *Pag Island* but a weak bridge made it a no go for the trucks.

At a checkpoint we asked advice, the police told us that the main road was now open. We had known that the *Meslenica Bridge* had been destroyed, which had been the reason for using the ferry. We carried on not knowing what to expect. From there on police and army personnel were much in evidence. We received a few curious glances but we were not stopped.

Soon we were passing badly damaged houses and buildings. A detour took us from the main road to where there had been a ferry crossing, we drove down the road which had been used by the ferry passengers in better times. Passing a row of damaged houses with roped off areas and small piles of earth here and there. Above these were hung signs saying 'MINE' or 'MINA'. Signs of a camera with a red line across it were along the roadside every few yards, NO PHOTOS. What was left of the ferryboat could be seen half submerged, close to it was a makeshift structure of concrete slabs on pontoons, edged with hundreds of motor tyres. Plenty of heavy traffic was using this bridge so we ventured across. Metal ramps between the slabs made a great deal of noise as we rattled and bumped our way across.

101

High above us were the remains of the original bridge, just a few yards of the structure hanging suspended from the cliffs on either side. We found out later that the tyres were in place on the temporary bridge, to protect it by deflecting bombardment.

On through *Zadar*, passing a bus depot with burned and smashed vehicles scattered around the compound like a child's discarded toys. In spite of the warnings not to take photos in the restricted area the temptation to bring home evidence of wanton destruction was too much. I for one took a couple of sneaky pictures.

Watching a glorious sunset as we travelled, we arrived in *Split* and made for the docks, it was hard to believe that we were in the same country. Massive sky scrapers and well lit shops were a great contrast to towns we had seen.

At the docks we settled in to wait overnight. We were to meet with a convoy arriving on an early morning ferry from *Ancona*. Fifteen vehicles travelling under the name of 'The Medugorje Appeal', were from Godstone in Surrey. We had been informed that their aim was to bring injured children out of the besieged town of *Mostar* and hoped to assist in this operation.

We watched as the vehicles disembarked. There were ex-army trucks, old ambulances, Land Rovers and an elderly battered coach. After an exchange between their convoy leader and ours, they led the way out into the morning traffic and onto the coast road. Through pretty seaside towns and villages, skirting harbours with fishing boats bobbing at their moorings. Then we took a turning inland onto mountain roads for a change. The weather changed too, mist which turned into rain.

With a sheer drop to one side our drivers took the twists, turns and hairpin bends very slowly. At times we had a good view of all the vehicles strung out along the mountain ledges. There were a few hold-ups when the old coach made heavy going on a couple of the steep turns. After an hour of the slow and steady pace we started to descend, passing through scattered villages and stared at by curious kids.

Arriving at the Bosnian border, we were called to a halt. The trucks and our two lorries were opened up for inspection by customs officials, papers were examined and we were through.

The Godstone crowd had passed through this way many times before. They led us to a restaurant which provided us all with a very good meal. Mixed grills with a choice of wine, beer or a soft drink for ten marks a head, about £4. Our two groups mingled, chatting and socialising.

Fed and rested, we drove the short distance to *Medugorje* where we parked in the main street. We were all informed that bed and breakfast accommodation was available to those wanting a comfortable bed for the night. *Medugorje*, the name means a village surrounded by mountains, was virtually unknown until in the 1980's. Then a vision of the Virgin Mary was said to have appeared to six young people on a hillside near the village. Since then *Medugorje* had become the most visited town in the Christian world.

The town itself seemed to us, to be a weird mixture of very quaint old mountain village with very modern villas. Souvenir shops, bars and bistros, looking as though they had been thrown up in a hurry along the rough and unmade roads. Almost opposite our parking spot we could see a warehouse, the story was going around that the 'Medugorje Appeal' people were expecting our convoy to unload all our aid there. None of our drivers were happy about this, the feeling was that we had not come this far to leave our goods to sit in a warehouse for weeks. It must go to where it was intended, which was to *Mostar*.

Having time on our hands while the situation was being sorted, we locked the vehicles and took a stroll round the town. We found that many of the souvenir shops selling rosaries, candles and statuettes of the Madonna would accept dollars and sterling and the assistants spoke English. At the far end of the village was a pretty church with twin towers. To one side of the entrance stood a statue of the Virgin Mary in pure white stone. In front of the figure was a bench where local ladies sat in silent prayer or meditation.

Nearby was a large information board showing a map of the area, with a pathway to 'The Hill Of Apparitions', the hill is topped by a very large cross. A legend tells that way back in history, local Christians would take unbelievers to the top of this hill and throw them to their deaths. The villagers put an end to the practice and built the cross. The women had carried buckets

103

of cement and water up the rough track and the men fashioned the sixty foot high cross. The legend tells that at times THE CROSS GLOWS.

Some of our group were keen to make the climb, which they were told normally takes one and a half hours. I knew that I was not up to the challenge, Denys thought that it would be too strenuous after a long day of driving. Mike decided to give it a go along with our friend Rev: David. They dressed up warmly and set off with torches in their hands. They returned a couple of hours later to say that they were unable to find the path in the dark.

Sunday morning and we awoke to the sound of the church bells, later we took a stroll to take photos of the church. As we returned we met up with an English lady, at first we took her to be local because she was all dressed in black. She explained that she had been expecting a delivery of aid which should have arrived on the convoy to which we had become attached. No one had been able to tell her the whereabouts of her goods. They were labelled 'The Don Ivan Marko Trust'.

She left us then to talk to Tony B. Not long after their conversation a message came over the C.B. "We are moving out, destination *Mostar*."

The lady named Sheila and her friend Mary, had offered to be our guides into the city. They assured us that they knew the area well enough and that we would not be in danger from snipers as long as we kept clear of the Moslem part of the city. Only fifteen miles from the quiet and peaceful village where pilgrims still arrived by coach, to the active war zone. One mile before the town we arrived at a police checkpoint, all the vehicles were opened and searched, for weapons.

The guards were a very friendly and cheerful lot, one policeman exchanged hats with our lorry driver John and invited us to take photos of them together. Satisfied at last that we were only carrying what was stated on our lists, we were free to go on. The road took us down a very long and winding hill, giving us a bird's eye view of *Mostar* in the valley. In a 'no photo' area we could see a great deal of damage as we drove through the streets.

Hearing the sound of distant gunfire, we each got a little closer to the vehicle in front, while hoping that our guides would not take a wrong turning. I didn't think that a cheery wave would have got us out of trouble this time. Sheila had decided that the best place to take our goods would be to a hospital on the outskirts of town. This was a huge square building and named The White Hospital on the Hill. From a distance we could all see that a huge hole had been blown through the front of the building, damaging two floors.

We were introduced to the doctor in charge, Doctor Ben was a big, cheerful black doctor from Ghana. He spoke English and Croatian. There were plenty of staff to help us unload, some one found a couple of wheelbarrows to help get the job done. All the food, toiletries and medical items were stacked in the hospital storeroom. On seeing the toys we were carrying, Doctor Ben invited us into the children's wards in a separate building. Twenty children in wards equipped to take one hundred patients. We were relieved to know that none of them were injured from the war.

We met a couple of newborn babes with their proud mums. A sweet dark eyed little girl of about one year old who had been abandoned by her gypsy family because she had an eye defect. A lovely little lad with cerebral palsy, he looked so happy in his mother's arms and gave us a chuckle when I gave him a soft squeaky duck to cuddle. Each cot and bed had at least two new toys, large teddies and cuddlies had found loving arms. All the time we were there we did not hear one child cry.

Anxious to leave before dark, we dragged ourselves away, although the hospital seemed miles from anywhere, there were the usual crowd of youngsters hanging around the vans looking for sweets and goodies.

Back at *Medugorje* there was no sign of the Godstone convoy and we were not sure what they had planned to do. We were all satisfied that we had completed our mission into *Mostar* and planned to leave first thing the next morning. We retraced our journey and arrived at *Ad Turres* hotel some ten hours later. Some of the drivers decided to press on after a meal. With two drivers to each vehicle they would be home in twenty-four hours.

We stayed on overnight to visit Nada and friends before leaving. Dave and Paul in the transit decided to tag along with us because they had not been able to meet any refugees on the trip. An hour at *Odmaraliste* gave them a chance to hear some of the stories of *Vukovar* and its people. Then it was time to hit the road for home. With two days of bitterly cold weather we crossed the continent to arrive home on the 20th January.

MARCH 1994

Elisabeth, a friend from our roaming days, owned a farm in Buckinghamshire. She had envied our free and easy life travelling in a motorhome and had decided to buy one for herself. She had never been out of this country before. So we thought it very courageous of her when she decided that she would like to fill a trailer and join us on the next mission. A couple of her cousins offered to run the farm in her absence. She came to Bournemouth to fill her trailer from our stocks ready for take off in early March. Jack, our warehouse manager, had volunteered to be Elisabeth's second driver.

With her Autotrail and our Autostratus both tugging trailers packed with supplies, we drove to Kent. We were to pick up a passenger for the trip. Mike an old R.A.F. mate of thirty years standing had been waiting a chance to join us on one of our missions. He and his wife Anne had collected some of the goods we had taken to the camps on previous trips.

Elisabeth and Jack had gone on to Ramsgate. We spent an hour with Mike's family and spent the night on a nearby layby. In the morning we picked up Mike and his gear along with a couple of pies that Anne had made to keep us from starving en route. At the docks we found that our friends were having problems.

The tow bar was coming adrift from Elisabeth's camper, and two wheels on the trailer had seized up. The A. A. had been called. The chap said that he could weld or remove the tow bar, whichever they did, the trailer was still out of action. After discussing the situation they decided to go back to Christchurch. No point in going on without the aid.

One other vehicle was a 'no go'. While the drivers were at a B & B. for the night their vehicle had been vandalized. It was unsuitable for a long journey. We renewed friendships and met new faces. Robin and Lut (Loot), Tony B., Patsy and Bryn, Steve and Sharon, Denise and a couple of lads. Rachel and Wendy, two nurses from Canterbury, Mike, Pauline and George in an A.A. van. We were to meet Chuck and Iris, on the other side as they were travelling across the channel by Hovercraft from Dover.

At *Ostende* we pulled into a lorry park to regroup into our travelling positions. Tony's transit and trailer leading, Rob and Lut with the Land Rover Discovery and trailer, five assorted transits, our motor home and trailer and the AA van bringing up the rear. For the first time every vehicle was fitted out with a C.B. radio. which made things easier on a three thousand mile trip. The *Brussels* bypass in the rush hour split us up from time to time but the contact on the C.B. was still there.

Travelling across the continent was second nature to us by then. Anne's pie and coffee from the flask kept us going. With Mike as navigator I was able to relax. We arrived at *Hockenheim* around midnight. I stowed away all the loose articles which had been thrown on the back seat, this was to be converted into Mike's bed. We turned in, snug in our beds, while those in the vans made themselves as comfortable as they could.

In Austria, it became very cold in the mountains, with traces of snow in the fields and forests. Racing on through tunnels and paying at the tollbooth, while our colleagues had to get documents stamped, gave us extra time to stop and have a hot meal. Then onto *Gralla Services* for our second night stop.

In the morning all were ready at 10am. We headed south for the Slovenian border. As usual Tony took the paperwork for all the vehicles into the customs offices. We sat in the sun and waited. There was quite a pleasant atmosphere until Tony walked past our van not looking too pleased. He came to tell us that the Slovenians were demanding half the load from each vehicle or 5000 marks, to allow us to drive the 30 miles across their country.

We waited while our convoy leader talked them out of the idea. They settled for 25 marks for each vehicle after a lot of argument. They seemed to change the rules every time we passed through.

Our refuelling stop in *Maribor* with petrol and diesel at

£1.40 per gallon. On to tackle the border from exit Slovenia and entry Croatia. Then the long road to *Slavonski Brod* and the *Antun Mihanovic Centre* where a group of cheery women came to meet us. Out came the coffee and the slivovic, home made plum brandy. We had acquired quite a taste for this spirit over the past months. A social get-together to welcome us back, the unloading could wait until the morning.

Some of the young refugee lads from the flats came to see us, one of them called out, "Where is Tim Fail?" We had to explain that Tim, our son, had not been able to join us this time. He had made many young friends and received some startling souvenirs at times. The young lad wrote Tim a letter saying how he was sad that he had not come to Croatia.

Some of the convoy members had made friends with families in the flats on previous visits and now had time to relax and socialise with them. The slivovic and the warm welcome had put us all in a happy mood. Part of the aid we brought to these lovely people is the ability to make them laugh, We did not have a problem with the language as laughter and tears are universal. We learned words as we talked together, local teenagers were a great help as they were learning English in their schools.

We spent a fairly quiet night in our own bed, the constant drone of machinery from the nearby gravel pit was the only sound. Some of our people had been offered accommodation in various forms, some on the floor in the hall, others in the flats. We woke up to rain and around ten o'clock got the vehicles sorted and ready for unloading. Each vehicle was to leave what was deemed to be most useful at this place. When it was our turn we unloaded food, toilet rolls, soaps and toothpaste, baby milk and Pampers.

I had made up personal gift packs for the ladies who entertained us so well. Magdalena, Gloria, Nada, Meira, Maria and one or two I could not pronounce, let alone spell. Little presents such as perfume, note pads and cosmetics. After the work we were invited for refreshments in the hall. A chap came in with a large bag, from it he produced a number of small packages rather like fish and chips. All 21 of our convoy members were given one of the parcels, inside each was a large bun with a filling of small spicy sausages and raw onion, very tasty and filling.

Coffee and Coca-cola, and slivovic for those with strong enough stomachs after the night before. This local brew was very cheap to buy in the market at 20,000 dinar a bottle, less than £2. The plan for the afternoon was to visit the convent, as we left the hall we were asked to return at seven for supper. The *Antun Mihanovic Centre* was run by local folks, not refugees and they were trying to support those who were.

The convent stands on the banks of the River Sava, which was the front line and the border between the Serbs and Croats. The buildings were pockmarked by mortar shells and bullets. Every member of the convoy found bits and pieces for the Sisters who were always pleased to have us drop by. Soaps, toilet rolls, rice and a couple of sacks of potatoes were warmly received by the nuns. We were entertained in one of the long rooms which overlooked the river, it was good to see that glass had been replaced in the windows and that the shutters were open, a good sign.

Home made wine and little cakes were laid out for us. Later we took a few quiet moments in the church. Then a look in the vestment room so that the new ones with us could admire the magnificent piece of furniture, which we had been told was carved from one gigantic block of wood. A couple of our group asked when the church was built, a lady with the help of a priest gave us a brief history.

The Church Of The Holy Trinity was built in 1639 in the Baroque style, I could not hope to remember all that we were told. Some of the religious statues and paintings had been stored away for the duration of the war but we could admire the wonderful intricate carvings. From the convent we drove to the worst hit part of the town, giving the new ones among us a few memories of a city ravaged by war, with warnings not to take photos near the river.

Back at the flats, and a good old cup of English tea, then decided to get an hour's rest. We dozed a while but children kept knocking on the vehicles or looking through the windows. At seven on the dot, we were called on the C.B. to ask if we were going to the hall. Tony, Robin and Lut were there but no one else had turned up. We arrived to find a table loaded with local delicacies prepared by the ladies for all of us. Our hosts Antun and his son, Tomislav were very entertaining, while we were pressed into trying some of the cold buffet. Cheese, spiced meats, pickles, little spiced sausages, crispy bacon pieces and loads of the fresh bread that we all enjoyed so much. We tried to make up for our missing mates, the food was tasty, the company great. Tony told some of his jokes with Tomi helping by translating them, line by line.

Mostly the expressions and sign language alone were enough to get the company in hysterics.

Chuck and Iris turned up with apologies, they had been entertained in a refugee flat and hadn't the heart to leave the family with whom they had become involved. Later a few more members turned up, the excuse was that they thought that it would be like an English party, where no-one turned up early. We found out that Tomi, was a disc jockey on the local radio, playing British music of the sixties. In all we had a great evening.

Another night in the car park of the flats, we were beginning to get used to the droning machinery. Denys took the chance to fill our water tank from a tap in the hall, most of the external taps were shut off at this time of the year. While this was going on the ladies started to arrive for work. They would distribute the goods we had brought to the needy families.

Nada had brought presents for us, a bottle of wine and crochet tablemats which had been made by her mother. The sound of 'Echo One's' horn got everyone into the vehicles and we set off. As we travelled towards *Kutina* I found the local station on the radio, heard Tomi's voice as he introduced an Elvis record.

Tony was telling our newer convoy members over the C.B. how we had taken what we had believed to be a short cut to *Pakrac*, he laughed and said that we wouldn't do that again in a hurry. This time we followed directions given by a couple of drivers and navigators who had checked with friends before leaving *Slavonski Brod*. These friends had said not to go through *Nova Gradiska*.

Travelling from *Slavonski Brod* was not as simple as it

seemed from looking at a map. The Serbs had control of a wedge shaped territory and we had to skirt around that area. After taking one road we saw signs pointing ahead for *Nova Gradiska*, then we turned off in what we hoped would be the right direction. Then Denys and Tony started to recognise some of the scenery. Yes, we were on the same route as before!!

Before long we started to see soldiers in the blue/grey uniform of the Serbian troops squatting behind sandbags among the blitzed houses of what was left of the village. What could we do but wave as we passed? Well, it had worked before! We would soon be on first name terms if we kept passing through their lines. At the checkpoint, nothing was said about our being there. The shortcut had reduced our journey by about three hours.

In *Pakrac* we parked next to the office blocks, closed as it was Saturday. Some of us went into the Faroan Bistro. Emira, daughter of the family running the bar, had been very kind and helpful when I fell on the ice in December. She had been with me at the hospital to act as interpreter while I was X-rayed and treated for a dislocated elbow. We had brought a large hamper for Emira and her family as a thank you.

Chuck and Iris had befriended the family some months before. They had told us that Mama was Serbian, Papa was a Moslem and their three daughters were born in Croatia. At the time of the battle in *Pakrac*, Fikret had defended his home and family. He had slept on a table in the bar at night to keep the invaders at bay. A bullet hole in one of the plate glass windows could tell a story. The bistro was right opposite the burnt out shell of a building where we had parked on our first visit to the town just one year before. Since our last visit the bar had enjoyed a face-lift, with red seating and coloured lights in the ceiling.

While those who had medical aid to unload were coping with the job, I took Mike inside the deserted hospital. We walked down the empty corridors, on one door was written in English 'The only good Serbs are dead Serbs.' That evening, as usual we were fed, chicken stew and a jug of sweet tea. On the table a couple of large plates were filled with little jam pastries. After the meal we drove into town, anxious to meet some of the young volunteers, we found the house where the group were living and to our surprise found Emira visiting as well. A nice young lady made us a cup of tea then one of the chaps came to tell us about the work they were doing in *Pakrac*. From clearing rubble to cleaning bricks for re-use, helping the elderly in their homes and children in the schools. The town had a dividing line, not only did the volunteers help on the Croat side of town, They were helping the Serbian families as well.

They were partly responsible for the cease-fire. Unofficially, *Pakrac* had been peaceful for the six months that the volunteers had been in residence. Most of the young people stayed for three weeks then were replaced by others. They were of many different nationalities and used English as their common language. We had brought some early learning books for use in their school projects.

The house they were using at that time had been damaged. In their spare time they were repairing walls, making it suitable for a family to live in. Then they would move into another damaged property to do the same. We were taken to the second building which was being used as an office and sleeping quarters. One room was labelled 'SNORING' and another 'NON-SNORING'.

We asked if it was possible to get a picture of the washing machine we had brought in December, it was in the bathroom and a young lady was in the tub. She just drew the shower curtain around her and allowed me to get the photo of the machine. We were assured that it was well used. Some of the resident volunteers were away on a day off. We did meet with another visitor, a little lad by the name of Sascha, he was from a very poor family with seven children and he had made himself at home there.

Our friend was very pleased at our interest in their group and gave us a couple of their *Pakrac* sweatshirts for souvenirs and a copy of their newsletter. It featured the story of Emira from the bistro. It was titled 'A TEAR FROM PAKRAC' It read: -

Her name is Emira, she is sixteen and attends secondary school. *Pakrac* is divided on two sides, Her Croatian and the Serbian. She doesn't know the statistics like, how many people lived in the town before the war or how many of them were killed. She does know that too many died in a war that nobody understands. She could tell you the story of her life since the beginning of the war because a friend once told her that she should share the things she feels. He was her best friend, she could tell you about him.

"I woke up that morning just like any other day, I even remember that I had milk, bread and butter for breakfast. I noticed strange things, a lot of people were leaving in cars, more than usual. They had baggage, I could not understand what was happening."

"A few days later I went to visit a friend, she was Serbian. I knocked on the door but no one answered. The woman next door came and said that they had left without saying where they would go. Then I decided to go and see my best friend. I was at his house about 5pm. he looked stressed and said that there was trouble at the police station, he must go there. I went home to my parents' shop and then it started, for the first time I heard shooting."

"I was so scared, I didn't go out, I could not sleep, grenades and bullets were flying everywhere. I felt fear and physical pain, even my bones were hurting. The next days were like a nightmare, I couldn't stay in the house any longer. I had not seen my friends for so long. In the street, my God, what a sight. This could not be my town. An explosion brought me to my senses, I could smell smoke and people were screaming."

"Dead animals were lying in the street and the smell was awful. I saw a wounded soldier, others were taking him away, he was screaming in agony."

"Fear overcame me totally, I was near the big supermarket when I saw my best friend. He was waving to me and shouting 'GET DOWN'. A second later a grenade exploded and he was gone."

"Other people came and collected what was left of him. I heard my own screaming and it all went dark. I woke up in hospital in *Zagreb*. My mother was there and she looked so frightened. I was afraid to ask, I could not cry."

In the months that followed fourteen of her school friends were killed in this senseless war. She was taken to *Podravina* on the Hungarian border to convalesce. From there she went to a school in *Zagreb* on a language course. She became sick and could see blood everywhere. She stopped talking and withdrew into her own world where she felt safe. She was sent to a phycho hospital where she was given many pills, Moditen, Akineton and Nozinan. She is now back in *Pakrac*, although it is now peaceful, she is still a victim of the war...

Back at the bistro we met up with Iris who told us that Mama Javanka, insisted on cooking us a meal. Iris and I sorted out a dozen eggs and two tins of ham to help out with the meal for the five of us. Emira was the eldest of the daughters, she was seen on the film of Anneka's visit to the school, Edina was the second daughter and Emina was the youngest. Edina was so like Mike's own daughter, Katie, that he could not get over the similarity. We handed over the provisions and sat in the bar talking to the girls. They were going to a disco that evening in *Lipik*, the next village. We thought that very strange as *Lipik* was in a worse state than *Pakrac*. Most of the houses were piles of rubble, one thing was for sure, the disco wouldn't annoy many neighbours.

Emina the nine-year-old, kept us amused by drawing portraits of us, she had a very good eye for detail. Then the meal arrived, we had expected cold ham and chips. The eggs had been scrambled, chunks of ham were added, with local spiced sausages and chips. Beer for the men and Coke for the ladies.

Some of the convoy were leaving for *Zagreb* to be *at Rangi Nekova* in the morning. We stayed on for another night in the shelter of the hospital to guide the rest of the vehicles to the camp the next day. As we got near the camp we gave a couple of calls over the C.B. They had been hoping to press on to get home for returning the hired vans. At the entrance to the camp we were met by a Red Cross representative, He asked if we would take our goods to the second section of the camp as our friends had left their goods on this side earlier.

I was trying to trace a family which Jean, with us in December, had met and befriended. They had entertained her and given her a rosary. Their kindness and the plight they were in had touched Jean's heart. She had asked if I could obtain their names and address for her, to write to them.

I carried a photo of Jean with me and asked a few people

115

before I found a young lad able to speak English and he told me that it was his family that I was looking for. He took me into one of the wooden huts, down a corridor and into a neat and tidy room. He explained to his parents and showed them the photo. They made me very welcome and I heard how they had lived in *Doboj*, near *Sarajevo* in Bosnia. They had two sons, the one who had found me and was about twelve years old, the older one was twenty and training to be a policeman. There were also two daughters who were still at school, they all lived in two small rooms.

I gave them Jean's address and they wrote theirs for me to take home. Ruza the wife gave me a beautiful lace table cloth to take for her friend Jean, it must have taken many hours to make. The family asked if we could get them a 'camp house'. I guessed that they were asking for a tent possibly for the boys to sleep in during the summer.

The work of unloading had been done while I had been visiting. There was only one more drop to make, the two hundred mile round trip to *Crikvenica*. Just Chuck and Iris were going with us to visit special friends in the two hostels on the coast. We had coconut oil for Ivana, English cereals for Boris, a dozen Barbie Dolls for the little girls, colouring books for the boys, rice, pasta and noodles for the kitchen.

We sat outside talking with Nada until the sun had set. Boris was due to leave school that year and would have to enlist into the Croatian army. They were all worried and we said that we hoped the war would soon be over, not only for Boris's sake. Chuck and Iris had been persuaded to spend the night with their friends so we stayed on to be company for them on the return journey over the mountains.

In the morning a four-hour journey to *Zagreb*, we were going to try to find the *Caritas* warehouse in the city. A lorry load of goods had been sent out to the centre from our Somerford warehouse in February. We just wanted to make sure that it had arrived safely. Finding a *Caritas* centre, we soon discovered that it was not the right place. We were informed that there were many *Caritas* centres in *Zagreb*.

It was late in the afternoon, we didn't really want to spend another night to go hunting in the morning and waste another day.

We made for the border and the road home. There was a problem in getting off the ferry at Ramsgate, a lorry in front of us had its gears stuck in reverse and had to be towed off. Mike was delivered to his family and we collected bags of clothing from his garage, before going home.

APRIL 1994

Our old camper had a great heart and did not often let us down. We had the load ready and the paperwork done to make yet another trip on Tuesday April 5th. The day before, disaster, we had a problem with the gearbox. The whole unit was taken to a specialist and he was informed of the urgency of our situation. The convoy sailed without us. Tim M. was to travel with us as a second driver, he had raised a fair amount of funding for the journey.

We kept in contact and promised that if we had the gearbox back and in place by the Wednesday night we would still be making the trip. At 1pm. on Wednesday the gearbox came home, Denys and Jack made a start in putting it together. Daughter Marion and her husband came to see if they could help. Marion had achieved unasked for fame when a reporter had interviewed her for a local paper, asking what it was like having a reversed role. The child wondering where her parents were and worrying for their safety.

Their two kids were no trouble in the warehouse, they were having wheelchair races around the huge building. A missing bolt held up the work, Marion chauffeured me to three different workshops to find a replacement, no one had the right size. I couldn't do much to help the men so I wandered around our bric-a-brac section, or car boot corner. I found a bag of odds and ends and among them were two bolts. I kept the tea flowing then sat with a book in the rest area to keep out of the way. Jack went home at 4pm. and then the cavalry arrived, son Mike and his lady, Jean. They swallowed a quick cup of tea, donned boiler suits and got to work.

Tim M's wife Jill, brought him over from Wimborne as soon as we told him that there was hope of us getting away that night. Their daughter Susie came along for the ride. Tim and

Susie had been with us on the October trip one year before. Jill and Susie left, hoping that they wouldn't have to come back for Tim the next morning. At six I went to the nearby shopping precinct to buy chicken and chips for the five of us. A break to eat, more tea, then the mechanics got back to work. At 9pm. I saw the wheel being put back on and kept my fingers crossed.

Trying not to look too obvious, I started putting things in order inside the camper, stowing bottles of drinking water, the generator and Tim's gear. Denys started the engine, it sounded good. A rush then to pack up the tools and hitch up the trailer. With good wishes from our mechanics we hit the road. A quick phone call to Tony B's wife Val, she would tell him of our progress when he next phoned her. As we were passing daughter Chris's house in Christchurch, a knocking noise had us worried and we made a stop. The exhaust pipe had become loose. Son Tim just happened to be passing and gave a hand to secure it. There was quite a family gathering outside Chris's house.

Forty-eight hours behind the convoy, our drivers did their best to make up the time. A clear road all the way, we had thought of spending the night in a lorry park but decided to press on to the docks. Refuelling at an all night services we then drove on to the ferry terminal. Denys and Tim went to the office to get us booked onto the first ferry next morning, while they were away I got the camper sorted and made up the beds. The men came back with the news that we did not have time to go to bed, there was a 4.30am. sailing and we were on it.

Moving into the boarding lanes at two thirty, we dozed while waiting. The boat was late in and it was 5am before we boarded. Feeling very tired by this time we settled in one of the lounges and did our best to sleep. We woke up to hear an announcement apologising for our late arrival at *Ostende*, 10.15 local time.

While we were waiting to go down to the car deck a chap came to ask where we were making for. He was on his way *to Zagreb*, he and his wife were from Derby Road in Bournemouth. We wished each other luck as we parted company.

On a very pleasant morning, we drove on until finding a parking area for breakfast and a couple of hours sleep. A cup of tea and a quick wash and got down to some serious travelling.

Denys driving, Tim navigating and I settled to starting the diary. The camper was going great as mile after mile slipped by. Into Germany, then Tim took the wheel while Denys rested, he slept for three hours. Sandwiches and coffee on the wing meant that no time was wasted.

Rain as we stopped at five for tea and refilled the flasks to keep us going later. At *Hockenheim*, our usual night stop, we parked up long enough to heat up canned meat and vegetables for our first hot meal in 24 hours. Then with Denys at the helm and Tim resting we carried on until 10.30. The night was spent in a layby with a couple of trucks for company. It felt good to remove some of my clothing and get into bed.

We were awake at 3.30am., took our time over a cup of tea and our ablutions, such luxury. It was still dark and raining as Tim took the first shift, driving us out into the early morning traffic. Heading for *Passau* and the Austrian border, we gave a thought to the convoy already on the Adriatic coast by this time. With chocolate to keep us going we reached the border at 9am.

While Tim was refuelling Denys tried to phone Tony at the *Ad Turres Hotel* to let him know of our progress, the number was unobtainable. On through *Wels* and then the old roads, as pretty as a Christmas card with snow capped mountains and villages too neat and tidy to be true. We passed a couple of vehicles with Red Heart stickers. Denys talked to them on the C.B. they had left their load at *Crikvenica* and were on their way home. They told us that our convoy was only 200 miles ahead of us.

Tim rested as the camper ate up the miles, at the Slovenian border we expected problems but to our surprise we were waved through, no hold ups, no charge and no aggravation. The Croatian border was the same. Following the route to *Zagreb* motorway then mountain roads we made it to the *Ad Turres* and treated ourselves to a hot meal in the hotel. Denys phoned Tony's wife in Canterbury in case he called to check on us. A can of beans paid for the call, the receptionist had a weakness for the humble beans.

We settled then for a good night's sleep to be away before 8am. Refreshed and refuelled we followed the coast road south, reporting at the police checkpoints before crossing the pontoon bridge. Tim was seeing this part of the country for the first time. With Denys driving I kept the coffee flowing. We didn't have to make many loo stops as we carried our own toilet. On reaching the city of *Split* we missed a sign somehow and had to ask the way to *Dubrovnic*. The young man wasn't much help, and he asked for money. Coming across a roundabout we retraced our route and soon found where we had gone wrong.

On the right road we soon made up the minutes we had lost. From there on we had to go by a map and rely on our memories of the January trip. From *Metkovic* we recognised the scenery and villages that we passed. Trouble came when we found ourselves in flat and unfamiliar territory. After passing through two tunnels we agreed that we had not been there before. Arriving at a border post, the men went into an office with our paper work, they returned to say that we could not go into Bosnia. We hadn't realised that Tony was carrying the papers giving permission for the whole convoy to enter the country with goods. The trailer was the problem. As we prepared to go back to *Crikvenica,* we discussed the possibility of leaving the trailer at an aid warehouse in *Metkovic.*

Back in January we had met with some members of a German organisation, at that time they had mentioned that we should look them up when next in the area. It was worth a try. A chap at the warehouse said that he was sorry but he couldn't take responsibility for our goods. He suggested that we try an organisation called CARE, just down the road. In the yard of the CARE building we were greeted by a large fierce looking dog as we stepped out of the camper. At his barking a young lady came out to see what we were about. We thought at first from her accent that she was an 'Aussie' but she soon put us right, she was from New Zealand.

We explained our predicament, she said, "No problem." We were welcome to leave the trailer against a wall of the building, the dog and a guard on duty would keep it safe for a couple of days. After thanking her we made back to the border. We thought that we would be let through by just showing our British passports. Not so, a customs officer asked to look inside the camper, he didn't say a word as he peeped into cupboards with his torch. He inspected Tim's hold-all, even checked Denys's video case. We had some sliced English bread wrapped in newspaper, he unwrapped each loaf. At last he seemed satisfied and allowed us to go.

Sure then that we could soon join the convoy, we were still puzzled over the fact that we had not found the twisting mountain roads that the *Medugorje Appeal* had followed in January. Also puzzling was that *Medugorje* was not marked on any of our maps. On rounding a bend we came upon a police and army checkpoint. We were stopped and asked where we were going and why. On hearing that we were trying to get to *Medugorje*, we were advised to turn around and go back about 10 km., we had missed the turning to the village and were heading for Mostar.

Turning around was easier now without the trailer. We drove back about three miles with three pairs of eyes straining to find the right road and a sign that we might have missed. At about the right distance we found a rough, narrow, one-track road with no signpost. Denys reckoned that it must be the one and soon we were on familiar territory, the steep and twisting mountain roads that we both remembered. Although Denys had been driving all day, he and Tim were happy to leave it that way on the narrow roads which were no more than goat tracks with steep drops to the valley below.

Listening out all the while for voices on the C.B. we travelled on, arriving in *Medugorje* to see a row of the convoy vans parked along the street. Then familiar faces emerged to greet us, we were told that they had been into *Mostar* that afternoon and that Tony could be found at one of the B and B houses nearby.

No one was surprised to see us turn up, Val had been passing on our messages. As we explained the absence of our trailer, Tony thought that he might be able to get it through the border on his paperwork. Elisabeth from Buckinghamshire was on this trip, after having sorted out the problems she had with her trailer in March. She had made it this time with co-driver Alan, his wife and a lodger, Derek. He was a photographer from a Kent newspaper. Tony had planned to put Derek in with us until he had heard of our problems.

At a get-together in a cafe not far from the church, Derek

122

and his co-reporter Rosemary bought drinks for everyone. A lively crowd, Chuck and Iris from Dover, Dave and partner Elise from Bournemouth, Hugh from Weymouth, Father David with Nick, Peter and Ray from Huddersfield, Terry and his lady, Gwyllym from Wales. He would have been with us on the January trip but his van was damaged on Ramsgate docks while he was in a B and B. Sheila with three drivers, one of them Mike, had a very deep and slow drawl, they were in two London hire vans, Ken and Rosemarie from Folkestone, Patsy and Bryn from North Wales and of course Tony.

Those who had not met us before had heard of us. A gentleman had seated himself with a sandwich and a drink at a nearby table. On hearing our conversation he introduced himself as Dean and he was from Switzerland, he said how he loved to hear the English language spoken by Englishmen. He told us that he had been working with Franciscan monks in *Medugorje* for the past three months.

Some of the convoy members including Elisabeth, were going to make the trek up the *Hill of Apparitions* the next morning which was a Sunday. Taking the narrow path up the hill which was almost a mountain, was looked upon as a task of faith and endurance by the local people. At the top was a sixty foot cross which was supposed to glow at times. *Medugorje* was steeped in mystery and legend.

We woke to the sound of the church bells and of rain. The wet did not put off the pilgrimage to the Hill of the Cross, Elisabeth and some of the more adventurous of our colleagues set out in raincoats and carrying brollies at around 9am. Some of we older folks, not fancying the one and a half hour climb, took a stroll to the church with its twin towers.

We took photos and video footage of the building. As people were walking through the doors we thought that we should have a peep inside.

We sat in a pew at the very back of the church and took in the scene. Dedicated to St. James, the church was pure white, very simple design and quite beautiful. Where most churches we had visited had stained glass windows, behind the altar were three small, plain, deep set windows which caught the morning light. About twenty or so people were sitting like us but suddenly the church began to fill. A group of young people walked to the front of the congregation, one of them was carrying a guitar. A priest in white robes started a service, after listening for a while we realised that he was speaking Spanish. We stayed on not understanding what was being said, sitting and standing and following the example of the worshippers. Hymns were sung by the group with the guitar. The church was pretty crowded with folk standing at the doors.

Then as Holy Communion was about to take place, people were moving around so we decided that it would be a good time to make our exit. As we left the priest was raising his hands to bless the bread. On our way back to the vehicle we took a look in some of the souvenir shops in one we were persuaded to buy a video of the Story of *Medugorje* and the visions of the Madonna. The hill climbers were back very wet but looking pleased at their achievement.

A message was put out that we were leaving at 2pm. We were to be visiting refugees who had been living on a train for some years. Everyone grabbed a snack lunch. Our guide was to be a priest, Don Ivan, a friend of Sheila whom we had met back in January. About eight miles from *Medugorje* we took a rough track to a disused railway siding. Three trains, each with about ten carriages looked at first to be deserted, until the children came out with the adults following.

A chap in charge of the food stores opened up one of the coaches which had been locked, we unloaded all the food supplies first into the secure store room. The rest of the goods were put into the hands of the people who had lived in these conditions for more than three years. In no time at all the area looked like an open market. Eager women collected piles of clothing and bedding, making personal heaps of goods along a fence and placing a child on top to guard her prizes. Then mum would go off to see what else she could collect for her family.

All the children were sucking on lollipops and carrying new toys. Cameras clicked and flashed from all directions. Proof to be taken home to the good folk who gave the goods for us to bring.

All we had to give were two large packs of Pampers, which had been hidden in our Luton area. One lady with bare arms was pulling at my coat, asking in a silent way for a coat of her own. At that moment, Terry's wife had found a leather coat in a bag of clothing that she was handing out.

Denys went to the camper to collect some disposable razors for one old man and an electric shaver for someone else. An electric cable had been connected to the carriages giving enough electricity to supply lighting. We were always amazed that refugees living under such conditions were so clean and tidy. The site around the train was bare of litter. On a raised platform, tables and benches had been set out under a plastic awning for their meals.

Tim's wife was head teacher at Hampreston School, her pupils had written letters to refugee children as a school project. Tim had the letters with him hoping to pass them on to a school in Bosnia. Until then there had been no opportunity. Don Ivan found a child from the train who could speak a little English, she promised to give the letters to her English teacher. This might start a series of pen friendships. All the convoy members were happy that their loads of aid had found a place of great need. As we moved out, those with blankets and clothing still on board were going on to a Moslem settlement. Others were going back to *Medugorje*, we were to make for *Metkovic* to collect our trailer, then follow the coast at a steady pace to meet up with the rest of them in the morning.

Taking a road down a mountain we could hear the voices of convoy chat coming over the C.B. Then as we rounded the corner we come upon them stopped for loo and refreshments. They were telling us that as they pulled into the parking area, there had been a burst of gunfire from the hills over looking that stretch of road. The brave Brits were standing out in full view of any sniper, pointing to where the firing had come from. 'Some mothers do 'ave 'em'.

Don Ivan had been impressed by my husband's famous RAF type moustache, he said that he would like us to meet his friend Matthew, who also had a magnificent moustache. The friend lived near *Dubrovnik*, Don Ivan was so insistent, that we gave in, having a free evening. First though, we had to pick-up our trailer at the CARE warehouse. While we were expressin' our thanks and hitching up the trailer, Don Ivan parked his car. He and Sheila joined us in the camper, the two London hire vans followed behind. While we were heading towards *Dubrovnik*, Don Ivan chatted away like an excited child in his cute broken English.

He reckoned that he should have a camper and trailer like ours, he would have the trailer converted into a mobile church, then he could visit all the refugees in outlying villages. As he directed us inland we realised that we were heading for the Bosnian border. Denys explained to our priest that we did not have the papers for taking our loaded trailer into Bosnia.

Don Ivan already in the passenger seat, said, "Leave the talking to me." After a short conversation, we were amazed when the guards waved us through. When Denys asked him what he had said, the answer was, "I told them that the trailer was empty." Denys, was a bit taken aback and said, "You are a Priest, and you lied?" Don Ivan chuckled and said, "Well, sometimes you have to." With the two vans still following we found ourselves on mountain roads until we reached a village called *Neum*. Following the Don's directions we parked in a narrow street and walked to a house which was dark and deserted. On looking at the time, Don Ivan realised that his friends would be in church and we should go to meet them. We were most surprised when he led us into another private house. He opened the door and allowed us to step into a room not much larger than an average sitting room.

At a table covered by a lace cloth, a priest in robes and vestments had his hands raised to bless the offering for Holy Communion. We had stepped into the secret church at the same point we had left the service in *Medugorje* that morning. We stood in silence during the prayers that followed, the ladies were kneeling on bare floorboards. We spotted the man with the large moustache. The priest disrobed almost as a ritual, laying each carefully folded garment on the altar table while the last prayer was being said. Then we were welcomed by the small congregation, they were mostly refugees and their religious meetings were held in secret because churches were prime targets for the enemy.

Matthew and his family invited all of us to his home, Sheila and her drivers had been there before. Cheese and bread was put before us as Don Ivan told us that Matthew had been twice a refugee, the first time during the Second World War and now in this conflict. As the men chatted, Sheila told me of how she had met the lovely little priest. She had heard of orphans left homeless by the shelling of *Mostar*. Wanting to help in the situation, the only way she could get out here was by joining a pilgrimage to *Medugorje*. Then as no one would take her to the Bosnian border she put a shawl over her head and by saying that she was a nun she persuaded a taxi driver to take her into part of the besieged city. By walking the rest of the way she went into the Cathedral.

There she met Don Ivan about to deliver hot meals to some of the desperate townspeople. He told her that if she really wanted to help she could go with him in his beat-up old car, with its doors tied up with string. From that meeting she created the Don Ivan Trust, collecting aid and money to help him help his people. We had met up with Sheila in January when she was waiting for a lorry load of aid. She had expected it to arrive from Godstone with the *Medugorje Appeal Convoy*. I asked her if she ever found the missing vehicle, she told me that the Slovenian driver had taken the truck home for the weekend and had helped himself to some of the goods.

Since meeting us in January, she had decided to bring her goods out herself in the two London vans on this convoy. Leaving our newest friends took a long time with so many hugs and kisses, Denys never could get used to the men kissing him on both cheeks. Don Ivan did his stuff at the border, on leaving us he asked that we didn't mention his name, as he helped on both sides of the conflict he could be shot as a spy. He and Sheila transferred to the vans the priest to be dropped at his car while Sheila and company would join the others in *Medugorje*.

Our route then was to *Makarska*. In this lovely seaside resort with a palm-fringed harbour, Denys found a good parking place near the water. The weather turned stormy, the fishing boats tossing at their moorings. We were quite cosy with the camper parked nose into the wind. We enjoyed a hot drink while talking over the day's events then dropped into our beds. The rolling thunder and the rain on the roof did not keep us awake. What a difference when we awoke, sunshine, blue skies and sparkling water.

We admired a handsome timber built yacht riding at anchor among the smaller boats. That was the scene only yards away from our window as we ate our breakfast cereal. People were going about their business and the traffic was building up as we moved out to find a good spot to meet the convoy. Driving along the coast we found a layby just around a bend at the bottom of a hill. A good spot to video the complete convoy as it came down the mountain.

Just after eleven, we heard Tony's voice as he led his flock toward us, they were still a couple of miles away. We drank coffee and sat in the sun until we could see Echo One's flashers coming over the brow of the hill. We had a great view of the vehicles along with a few locals who had got in between the vans. All the convoy members knew that they would be on film, they came by waving dusters, hats and anything handy, while sounding horns and shouting as they passed by.

We got ready to take off and slip in behind the last vehicle but Alan, driving Elisabeth's van, pulled in beside us thinking that we had a problem.

All on the road and heading for *Split*, with the familiar chat to keep us company and alert. Then on to *Zadar* where Tony suggested that we make a stop at *Dracevac*, for the benefit of the press. The rusting hulk of the Croatian tank made a focal point for the photographers. As our trailer was still full, we opened it up to give clothing and food parcels to the few villagers who came out from the ruins of their homes to see what we were doing there.

We opened boxes and let them see what we had, for them to take what they needed. An elderly man took an armful of shoes. A group of ladies who obviously had no little ones of their own, lifted baby clothes from a box, holding each one up then carefully folding them to put them back in the box. Children were loaded with sweets and the younger ones cuddling soft toys. The ladies accepted blankets. The press collected evidence in pictures and stories of the brutality experienced.

On to the pontoon bridge, as we approached the crossing the police stopped Elisabeth's van. Alan who was sitting in the passenger seat had his camera slung round his neck. The police warned 'no photos'. As we reached the other side Tim managed to get a couple of shots looking down on the bridge. The journey to *Crikvenica* was spectacular with a blazing sunset, as the sky darkened it became more red and dramatic.

A well-earned meal at the *Ad Turres*, then we decided to have the luxury of a room for the night. Before turning in we joined Elisabeth and her crew for a cup of tea. We had not had time to socialise with her, Alan and his wife Diane seemed to have enjoyed their trip and they were coping with their extra passenger.

By the time we settled in our room, the hot water was off so we put off having a shower until the morning. We spent the night cursing the hard beds and wishing we had stayed in the camper. In the morning the shower and plenty of towels made up for the discomfort. Breakfast of fresh bread with cheese, meat and jam.

Tony was going to Switzerland to pick up a load of aid to bring back on a second trip, maybe to drop it off at a refugee camp in Slovenia. He thought it might smooth our way at the borders on future trips into Bosnia. He had asked us to go along with him on this extension trip, we declined as it would mean another one thousand miles. We did not have the money for the fuel.

We still had a fair amount of goods in our trailer. While talking to the receptionist at the *Ad Turres* hotel, we were told that a group of refugees were living in the annex building. She told us that they had seen our convoy passing through without having a share of the aid that we were bringing to others. Chuck went to find out who was in charge of the group, while Denys reversed the camper and trailer down the steep slope to the doors of the building.

Soon willing hands helped to carry the goods into the storeroom which was just about empty. Keeping back just enough for Nada's group and medicines for the clinic we gave them food, toiletries, knitting wool and needles. There were no babies so we kept the baby items for the clinic. After unloading we were invited in for thick black coffee. The room belonged to a man called Josep, he spoke broken English and became our interpreter. While we sat on his family's beds he told us of things needed most by his group, food was high on the list, with washing powder, shampoo, toothpaste, milk and blankets. At present they had only one blanket per bed.

Josep was a very good-looking young man, tall with dark curly hair and bright blue eyes. A group of people edged into the room to look at the strangers. To amuse the children Denys did his disappearing coin tricks, making it re-appear from behind one child's ear. That started a magic session, Josep found a pack of cards and showed off with a few tricks. Denys was in his element then and took the floor. There was no language barrier with a pack of cards. Our hosts would have us stay on but we still had a couple of calls to make. After promising to return soon, we made for the clinic in town.

We parked in the grounds of the health centre, which was directly under a flimsy looking viaduct about 150 ft. above, which was the fly-over bypassing the town. The doctors were not allowed to use their medical supplies on refugees, only donated items could be used, to make sure that the local people should not suffer through the influx of so many 'outsiders'.

We gave surgical gloves, sterile needles, disposable sheets, bandages and burns dressings, oxygen masks, baby milk and food. Some of these would have gone to *Mostar*, if things had gone to plan. Chuck and Iris left us to visit their refugees, like us they had adopted a particular group of refugees. bringing them items that would make life a little easier. We made our way to *Odmaraliste*, to visit 'our' people. The men unloaded the goods brought specifically for our friends. We also brought gifts for Nada and her teenage children.

Nada had asked us not to bring presents just for her family because it was causing jealousy and ill feeling among the other residents. Then we decided that next time we would make up 30 family boxes, one for each room. With living in such close quarters for three years, there were bad feelings growing between the families. They had stopped eating together and were collecting meals from the kitchen to eat in their rooms. We hadn't intended to add to their problems.

On the quiet we had wondered about Nada's husband, was he one of the victims of the Serb massacres? Or away in the army? We hadn't liked to ask for fear of upsetting the family.

While chatting and drinking coffee in their room, Nada showed us photos of their happier life in *Vukovar*. Seeing a family group one of us asked Ivana about her dad, we were relieved to know that her parents were divorced 12 years earlier, Ivana said, "There were problems." We invited the family to come for a meal with us that evening. Nada was going to be busy, but the young people and a young lady taking on the job as housemother from Nada accepted.

Tim had wanted to buy a tape of local folk music. *Crikvenica* was quite a fair sized seaside town, once busy with tourists, mainly from Germany. We found a department store with tapes and books on the ground floor. We wandered around interested in the goods on display. Up on the first floor were household goods, the shelves were not exactly overloaded and prices were very steep. Children's clothes were expensive we worked out the price of a babygrow as £12.

A fairground was open close to the car park, with about six customers on the dodgems. Just before 7pm. we picked up our guests, going on to Mika's bar where there was a barbeque going on but the place was so busy there was no room to park. We asked the youngsters if there was any particular place they would like to go, they couldn't come up with a suggestion. We decided then that the *Ad Turres* would be a good choice.

First a drink at the bar and then ordered our meal, we were hungry and ordered mixed grill. No amount of persuading would tempt our guests to order more than a sandwich. Ivana and Jadranka fancied a cappuccino coffee, Boris joined the men with a beer. He was so interested in life in England, asking what people did in their free time and what we did for a living. We explained that we were retired from paid jobs, our time was filled with collecting aid and money to bring to people in need.

We took them home and said goodbye, we would not be seeing them for a few months.

During the night terrific thunder storms rolled around the mountains. The morning dawned dull and cool. Our trailer lights had not been working since leaving it at *Metkovic*, Tim and Denys spent an hour checking the wiring trying to find the fault, with no luck. We had planned to go on to *Zagreb*, hoping to find a chap called Mario. He was in charge of an organisation, which should have received a lorry load of goods from our warehouse in February. After hearing Sheila's tale about her goods not arriving at the destination where it was expected, we thought that a check at Mario's while we were in the area would put our minds at rest. A phone call from the coast as we left, had only connected to an answering machine.

While travelling over the mountains we discovered that quite a lot of snow had settled while we were in the sun on the Adriatic. About two feet of snow on the sides of the roads but the highway had been cleared.

Arriving in *Zagreb*, we made for the city centre, finding a yard full of U.N.H.C.R. vehicles, Tim and Denys went in armed with the address to ask for Mario's warehouse. I stayed with the camper to catch up with my diary. The men came back to say that we were miles away from that address. A lady in the office had tried to phone the number we had but again, an answer phone. We had directions and a sketched map, back into the city to look for the Cathedral. Found it down a series of narrow roads.

A priest pointed out a building across the road, a chap there knew Mario but he did not live there. We were given yet another address, we were beginning to realise just how vast *Zagreb* was. On finding ourselves near a railway station, we thought that we must be hot on the trail, as we had been told that Mario's place was near a station. Denys asked a taxi driver and soon we were in the right road. The men went to investigate, they found the warehouse which was completely empty. A chap working in an office phoned Mario's home number, Denys spoke to Mario's son who said that his father was in America. A dead end!!

Parked in the station yard, Denys and Tim decided to have another go at fixing the trailer lights, this time they found the fault, a broken wire in the connection to the camper. Then it was all systems go to get home. All plain sailing until we hit road works in Germany. Everything was down to a crawl, we travelled many miles with monster trucks on every side of us.

In a service station for the night we met up with a lorry driver who told us that the motorway to *Antwerp* was more straightforward and quicker than the *Brussels* route. We tried it but most of the way was so rough that it felt like travelling on cobbles, I was wishing that I had worn a stronger bra!

We did not have to make any specific time to get to the ferry. On the Sally Ferries deal we paid for the trip across the Channel to France, and had a free passage back on any boat that could take us.

A quick visit to the Collier household to pick up boxes and bags of goods collected from local folks from Beltinge. Time with them to catch up on news then to Wimborne to deliver Tim to his family.

The huge warehouse loaned to us by Pickfords the removal firm had been sold. Appeals put out by a local newspaper and the efforts of the Bosnian Crisis Appeal had failed to find suitable premises for us to continue collecting aid for refugees.

On May 18th a Croatian lorry with a trailer was organised to take four and a half tons of our remaining stocks, including 151 beds, 80 bedding packs of blankets, sheets, pillows and pillow cases, 4 prams and a large amount of clothing. The destination for this load was to *Zagreb*, to be distributed to refugee camps throughout the area.

Our trailer was filled with medical aid, toys and children's clothing. Elisabeth had come down from High Wycombe to fill her trailer with bedding, clothing and the last of our food stocks. A large foam filled play area given by Weymouth Council, boxes of oxygen masks and household textiles were stored in a friend's garage to be dealt with later.

MAY 1994

One afternoon on a local radio station, it was put over the airwaves that a large amount of T shirts were being offered to any organisation that could take them out of the country for a good cause. Any takers would have to submit the name of their charity which would go into a draw. There would be only one lucky winner. Unknown to us five different people sent in our names to the draw and we won the T shirts. On being given an address we contacted the man in charge and arranged a pick-up day. We were just amazed at the number of boxes there were to collect.

The royal blue shirts had an anti smoking logo with a picture of a broken cigarette. Under this was a phone number, which had been wrongly printed. The shirts were of all sizes and still in their plastic wrapping.

We were in the process of getting ready for our next convoy. The plan was to take goods to a Moslem refugee camp in Slovenia. We made yet another street collection in the shopping precinct in Poole. Don and Rose, a very sweet elderly couple, held coffee mornings in their home. We would attend these get-togethers and tell of our experiences, receiving donations of goods and funds from their friends.

A phone call from Tony in Canterbury, asked Denys if he would be prepared to lead that month's convoy. He would send all the instruction and necessary paper work for the borders, the rest should be plain sailing. Promotion at last.

Shirley wanted to make another trip but she was in need of a co-driver, Kelly was keen to go and agreed to travel with us as far as Ramsgate, then she would transfer to Shirley's van. Shirley's brother was to join us with a Luton van together with two lads in an old ambulance. After driving some distance the lads in the old ambulance had a problem when it became unstable. On our first night stop we decided to examine their load. Some large sacks of flour had been loaded to one side of the ambulance, the load was then spread evenly in the vehicle and things improved no end.

All went well until we were to exit Austria, we discovered that we were a van short. A message over the C.B. told us that they had taken a wrong turning and they would catch up with us later on. Five vehicles made it to the first of the borders to the former Yugoslavia. As Denys handed the papers to the customs, he explained that we were expecting one more car (all vehicles are referred to as cars). With no further problems we went on through entry Slovenia border with the same explanation. We could hear from time to time the voices of our lost colleagues. We kept going, according to our instructions the camp was almost under a large TV and radio mast. We headed in the direction but could not find an obvious entrance to a camp. On turning the convoy around we had another go at finding the gate. We found ourselves at what looked like a military establishment. On enquiring from a passer by we discovered that this was the camp. Through a gateway in a high wall, passing various low buildings, through a second gate and came upon a huge barrack block. We were concerned that our missing drivers might miss the entrance, Denys got a lift in one of the vans to wait at the aerial. The voices on the C.B. seemed to get nearer, then they would fade away, until at last they found us.

By this time the women and the children had come from all directions, clamouring to see what we had brought, there seemed to be no one in charge and hands were trying to grab everything in sight. Denys advised all the drivers to keep their vehicles locked until we knew where we were to unload. I was just getting out of the back door when a group of kids pounced, their arms were thrust into the doorway trying to reach what ever they could, we almost lost our blankets from the bed just inside the door.

Youngsters were climbing all over the ambulance, one had control of the horn and was blasting the ear drums of all around him. The best thing we could do was to start unloading, if anything was swiped it would only be items intended for them anyway. Soon an office was opened for the goods. When our turn came the Tshirts caused great excitement. To get the best possible photos of the shirts, we handed them out to the eager hands coming from all directions.

Box upon box was emptied, every child and adult was walking about as pleased as punch with their trophies. Women in headscarves and long dresses were wearing them, children were showing them off to others who were still waiting. We noticed that a lot of women were wearing odd shoes, down-at-heel men's shoes or trainers without socks or stockings, slippers with the toes torn away. There were many boxes of shoes among the supplies taken into the storeroom.

We had a large amount of rock from a local factory in our area. Most times when they knew we were about to make a trip to the camps, we could be pretty sure that we would take some of their sweet products with us for the children. In most camps the children would wait very patiently to be given sweets or chocolate. Not so here, the boys would grab whatever they could, some of them stuffed sticks of rock under their shirts and ran off. Some of them even had the nerve to come back for more after hiding their spoils in a safe place.

A lady from an office in the building asked if we would go with her to some flats near by, she had a request, She was a refugee from *Sarajevo*, as were many of the families. She asked that if we could get into *Sarajevo*, could we take some parcels for their men who were still in the city. We had to refuse her at that time, but promised that if we did go there in the future we would get in touch. While we were there a young lad asked us if we would come and have tea with his mother and grandmother. A lovely family but like so many others not knowing if they would ever see their men again.

The main convoy split up here and most were heading for home. Once the vehicles were unloaded they were free to go home. We ourselves had one or two personal gifts for friends we made in camps on previous trips. Shirley and Kelly said they would like to come along with us. Making for *Zagreb* next we were to visit a family at *Rangi Nakova* camp on the outskirts of the city. Jean's friends, Ruza and Anton with their family of four children. had asked us if we could get them a 'camp house' we had taken this to be a tent. Mike who had been with us when they asked said he had a large tent in his garage. His family had grown and left home and now the tent was standing idle. He donated it to this family that he met on his first visit with us. The whole family were over the moon with the gift.

Their youngest daughter had just made her first Communion and she dressed up for us in a long white dress, hand sewn by Ruza from one of their precious sheets, a coronet of flowers and holding a candle, for a family photograph. Life still goes on.

Leaving the camp and taking the motorway to *Kutina*, and then on country roads we made for *Lipik*. As we drove 20 odd miles past devastated villages and dodging craters in the road, Shirley became very emotional. Her voice over the C.B. came between sobs, with expressions of pity and anger that humans could do this to their own kind. *Lipik* had been a well-known spa town before the Second World War. There had been a lot of destruction in this civil war but now there was rebuilding by house owners over the past year. While we walked in *Lipik* to stretch our legs, we passed a house under repair. Denys called a greeting to some men who were round a concrete mixer and we received a cheery *Dobar Dan*.

A bottle of wine and some glasses were on a table in the yard. We were called to come and join them in refreshment. One of the men said he had met us at the hospital in *Pakrac*. We drank to their health and success, Denys remarked how brave they were to be rebuilding their house in sight of the *Chetniks* (Serbs). The front line was no more than half a mile away. At that our friend beat his chest, saying loudly, "This is my house, my home, my town."

On then to *Pakrac*, a quick visit to Anton the shoemaker. He and Maria would never forgive us if we should be so near and not find time to visit. Shirley came with us while Kelly, not feeling too well, stayed in their van sleeping. While we struggled along with the language problem, Anton was asking if we could get him some leather for shoes. He insisted, "Not this" pointing to the soles of his shoe, "This," he said pointing to the uppers. It never ceases to amaze us how things worked out. Shirley said that she might be able to get leather from a college in her home town

The work all done we popped into the bistro to say a quick 'hello and goodbye' before leaving for home. A few of the volunteers were chatting in the bar L. J. (Little John) offered to buy us a drink, and asked if we had any brown sauce to spare. He had a weakness for the spicy sauce and it couldn't be had in *Pakrac*. We handed over the remains of our own bottle.

Shirley rejoined Kelly in their van and our two vehicle convoy hit the road for home. The weather was nice enough for a picnic on the way through Germany. With plenty of eggs on board we cooked omelettes for lunch and sat in the sun at a rest area. Our journey home was pleasant and we enjoyed the restful channel crossing. Shirley left us near Sunbury and Kelly came aboard to be our passenger as we travelled the last leg home

JUNE 1994

Andy a friend of our free ranging days, was at a low stage in his life. Denys was giving him a pep talk and said jokingly, "What you need is to come with us on one of our trips." A short while later, Andy rang and asked, "Did you mean what you said about my coming with you on a trip?" We did. Elisabeth from a village near High Wycombe was to make her second mission with us, her co-driver had backed out at the last minute so Andy was volunteered for the job of driving the Autotrail camper with trailer. He agreed as long as his sleeping quarters were in with us.

Chris from Weymouth, towing a horsebox, was taking Mike from Brighton as his passenger. Tony B. with his transit and trailer, Denise and Steve, Dawn and Dave in two transits from Kent. The two of us in our old faithful Autostratus and trailer and Elisabeth with Andy. The four hour crossing gave us all time to mingle and get to know each other.

Across Belgium and into Germany where at *Hockenheim* we met up with Chuck and Iris, this time in a transit van. They'd had a lot of mechanical problems with their camper on past convoys. They had made the channel crossing on the Hovercraft.

It was about midnight when we found parking spaces among the lorries for the night. While we talked together we asked Andy if he was happy driving the Autotrail, he admitted that he was happier being involved rather than sitting back as a passenger.

The next day as we were heading for *Cologne, Nuremberg* and *Regensberg*, we passed through lovely countryside, the banks of the motorways were a riot of colour.

Wild blue lupins, red poppies, red and pink dog roses and white horse daisies. The woodlands and fields were lush and green. We passed acre upon acre of vines all in neat lines.

At our lunch stop I cooked sausages and eggs while Elisabeth heated baked beans and made a pot of tea. We put it all together and ate in our camper. Later while the rest of the convoy spent time in the toll offices having loading sheets stamped for free passage, we knew from past experience that we had to pay so we got a head start on our colleagues. Then as they had faster vehicles than our old camper, which was built for comfort rather than speed, they would catch up and overtake.

While this game of tag was going on, we made contact with an English driver on the C.B. radio, travelling with his daughter and in the same direction as we were. We all joined in on the conversation. Pat was making for *Graz* and was carrying a brand new British car on his truck. We had planned a comfort and cup of tea stop in the next layby so invited them to join us. Elisabeth and Andy pulled in, along with Chris and Mike, Pat with his daughter Karen came to join the party. The rest sailed on by, hoping to make the services at *Gralla* before the bar closed. Pat left us to turn off to *Graz* town centre, wishing us all luck as he vanished out of sight. At *Gralla* services we joined the rest of the team for a nightcap before retiring.

It was warm and sunny as we moved out to do the business at the borders. At Slovenia not too long a wait but going into Croatia, a problem cropped up because three of the vehicles were carrying medicinal drugs. A chap in the customs office had to keep altering the paperwork until it satisfied the customs requirements.

It was very hot in the sun as we waited, some strolled around or smoked. I took the chance to make up a pile of sandwiches for later. At last we were away. By the time the convoy reached our usual resting place, *Virovitica* bus station, we were more than ready for a cup of tea and a meal. The roads from here on were very rough and narrow. Our drivers needed to watch out for wobbly cyclists, tractors with trailers and speeding trucks. The Croatians are not known as the world's best drivers.

We were heading for a centre for refugees in *Slavonski Brod*. One that we had not visited before. The address was The Church of St. Dominic Savio which we had been told cared for one thousand displaced persons. At a filling station outside town we pulled in to ask directions. A phone call was made to let the organisers know that we were near. A car was being sent to guide us to the church While we waited, Tony and Mike decided to liven things up with a bucket, a sponge and some water.

The car arrived, a priest stepped out and introduced himself as Father Peter. As Tony introduced himself, Mike leapt forward saying "Pleased to meet you, I'm Mike, soaking wet." We were then led about half a mile or so to the church. As it was 10pm. we felt it was too late to unload. We were all taken into a long room where supper had been prepared for us. Bread and cheese, coffee and Coca-Cola. Father Peter did not speak English but his friend managed well enough to be our interpreter.

Accommodation for the night was offered, Chuck and Iris accepted. Denise and her crew left us then to spend the night with friends near the hospital. They had medical supplies and would unload there. The rest of us were shown into the church which was a really beautiful modern building. We each took a quiet moment to take in the peaceful atmosphere admiring the frescoes and decorations.

The church bell woke us at 6am. we soon realised that it was a recording played over speakers. Some of us turned over and enjoyed another hour before facing the day. The unloading was scheduled for 9am. It was raining as we started carrying the boxes into a storeroom beneath the church where there was a very strong and peculiar smell. We soon discovered that it housed two very large pigs in one corner.

A large amount of our load was a collection of shoeboxes made up by school children from Hertfordshire. A lady named Dawn had collected these from sixteen schools in her area. She had contacted our charity and asked us to deliver them to the church after asking Father Peter to distribute them to the refugee children. We had travelled to Dawn's home at Hertford Heath along with Tony, Chuck and Iris and Elisabeth. Each taking a large amount of the boxes for this trip. The press had taken photos of us with a banner 'CONVOY OF HOPE' for the local papers.

There were plenty of volunteers to do the work, I took photos with Tony's camera and my own. Dawn had asked for pictures to pass on to the schools involved. Then I gave a teddy to a small girl in her mother's arms, they were watching the proceedings with great interest from a balcony nearby. A group of children hanging around the gateway were each given a shoebox to take home.

Later in the day we moved on to the *Antun Mihanovic Centre*, Denise and her friends had arrived there before us so we were expected. We had not brought a great deal to them this time but we received a very warm welcome with slivovic and coffee. When things settled down a little, Chris W. stood up and started to make a speech. To our surprise it was directed to us.

Last November our convoy had been the smallest yet, four vehicles. This had been just after our Ruby Wedding Anniversary. At each stop on the journey, we had brought out the remains of the celebration cake that daughter Chris had made for the party, to be eaten with our cups of tea. Chris. W. had drawn a cartoon picture of the trip, the monster cake set on top of our trailer and it being refused in all different languages as we crossed the Continent. After the speech he presented it to us.

We gave the ladies who worked at the centre a photo album containing pictures taken on previous visits. Tony had a special box for a lad called Addis, the last time we were there Tony was told of this boy. His father had been killed and the boy waited every night for his Daddy to come home. Tony had not been able to forget the story and had brought roller skates, books and games for him. The lad's mother looked on with tears rolling down her face

A refugee mother of ten children arrived, Dawn had specially asked that some of her boxes be given to this family. She had been involved with them for sometime, which had motivated the school collection. She had given us a photograph of the family so that we would recognise them. The next call on our list was to a hospital school outside town, where Father Ilya made us welcome and showed us around the building. The children at the school were suffering from traumatic conditions caused by the war, three of them were unable to speak. The children's ages ranged from five to ten years old. We had arrived just as the children were getting up from their after-lunch nap. While they were having orange juice and biscuits, they were encouraged to sing for us, "If you're happy and you know it, clap your hands," in Croatian.

A little charmer named Marina took a fancy to Tony, she had a disability in that her legs were very deformed but that didn't stop her from running down the corridors after our big, bluff convoy leader, squealing his name at the top of her voice. We saw the classrooms, play rooms and physical exercise rooms with all new equipment. We were invited to take coffee in the dining room where there seemed to be a meeting going on. Father Ilya told us that the school was well supported by local businessmen and doctors who funded the project. They really needed nothing that we could give but we were told that the school was looking for an English teacher to join the team. A good opening for someone with no ties.

On earlier visits to *Slavonski Brod* one of the ladies named Nada, which was a very common name in those parts, had asked us to spend a night at her home.

We had declined her offer before, mainly because of leaving our vehicle unattended. Our home on wheels always raised interest in the towns and villages because it was a little out of the ordinary. On this trip we had no excuses not to accept the invitation as Andy offered to 'house sit' for us.

We had a box of personal gifts for Nada from both Jean and Jack, guests of ours on previous visits. Jean had carried on the friendship by mail. Leaving Andy in charge of the camper and the teapot, we set out for Nada's flat. There we met her son, Ivan and daughter Meirta both, glad of the chance to practice their schoolroom English. We discovered that they were a very musical family and we spent an interesting evening. They were not refugees but have had some amazing experiences, one of them when Nada was on her balcony and narrowly missed being hit by a sniper's bullet. The children had been sent to relatives during the nightmare of the war years. They had very little money to live on but Nada had a job in the bookshop of the Holy Trinity Church, which was part of the monastery.

We spent a comfortable night on a bed settee in the small lounge. For our breakfast our hostess had already been to the market for fresh baked bread and the local smoked fat bacon. The young people had already eaten and left for school at 8am. Nada handed over a couple of small gifts for her friends Jean and Jack and then walked with us back to our camper. At

143

intervals she would stop to greet friends with, "These are my friends from England." After fond farewells, and retrieving our house keys from Andy, we moved out with the convoy to make a stop in town for one of Tony's 'Front Line Tours.' This was for the first timers to take evidence home of the destruction of a fine city.

After a walk-about and as we were about to return to the vehicles a lady with a very strange accent came to talk to us. A local lady who had lived in Australia for some years and she was at present visiting family. She just wanted to thank us for helping her country and wished us luck for the future. We had kept back a few items of toiletries for the Sisters at the monastery, where we made a tour of the church and vestments room. A new addition to the church since our last visit was a huge brass plaque, depicting St Francis, which had been brought from a destroyed church in Bosnia.

Outside, a couple of policemen were taking a great interest in ours and Elisabeth's campers, one of them was a C B enthusiast and gave Denys his card. his C.B. name was 'Dragan', the second chap was armed.

A little later I spotted him talking to a small girl on a bench, I took a soft toy to the child and asked permission to take a photo. The policeman stepped back as he was not allowed to be photographed. I got my picture of the girl sitting next to the gun which was still leaning against the seat.

As we left the city and headed to *Virovitica*, it was to be a parting of the ways. While driving through a village we found ourselves in the midst of a wedding celebration, the party had spilled out onto the road. As we drove slowly between the revellers, bottles of local brandy were thrust through our windows for us to drink to the happy couple.

Chris and Mike were going on to *Ljubjana* to visit friends, Tony, Chuck and Iris were heading for home. Two transits and Elisabeth were following us to *Pakrac*. From there on, our companions were getting their first sight of truly devastated homes and villages. We had saved our medical supplies for the emergency hospital at *Pakrac*. Denise and friends left us to find Dragitsa who was a doctor from the hospital. They would be spending the night at her home.

After taking our contribution of medical items to the hospital, we visited the family at the Faroan Bistro, personal friends now after so many visits to their town which was badly damaged in a battle two years before. No refugees there but just local people trying desperately to survive. Soap and shampoo for Mama and the girls, and a Wombles tape for the youngest, Emina.

We took Elisabeth and Andy for a tour of the town, to see the dividing line separating the Serbs and Croat territories where a U.N. checkpoint was set up in the middle of the street. Then to the Anneka school for our friends to take a couple of photographs.

Later we drove to the ghostly hulk of the hospital to park up for the night, our two campers were parked side by side, door to door. In the morning we made a visit to the young volunteers, they were a great bunch. We helped them by bringing books, football kits, leotards and other items useful to the schools. This time they had just opened a youth club, we passed on some of own playing cards and a game of Scrabble.

In our trailer there just happened to be a bicycle, which had been donated from an RAF Officer in the U.K. We passed it on to the volunteers asking them to find a good home for it. Denise and her crew caught up with us and we were all ready to hit the road. A call at the bistro to say goodbye, Mama had made up two Bosnian Burgers to keep us from starving on the way.

2 miles to *Lipik*, a town as devastated as *Pakrac*. Almost as famous as the Anneka School is the Mark Cook Orphanage. This children's home was rebuilt by Englishman, Mark Cook with a great deal of help from publicity by the BBC and the 'Hearts of Gold' team. It was not too difficult to find, for it was a large beautiful pink building among blitzed homes and hotels. We had one box of toys that we had been asked to deliver to the home. Denys went in alone to check that the gifts would be welcome. He came back with a very charming lady who introduced herself as Anna from Lincoln.

We were a little embarrassed at the fact that we only had one box of gifts but Anna told us that they had more toys than they could handle. We were all invited to look around the complex. Our guide Nina, was an orphan herself, nineteen and soon expected to leave and make her own way in the world. She took us first to the girl's accommodation. Each room was fitted out for three girls, with beds, wardrobes, lockers and chairs, bright and cheerful bed covers and decor. On the top floor was a large playroom.

On the wall outside the door of each room was a plaque showing the name of the sponsors who had given cash for the project. Anna's family name was outside the playroom. We were served with coffee in the dining room while some of the children were having early lunch. The children go to school on a shift system, older children in the morning and the younger ones in the afternoon, no babies in this home, all children over 5 years old.

We made a move then, I cut the huge burgers into eight pieces to keep us going until our lunch stop. Onto the motorway to *Zagreb*, a short visit to *Rangi Nakova* to leave the last of the food and clothing from the transits. All we had was a packet of broad bean seeds, they were well received. Passing through the outskirts of *Zagreb* we picked up the road to *Maribor*. We arrived in the U.K. on the 15th June.

JUNE\JULY 1994

With no longer a warehouse full of goods from which to choose a suitable load, we picked up the stored boxes from Tracy's garage along with medical supplies donated from the new Royal Bournemouth Hospital. We were able to make up about half a load. We then received a call from our friend Robin who lived in Havant, he with his wife Lut were veterans of many aid convoys, like ourselves. They had more goods than they could take on the next trip so offered some of it to us.

Tim M. who had travelled with us in April, was keen to come with us on what we hoped would be the first private convoy to make it into *Sarajevo*. With Tim on board we left for Havant on Sunday 26th June. As we neared the town, while making a turn, Denys looking in the rear view mirror, noticed that we were short of one trailer wheel. None of us had noticed it leaving us. Hoping to find it Denys drove all the way back to Ringwood, as that was the last place we could be sure we had four wheels on the wagon.

Most of the road was dual carriageway so there was no hope of spotting the wheel until we turned back towards Havant. Three pairs of eyes scanning the verges and central reservations brought no sign of our missing wheel. There was no hope of getting another wheel as it was a Sunday. Denys put the spare wheel on and just hoped we would not get a puncture. We got all Robin's goods into our trailer with room to spare.

On the Monday morning Rob had a phone call from the local Tampax factory offering a load of their goods. We went along and took enough of much needed ladies' items to make a full load. With a full crew and a full load we drove on to Ramsgate that night. Our sailing was 10.30 the next morning.

Shirley from Sunbury on Thames, in a transit, was minus a second driver, Although Denys usually did all his own driving we recommend that a second driver is necessary on long hops. Tim volunteered to drive with Shirley. Our passengers often came in useful. On the channel crossing it was more like a Caribbean cruise, the decks were awash with sunbathers. Everyone was making the best of the glorious weather. At *Ostende* the convoy was regrouped after leaving the ferry, transits and small vehicles were to follow Tony. The large and slower vehicles would be under our care. With us were a seven and half ton truck driven by Graham and Sue, Chris from Weymouth with camper and horsebox trailer, and a Talbot van, the drivers Joyce and her brother Derek.

While driving across Belgium, the Talbot van gradually became slower holding us back some miles behind the main convoy, until it stopped altogether about 20 miles short of *Aachen*. Chris called over the C.B. that the van had broken down. He stayed with the van while we went on to let the rest of the convoy know what was happening. We were fortunate in that we had two A.A.vans with us. They went back to sort out the problem, soon they all rejoined us at the services.

We still had a long way to go to our night stop at Hockenheim, we made it at 2.45am. After breakfast we sorted some of the loads around, some of the trailers were over loaded and the seven-ton truck was half-empty.

With a late start we moved on to *Hohenlohe* services for refuelling. A coach load of German tourists looked on with interest as our happy gang filled vehicles with diesel and bought sweets and drinks from the shop. The lady bus driver came over to us and asked questions about our journey, and how long it takes to get from our homeland to the refugee camps. She then went back to her coach and passed on the information to her passengers in German. We did wonder if they might have a whip round for us, no such luck.

In hot and sultry weather, we and our charges were some way behind the rest of the convoy but still in radio contact. All of a sudden we heard Tony pulling all the vehicles onto the hard shoulder. They had been caught in a heavy storm, suddenly we were in it ourselves. Seeing the hazard lights ahead we pulled in at the tail end of the convoy. There we sat for half an hour with banter and jokes flying over the airwaves.

Then a decision to pull out as we could just as well drive out of the storm as quickly we drove into it. We in the camper closed the back door. This expression means that as we were at the rear of the convoy we would pull out into the road first. Thus blocking the lane of traffic, then the vehicles in front could all pull out together. The rain did slacken off but we were well behind schedule with one thing and another.

Lunch stop 3pm. Problem! The lorry had a puncture and no spare wheel, George and Mike the A. A men did what they could but a new tyre was needed, this would have to be done at a garage. The nearest town was *Nuremberg* which was some miles back. One A.A. van would go with the lorry and see the repair done while the rest of us pressed on, they would meet up with us at *Gralla Services* that night.

At *Passau* a great many lorries were waiting to clear customs, we hoped that it wouldn't be so busy when our lorry came through later. In Austria, the weather was still stormy, it turned to thunder and lightning as we travelled on the old roads. Quite spectacular streaks and flashes over the mountains. As we passed through the tunnels we stayed with Chris and his horsebox while the others sped on. When they had to stop at the toll for a free passage ticket, we caught up with them. The rain stopped and the weather was cooler as we reached the last stretch to *Gralla Services*.

On waking the next morning we saw that the lorry and its escort had rejoined us. They'd had a problem at the border caused by the extra weight of the loads from the trailers. They had more weight than stated on the T forms and loading sheet. Their explanation was accepted.

A meeting was held to brief the new members on driving in Croatia, then we moved on to the borders. An hour wait in temperature of 90deg chatting and resting in what little shade could be found. At last we were cleared but an emergency meeting was held in the car park. The police had requested that we split the convoy up for the drive through Slovenia so as to minimise traffic hold ups.

With three groups of five and one of six vehicles, we left at five-minute intervals. On to the Croatian border and another long wait in the blistering sun. Two hours later we were heading to *Zagreb, Karlovac* and the Adriatic coast.

Tony led the main convoy, 'the hares', we took care of 'the tortoises'. Some of the drivers not used to the C.B., were causing confusion by talking over the messages from the lead vehicle and other drivers. On the mountain roads shady patches gave relief from the blazing sun. As we reached the top of the hill before the long steep descent, we pulled in to regroup and to prepare everyone for the 20 mile down hill run. We made it with no mishaps, each driver making the twists and turns at their own pace.

At this part of the journey Tim and Shirley were a little worried about the mountain roads. At the fact that there was no barrier between the road and the drop on our side of the road, Shirley asked Ray to drive her vehicle down the steep hill, while Tim rode with Uncle George. We arrived at the *Ad Turres Hotel* at 8 45pm.

Tim treated us to a meal in the dining room of the hotel, the three of us ordered a mixed grill, Shirley ordered scampi, she was most surprised when a large covered dish was set before her. She lifted the lid to find four large lobster-like creatures complete with claws in a very rich sauce. Tony helped Shirley out by peeling the shell from the fish. Then he mopped up some of the sauce with local bread, while waiting for his own omelette and chips. We all enjoyed our meal, then relaxed.

A party of us sat outside on the patio, a gorgeous night with bright stars and a slight breeze. Shirley took a room in the hotel, special rates for convoy members. In the camper we found it really too hot to sleep. I opened all the windows and the half door. Then sometime in the night the wind got up and blew the curtains about and the paperwork was scattered all over the place.

In the morning a briefing on C.B. usage. At 10am. we moved off heading south on the Adriatic Highway. For the first couple of hours our vehicles were buffeted about by the strong, hot and almost gale force winds. At lunchtime we took a break by the sea, a chance for those with the energy to have a dip in the inviting blue waters.

The temperature was about 90 degrees in the shade. Setting off once more, it wasn't long before Chris shouted 'Mayday-

Mayday-Mayday' over the C.B. The brakes on his van were failing, we were on a long down-hill stretch at the time. When he could Tony pulled us all into a layby. Mike and George got busy. The heat and excessive use of the brakes had made the oil in the system boil, more fluid was added. One of the Verwood vans took on the towing of the horsebox, to make things easier for Chris.

A few more miles and Robin had a problem with his Land Rover, the clutch had gone. Again we pulled into a layby close to the sea. Once again, all but the chaps from the A.A. took time out to relax and wait. But it seemed there was no chance of getting this job done on the roadside.

It was decided that Shirley's van should take Tony's trailer and Tony would tow Robin's Land Rover until they could get it to a workshop where it might be possible to get the clutch repaired. Close to where we were parked, it was noticed that locals were bringing bottles and other containers to a stream of water emerging from a wall and into the sea. We soon discovered that the stream was from a fresh water spring and it was ice cold. While we waited, we watched as soldiers and truck drivers refreshed themselves in this water. Some even came to dip crates of beer or mineral water into the pool which was being fed by the spring. It was not long before we too filled every available container and refreshed ourselves with this icy water.

On the road again and heading for *Zadar*, passing through the *Meslenica* village and crossing by way of the pontoon bridge. The road down to the sunken ferry had been resurfaced. On the other side at the police checkpoint, Tony and Robin asked where they might be able to get the towed vehicle fixed. We waited while phone calls were made. Then it was suggested that they try the U.N. base in *Zadar*.

We parked as usual at the *Kalovare Hotel*. Refugee kids were soon swarming around our vehicles looking for 'bon-bons' and 'chocolad'. Tony, Rob and the boys went off to see what could be done about the Land Rover. The rest of us just sat, talked, wandered and waited. We seemed to be doing a lot of that on this trip. A group of us decided to take a walk down to the sea, only a matter of yards from the vehicles. On the way we found a nice little ice cream stall with tables set under shady trees.

Surrounded by local families, we sat a while with ices. After cooling off, we walked along the beach until we felt we ought to get back to find out what was happening. There was no news, but Denys found that some U.N. troops in a truck parked beside our camper were Malay's. He was in his element, it was the first chance he'd had to practice his knowledge of their language in many years.

George, known as 'Uncle George' to all convoy members, started a game of horseshoes, our drivers and the local kids all had a go, it was going in full swing well after dark. There were no 'fireworks' or 'bumps in the night'.

Saturday morning and the news was that nothing could be done about the Land Rover until mid-day. Making the most of our free time, most of us went to the bar by the sea. The owner seemed very pleased with our orders of coffee, fruit juices, cokes and ice cream. At least we made the bar look busy. Locals came and went while we sat there and talked. Back at twelve, and still nothing happening.

After lunch of bread and cheese, the message came through that we were moving off to *Split*. It was hoped that the R.E.M.E. workshops there would be able to do the job. Some missing drivers were rounded up and we moved out at around 3pm.

Tim in Shirley's van and towing Tony's trailer, was finding it heavy going on the hills. The rest of the convoy sailed on and their voices on the C.B. gradually died away. It was not a problem as we knew the road, we had travelled it alone in April. We kept our speed to that which suited Tim, listening out and calling for 'Echo One' or the convoy at intervals. We arrived at the outskirts of *Split* at 5.30 and drove part way into the city and out again, calling until we were hoarse.

Following the itinerary, we were taking the road towards *Dubrovnic*, when we heard Uncle George calling 'Echo One', Tony's call sign. We answered George and he was able to give us directions to the R.E.M.E. depot. He said that we should turn left at a large crossroads where there were road works. Problem was that we had just passed that point and were bowling on down towards *Makarska*.

Suddenly Denys spotted Catweazel, a character from the

Canterbury area, he was standing beside the road. We did know that we were to meet up with him but our problems had delayed us somewhat. Finding a suitable place to turn round was not so easy with our 20ft. camper and 10ft. trailer to manoeuvre on the coast road. By using a slip road and stopping all the traffic Denys managed to turn our rig around.

We were soon heading in the right direction and stopped long enough to allow Catweazel's converted ambulance to join our mini convoy. At the crossroads Uncle George was waiting to show us into the narrow lane leading to an open air market, then on to a large lorry park which was almost full of heavy vehicles.

Just after this we could hear Tony on the C.B., we called back but all we got was Tony and Robin chatting to each other as though they were out on a Sunday afternoon joy ride. When they eventually arrived Tony was quite annoyed. He told us that the convoy had waited an hour for us. He had left the two A. A. chaps waiting in a layby in case we had broken down. The little 'Brett Hire' van had gone back as far as *Zadar* out of concern for our safety.

There was no way we could have passed them on the road. There was just no way we could have missed each other. Then the problem was solved, we had followed signs for *Split* and they had followed signs for *Dubrovnic*. Same direction, different roads. We had followed the itinerary, they had used instinct. The A.A. chaps were contacted, then we waited for Lisa who was in the Brett Hire van.

The Land Rover was to be left at the R.E.M.E. workshop, Lut and Robin would travel with Tony, there would be no problem with sleeping arrangements as accommodation was available at *Medugorje*. Lee and Lizzie came to ask us if we would recommend a refugee camp where they could take their load if they decided not to go on to *Sarajevo*. Denys gave them directions to *Rangi Nakova* near *Zagreb*.

A little later Lee had a confrontation with Tony saying he was not happy with Tony's leadership or the time wasted with the Land Rover. Tony told him he was free to leave.

We were ready to move out, waiting to hear from Lisa. Peter from Reading volunteered to go back a few miles to see if he could contact them. They could have broken down themselves. The vehicles were lined up along the lane, waiting. Catweazel came to complain that he was out of money and short of fuel. He told us that someone on the convoy had promised to finance his ambulance but had not kept his word. We ourselves were in no position to help him. He then said that the only thing he could do was to ask for help from the U.N. or to sell the goods that he was carrying in the market, to enable him to get home.

We waited, with ears straining to catch news of our missing vans. Then we heard Peter's voice telling us that Lisa was caught up in heavy traffic on the other side of an accident in *Split*. We waited. At last Peter was calling to say that they were all on their way back to us. The convoy started to roll out onto the main road. Some British lads in civvies walked past us on their way back to base. They wished us luck.

10.30, and it was a four hour journey to the border and *Medugorje*. Tony's trailer was now behind his own van, Tim and Shirley somewhere among the group of transits ahead of us. As we left the coast road and took to the mountains once more, we thought that it was probably a good thing that it was so late at night. Not much traffic about so we could travel down the middle of those rough and narrow roads, cutting corners with the drivers in front giving a warning of oncoming cars. Onward and upwards we rode through the night, arriving at the border at 2.30am. all very tired and tempers slightly frayed.

Leaving Croatia took twenty minutes at the customs post. On the Bosnian side no one to deal with us until 7.30am. There was room for the whole convoy to park in the car-park. We all settled down to a few hours sleep.

On waking at 6.30 on a bright and sunny day, more problems. The Customs there could not deal with us as an aid convoy. We were advised to try the *Metkovic* road, the border we went through in April when we were minus our trailer. 9.45 when we arrived there, in front of us were 50 lorries also waiting. This was Sunday, on Mondays and Fridays the border to *Sarajevo* was closed all day. Any other day the hours of entering this besieged city were between 10am. and 12 noon. If we did not make it that morning we would have to wait until Tuesday.

Tony left us, he dealt with all the formalities and paper work at the customs office, while we waited. Two hours passed and a message came that documentation had been changed two days before. At 12, Tony asked Irene from Reading to join him at the office. We were parked in a very narrow street, a family with a young baby were watching the scene from the balcony of their house. To break the monotony Graham from the lorry in front us gave the baby a teddy. I took a couple of photographs, then a lady from the family brought us glasses of lemon squash. I rummaged in our cupboards and found a couple of fancy soaps to give her.

These were not refugees but it felt good to give something to someone after so long waiting. Some of the crews had found an open air shower and had livened things up by giving everyone in sight a soaking. At 1.30 came the word to turn around and head back to the coast. As we travelled Tony told us that Irene had been very useful as an interpreter but the officials could not understand or speak English, German was their second language,

The spokesman had suggested that he could take Irene to the address in *Sarajevo* where we were to take the aid and to get a fax to verify that we were expected. This would cost 500.marks. 20 for each car and the rest for him and the service he was providing for our convoy. Tony had decided, enough was enough.

We were still free to take our aid to refugee camps or towns like *Pakrac*, where help was still badly needed. In the meantime we were going to the beach to relax after a frustrating day. While we were waiting at the border some locals had told Denys of a very good beach on the *Dubrovnic* road. But on taking this road we soon found ourselves at yet another border. The police allowed us into Bosnia just to turn the vehicles around. One of the policemen there told Denys of an Auto Camp that we could use, at a village called *Kiek*. He said we would be very welcome as a Humanitarian Aid Convoy.

On finding this camp we drove into a shady area under some trees. Although we were the only people parked there, it seemed to be a holiday camp, with a motel, bars and chalets. There were very few people about, a group of children were playing near by. As soon as we were all parked, a meeting was called. Tony was upset and apologised for our not being able to make our destination. A decision was made to rest up for the night and get an early start in the morning. There was some shunting around of vehicles and then Tony went off to rest in his van.

To give him his due, he was not 100 per cent fit having just recovered from pleurisy. We had just settled when Uncle George had a change of plan, he wanted to take six of the vehicles to one of his favourite villages, *Gospice*, not far from *Behac*. As Tony was asleep George gave Denys a list of vehicles he was taking with him. That was fine, but a little later, the Reading truck pulled out and just about every other van followed. Surprisingly no one said goodbye or where they were going.

From 21 vehicles we were now down to 3, Tony, with his passengers, Tim and Shirley, and us. We felt deserted. As Tony and Denys did all their own driving they needed a break after the disastrous couple of days. Rob, Lut and Shirley found themselves rooms in the motel, later we all took a walk to the sea. Near the beach we found a small cafe where a couple of pleasant young ladies served us coffee. One of them spoke English and told us that she lived in *Dubrovnic* until her home was destroyed. With the shortage of customers the girls played darts in between serving us. We found the dartboard very interesting. It was computerised, showing the scores and remaining amount that each player needed.

We sat at tables under shady grape vines. As the sun set and darkness fell we strolled back to the vehicles where we sat and listened to a recorded comedy show until each of us was tired enough to turn in.

The next morning we were moving out with Tim and Shirley following, heading for *Crikvenica*. Tony with Rob and Lut would be stopping at *Split* to check on the Land Rover. We were leading vehicle this time and Tony was following up the rear as tail end Charlie for a change. We made a stop at a seaside town, Tim needed to change some marks to local kuna. In the car park we met some interesting people from 'The Convoy of Mercy'. They gave us some information on entering *Sarajevo* if we were to make another try.

We travelled together until we reached *Split*, there Tony

peeled off to go and see about the Land Rover. Skirting *Zadar* we carried on up the coast road and watching out for the fresh water spring, it was on a bend in the road. We pulled in and watched as locals were filling bottles and chatting together. We stood back and waited for our turn to get to the water hole. Denys and Tim filled our water containers as we paddled to cool off.

The temperature in the water was 9 degrees, while the air temperature was 92. I used the pool to cool off a can of corned beef for sandwiches, our little fridge was unable to cope with the heat. The last lap to *Crikvenica*. The traffic was busy and the local suicide jockeys were out in force. The near misses we had were unbelievable. All thanks to the skill of our drivers we arrived unscathed.

We were too late for a meal in the *Ad Turres Hotel*. The receptionist told us of a restaurant just a few yards down the road. This time it was Shirley's treat, mixed grills for us while she fancied an omelette. We sat at a table under the vines, the scent of the jasmine in the air with cicadas making a din. A perfect setting for a holiday if you could ignore the midges and flying ants.

We walked back to the *Ad Turres* to spend the night. At a nearby bar a disco party was going on until the early hours.

While we were having breakfast a little white Escort pulled in beside us. It was from our former convoy and had contained two young men the last time we saw it. Now there was only the driver. Paul was so pleased to see us, he was on his way home with no food and very little money.

We gave him a breakfast, then Shirley and I gave him a few cans of beans, spaghetti, and soups with a can opener to keep him going across the continent. Fuel was not too much of a problem as an Escort will almost run on fresh air.

A social call on our friends, we did not have much to give them but we were welcome just the same. We mentioned that we were on our way to the clinic to leave medical supplies. Nada told us that her mother had a heart problem and that it took nearly all her father's pension to buy the pills needed for her. These families did get £5 a week pension but if they needed medication the clinic was charging high prices for drugs. Maybe they were making a profit out of the aid that we were bringing. Denys suggested that we take the goods we had and bargain for the pills needed by our friends.

We left some 'ladies necessities' then made our way to the clinic. We parked under the viaduct which carries the new bypass, and behind the clinic. Tim and Denys went into the clinic to arrange the unloading of the supplies. Half an hour later they were back pretty disgusted because they had been shown to a small room and asked to wait. They had not been able to find anyone who would talk to them. A little different to the treatment we had been used to.

Lee and Lizzie found us in *Crikvenica*, they told us that they were unable to find *Rangi Nekova* but the police had directed them to a camp near *Varazdin* which was not often visited by aid convoys. They were feeling a lot happier about the trip now they had done the job they set out to do. Hearing that we were making for *Pakrac* and *Lipik*, they decided to tag along with us.

We refuelled at Mika's, the ex world champion speedway star, then took the mountain road. At one point on this road for the return journey, vehicles had to take a one way system through a tunnel in the rocks. As our camper was too high for this route, we had to drive on the wrong side of the road around a blind bend to the right. Tim drove the van through the tunnel and blocked the road from oncoming traffic until we rounded the bend and got back onto the right side of the road. For lorries and coaches there was a detour on a longer route.

As we climbed into the mountains, the weather changed dramatically, lightning streaks bounced across the road in front of us. Terrific claps of thunder rolled around the mountain, then the rain, so heavy that we could hardly see. We knew from past experience, that we could well drive out of it in a while.

We did, coming out of the rain we found a bone dry layby. A good stop for lunch, cups of soup and the last of our local bread. A stray cat, thin as a rake came to join us. Lee opened a tin of tuna for it, the poor creature must have thought it was his birthday. TV Arthur did not have a thing on this little Kitty, digging the fish out of the can with its paws.

On our way again, the weather was still dull but we didn't

mind it being a little cooler. Travelling on through *Karlovac*, it seemed to us that there were more bombed buildings than we had noticed before. On the outskirts of town, high on a chimneystack, I spotted a stork's nest. They were quite a common sight in those parts. On to the motorway, showing our loading sheet got us a free passage through the peage. As we travelled Denys called Lee on the C.B. to point out the huts that made up *Rangi Nekova* camp.

On to the E70 road to the *Kutina* turnoff, as far as we could go on the motorway. From there on it was Serb held territory. On the country roads we admired the pretty villages, bright with flower decked balconies and window boxes. The villagers waved and called out as we passed, our vehicle was well known in the area. At the U.N. checkpoint, Jordanian soldiers had a portrait of their King on view outside of their shelter. I don't think they understood what we said to them and we certainly didn't understand their reply. They let us through the barriers. Over the C.B. I informed Lee and Lizzie that we were now on the front line of the war.

Tim and Shirley had been in these parts with us before. Everyone fell silent as we drove past the bombed and derelict houses. Among the ruins of so many, one or two seemed to be untouched and occupied. It must be quite eerie to live among the ruins of your neighbours' homes.

Then as we entered *Lipik*, we made a stop at the new orphanage, which had been rebuilt by Colonel Mark Cook of the Ghurka Rifles. The effort was helped by our own B.B.C. Hearts of Gold team and Woolworth's. Some homes in *Lipik* were being repaired with financial help from Italy, as some of the villagers had Italian connections. These houses could be recognised by a small blue pennant hanging from the building.

Two miles on and we were in *Pakrac*, we parked up in the main street and were met by some of the volunteers. We all went into the bistro to a warm welcomes and cool Cokes. Shirley told L.J., one of the British volunteers, about the sports equipment she had brought for the youth club.

Table tennis kit, a 6ft. pool table, baskets and basket balls, dartboards and rounders outfits, even posters for the walls, all generous gifts from the firm where Shirley worked.

If we had been able to get into *Sarajevo* as planned all this gear would have been left there. The customs would not have let us bring the goods out of Bosnia once they had been checked through their border. *Sarajevo's* loss was *Pakrac's* gain.

We had planned to stay only one day in the blitzed and friendly town. Our plans were changed on learning that the Volunteers were having a celebration for the anniversary of the start of the 'Pakrac Project'. We were invited to stay on, we had great admiration for the group. One or two of them like B.J. and L.J. stayed full time, others were replaced every few weeks.

The evening was spent with the family from the bistro, a dish of strange but delicious fish was put before us, Papa had caught it that afternoon. With corn fritters and fries we were urged to eat up. No matter how we tried we were not allowed to pay for the food. At 11 we retired to our parking place behind the hospital.

In the morning we woke to the sound of voices, Women were going into the hospital and men were cutting the grass and weeds in the grounds. Early signs that the townspeople were about to pick up the pieces of their lives. We had promised L.J., one of the English volunteers, that we would cook him an English breakfast that morning. The aroma of eggs and bacon floated down the main street as I got busy with the frying pan outside the bistro.

Shirley had brought a couple of sealed packs of bacon, it really needed using after all the miles it had travelled in the heat. Emira had arranged for Denys to meet the pharmacist from the town's clinic. He told her of our experience of clinics making money from our country's generosity and their own peoples misery. This lady was only too pleased to accept the medicines that we were carrying and promised that they would be given free to the needy. We had been led to believe that there were only 3 babies in *Pakrac*, later while we were in town we saw that many in half an hour. We loaded the surprised Mums with Pampers, baby clothes and milk powder.

On turning a corner we noticed Anton just about to get into his car. We had not met up with him for some months. He followed us to the house of the volunteers and waited. In this divided town there were many families on either side who were in desperate need through no fault of their own.

We decided rightly or wrongly that we would help by bringing food parcels to be distributed by the volunteers, to help ease the suffering. We could not do this ourselves without upsetting the friends we had made on the Croat side by openly helping Serb families. The volunteers had agreed to help by getting the goods where they were most needed. Leaving our colleagues to be shown the sights round the town by the volunteers we followed Anton's little car out of town. We stopped at a very smart little house and met his 'Frau' Maria, for the first time.

Anton told us that the house belonged to his son who was living and working in Germany. Maria served us with cold lemonade although they spoke very 'Leetle' English we managed to converse, a lot of it from guess work on both sides. Maria showed us photographs of their family, two sons and one daughter. Some of the pictures were of the old house as it was and some of how it is now. Maria gave a shrug of the shoulders and gave a big sigh, then put the photos away.

I fetched the albums to show them pictures I had taken of the town, among them were one or two of their old home and of when we first met Anton. Anton managed to explain that most of his albums had been destroyed with their home. I happened to have two empty albums in the camper, I gave them to Maria for her family photos. While we were talking our hostess had been preparing and cooked lunch for the four of us. A vegetable stew with baked mince and onions. While we sat in the garden after the meal, people would arrive at the gate and Anton would go off and deal with them. Then we discovered that he had managed to salvage most of his shoe making equipment and was back in business.

We were given a tour of his workshop set up in his shed in the back yard. On the other side of the shed was a pen holding a few turkeys and chickens to help out with the food situation. Fresh water was always a priority with us, Denys borrowed Anton's hosepipe to fill our camper water tank. The cat caused a few chuckles by trying to 'kill' a leak which sprayed out from the hose. At six we had to leave as we were expected at the volunteers' Celebration Party. Then we had a problem, the camper refused to start. Anton called a neighbour who had a tractor in his yard, he gave us a short tow and the camper burst into life.

At the bistro we met up with our gang and compared notes on our afternoon outings over cool Cokes. Then we went to the party venue, loud music and voices raised above it led us in the right direction.

Bosnian Zelika made sure that we had seats and a drink in our hands. The favourite seemed to be Sangria or the local rakia. A young lady with a very strong American accent came to talk with us. Although she was local the accent came from the fact that a lot of youngsters learned most of their English from watching American television programmes. Her name was unpronounceable but shortened to Schnezzy, it was a Croatian translation of Snow White.

We had a great evening and left when everyone reached the 'smoochy' stage. Once again our vans found shelter behind the hospital. After a guided tour of the devastated buildings in the morning, we moved out. One chap who was clearing weeds from the parking area, presented Shirley with a bunch of bright blue star-shaped flowers he had cut from a near by bush.

In town Shirley mentioned she had been given a box of costume jewellery before leaving the U.K., she really had no idea what to do with it. In the street she opened it on the bonnet of the camper, in no time at all women came to see what we were giving away. Shirley encouraged them to help themselves to the free goodies. I took a few shots with my camera through the windscreen of the camper.

Most of the volunteers were still recovering from the party as we called to say goodbye. Just as we were about to leave a young lady rushed from the house, asking for a lift to *Zagreb*. Lee and Lizzie took her on board. First a visit to the orphanage in *Lipik* just to say hello, the place was very quiet, a young lady came out and told us that the children had gone on a holiday trip to Italy.

Lee and Lizzie were to head for *Zagreb*, they intended to spend a couple of days in the city before going home. We and Shirley still had a quantity of clothing and bedding on the vehicles. We knew there was a refugee camp at *Maribor* in

Slovenia. A helpful chap at a filling station gave us directions and we arrived at a place that was once a military barracks. It was early evening and we could see by the mode of dress that they were Moslems. As soon as we stopped, the vehicles were besieged by children and young adults. They climbed all over the vans completely out of control.

We stayed just long enough to get all the remaining goods into the office, then we left in fear of damage to our vehicles. A pleasant journey home. In Germany we were driving past acres of sun flowers grown as a crop, probably for their oil. All the sunny faces were turned the same way. On the ferry the girls made up their diaries while the men rested.

Arriving in the U.K. Tim drove Shirley's van as far as the M3 near Sunbury then he joined us, making for Dorset.

SEPTEMBER 1994

At this stage, home for us was a field at Three Legged Cross near Ringwood, one of the Caravan club's five van-sites. Our landlord Phil was a chicken farmer and had a number of large sheds on his property. He allowed us to use part of one of these buildings for sorting, packing and storing the goods for our next mercy mission. Schools were still making collections of bedding and clothing, One Blandford school made a collection of just shoes.

Spetisbury School in Dorset more or less adopted us and we could call on their support at any time. The children looked forward to our visits after each trip and they always had questions to ask. One day as our camper entered the gate one lad was so excited, he ran into his teacher saying that "Menys and Dary were coming". Those names stuck. Even at their Christmas play, on our chairs were place names 'Menys' and 'Dary'.

On September 13th we joined seven other vehicles to make the long journey across the continent. On our July trip, Tony had given a young voluntary worker a lift home to the U.K. He asked us to take Emma on board with us to go back to Croatia, as he already had a passenger for this trip, Carolyn. We picked Emma up at Ramsgate along with a good deal of baggage.

At *Hockenheim*, Chuck and Iris were there waiting to join us. One of the transits, nick-named 'Yellow Peril', developed a problem with engine overheating. Denys removed a rubber washer from the filler cap, problem solved. In Austria as darkness fell, we were kept to a crawl by heavy trucks on the narrow mountain passes. As we pulled into the services at *Gralla*, the Yellow Peril arrived with a loud bang and seemed to give up the ghost. Two other vehicles were missing but turned up an hour later. They had taken a wrong turn and finished up in the town centre before finding their way to us.

The next morning, we gave Pete and Colin in the Yellow Peril an early call and a cup of tea so that they could have time to sort out their problem, Pete removed the distributor cap and found that the points required adjusting, it seemed to be okay. On then through the borders of Slovenia and Croatia, motorway to *Zagreb*. and mountain roads to the coast. The Yellow Peril coped quite well with the climbs but we stayed close behind in case of further problems.

At 5.30 we all had a break, to give those (like Emma) who were dying for a smoke, a chance to have a cigarette. New drivers were given advice using low gears instead of relying on their brakes for long steep descents from 4,000ft. to the Adriatic highway. Marie and Andrew had a May-day situation, their low gear would not stay engaged without applying constant pressure on the gear stick. They were advised to stay close behind Robin's trailer and use it as a buffer in an emergency. We all made it safely.

When all the convoy members were settled in the parking area of the *Ad Turrres*, we went on to visit our friends in the *Odmaraliste*. We had brought marmalade, sugar and soap powder. They had asked for specific medication for problems of the heart. We had been unable to obtain this; the items had to be on prescription only. The best we could do was to hand over 100 marks (about £80), explaining that it was for medical expenses. In torrential rain and hail, we made our way back to join the others for the night.

The next morning a visit to Josep's group behind the hotel. We had piles of blankets for them and gift packs of soap donated by The Body Shop. We took time to show them the photos that we had taken in July. By this time the convoy was pulling out to go on to *Zadar*. A lunch break next to the ice cool spring which we discovered on a previous trip. Then, bypassed *Split* and followed the coast road to a small town called *Dugi Rat*. This was where Emma was to leave us and where we hoped that the paperwork which would get us into *Sarajevo* would be ready for us.

We were at the base of the Convoy of Mercy. This group led us to believe that they could have the required documents ready for us on this trip. We went in to meet some of the gang, all of them British. Over a cup of tea in an assortment of cracked and chipped cups, we were told that the chap with the paperwork was still in Bosnia and was expected the next day. With a great shortage of parking space, we and a few other vans went on to a lorry park in the next small town called *Omis*.

Once we were settled I made a pot of stew for us and seven of our colleagues. It was still early evening so we all went for a stroll around the town before turning in. The next morning we noticed an open market in the street, we were tempted into buying some fresh fruit. Denys kept an ear open for the C B in case Tony should call with news.

Tired of waiting, Pete and Colin drove back to *Dugi Rat*, to find out first hand what was happening.

We received a message saying that the paperwork was still not ready and that we should have to wait until after the weekend. We knew from Uncle George that *Gospic* was badly in need of supplies, high in the mountains and only yards from the Serbian lines. A vote was taken and there was a unanimous decision to take our goods to *Gospic*. To make sure every one was ready, we arranged to move out at 3.30. While we sat waiting a young man arrived in a car and called out, "Where is Denys Fail?" Our camper was pointed out and he came to explain that he was Anthony Jefferies the brother of a man we had met in our warehouse at Somerford some months before.

He was working for an organisation called Newhouse Trust and had been in Croatia for over a year. On hearing of our problems in getting into *Sarajevo*, he told us that the young lady with him could have the documentation done in 20 minutes but not at the weekend. Anthony gave us his phone and fax number for future reference. He did not seem to have much faith in the Convoy of Mercy group, in his own words they were, 'Just a bunch of Yuppies on extended holidays'. We knew that some of our group had given the 'Yuppies' food supplies and a considerable amount of contraceptive pills in return for the 'favour' they were supposedly doing for us!!

At 3.30 we pulled out for the short drive to meet up with Tony and co. Then we made our way back to *Zadar*. The drive along the glorious coast road was livened up by the erratic driving of the locals. I lost count of the number of accidents we saw en route, some involving U.N. trucks and Land Rovers. At *Zadar* we made a detour to *Dracevac*, where a few items from each vehicle were given to the few remaining inhabitants of the village, some gave blankets, we gave Body Shop gift packs of novelty soaps.

In *Zadar*, we pulled into the *Karlovare Hotel*, the drivers parked in a wild west circle to keep out the refugee. 'Indians', as most still had full loads on their vehicles. In the morning as we prepared to leave, refugee children and women milled around our vans, hoping for handouts. Sweets, balloons and toys were passed over to the children, soap and Pampers for the mums with babies.

Time to move out, we headed for the pontoon bridge at *Meslenica*. On the coast road to *Karlobag*, there we turned inland to take the mountain road to *Gospic*.

Higher and ever higher, the road climbed, twisted and turned until we felt that we were on top of the world. We could see vehicles on the road far below us and others on the levels way above us, some of the passengers were checking their maps and passing on the information that we were at 6,000ft. above sea level. The view of the ocean and the islands was as if seen from an aeroplane.

At last the road levelled out and we were driving through mountain villages and countryside. Soldiers in camouflaged uniforms became a common sight. On our arrival in *Gospic* we were directed to the main hospital by local police. A group of our drivers went in to find out if we could give our goods to the hospital, remembering the experience at *Split*. As we hadn't been expected there was confusion and a lot of discussion.

Our loading sheets were scrutinised and the medical team picked out the items that would be of most use to them. All medical supplies and baby items, disinfectants and toiletries. Everyone opened up the vehicles and started sorting out the loads. Our medical boxes were right at the back of the rest of the goods so the lot had to come out. The temperature was a great contrast to that on the coast, 55 degrees and it was raining. The crew from each vehicle had to carry their contributions into the different departments, long corridors and dark cellars of the hospital.

One of the doctors offered to give us a tour of the blitzed part of the town, he travelled in the lead van. We drove in convoy while given a commentary over the C.B. We were told that just 12 months before, there had been hand to hand fighting in these streets. 130 people had been killed and many more injured. We drove to what had been the railway station, now just ruins. The enemy once were inhabitants of the town. The doctor told us that as the soldiers shelled an old folks' home, some of the relations of those soldiers were being cared for within its walls.

At the hospital a meal was waiting for us, cheese with bread and pots of strong, sweet, black tea. We hadn't thought of the fact that to have milk you had to have cows or goats, most of the animals had been slaughtered for meat. After the meal we were taken into the maternity unit, to meet two young mums with their newborn babies, one a boy and the other a girl. A couple of the team had brought some teddies, they were placed in the cots close to the sleeping infants. We all wished the mothers 'good luck'. They would certainly need it.

We were keen to get down the mountain before dark; it had been raining all the afternoon.

We slowly wound our way down the steep hills, most of the way through a thick mist, more than likely cloud. As we reached the coast the weather was clear and bright, such contrasts. We went on to spend the night at the *Ad Turres*. A drink at the bar while we discussed where best to take the remaining goods. With plenty of camps to choose from, it was decided to make for *Rangi Nekova*.

We ourselves still had goods on board that might be of use to our friends at *Odmaraliste*. We went into the building to be met by a new social worker, his name was Joachim. He did not speak English but his teenage son, Oliver did. They were pleased to accept men's clothing, canned drinks, soap and pasta. They did explain that relationships in the group were becoming very strained. Meals were being taken to their rooms instead of them eating together. It was suggested that if we brought supplies in future, it would be better to make up individual parcels.

On asking after Nada and her family, we were told that the young people were out. Nada greeted us in her room on the second floor, she told us rather coyly that she had a gentleman friend visiting. We were really pleased that she had found a companion. She told us that she was worried about Boris, he was about to go into the army and she was understandably anxious. We were invited to stay in the hostel for the night, usually we turned down offers of accommodation, for some reason this time, we accepted.

Joachim took us to one of the chalets at the back of the main building. The one we were to occupy had five or six rooms, a toilet, a shower and a mini-gym. We slept in rough blankets and during the night something had made a meal of my feet. In the morning they were covered with small, red, fleabites. Breakfast in the main building with Joachim, bread and honey and a dish of small cakes.

Pete from the Yellow Peril had been to visit a friend in *Rijeka* and stayed the night. He returned to meet up with us and Colin at the *Ad Turres*. We left then to follow the mountain road and motorways to *Zagreb*, following in the tracks of the convoy to the refugee camp at *Rangi Nekova*. We were soon surrounded by women and excited children as the boxes were opened up to reveal their contents. Our load by then was mostly clothing, canned drinks, soaps and shoes.

Jean's friend Ruza found us and took us to the small room that the family called home. I knew that Ruza was in need of shoes for herself. I had brought one of the sealed boxes marked shoes, with me into her room On opening it we were disappointed to find that it contained only children's trainers.

The shoes Ruza was wearing were too small and were cutting into her toes. I took off one of my own trainers for her to try, it was the right size. I had a spare pair in the camper so I collected them for her.

Colin had a bunch of letters with him, they were printed in Croat and in English for the refugee kids to send to children in England. We helped by addressing some of the envelopes to some of our many grandchildren. Ruza's son Mario said that he and his young brother Meroslav, would get the children to send off the letters. We and the lads left money to buy stamps to cover the postage. Our visits and the personal touch in camps like this one were so satisfying that we felt that we were doing

169

far more good than we would by making glory trips into Bosnia.

Saying goodbyes always took a great deal of time, eventually we were on our way to find The Holiday Hotel lorry park just outside of *Zagreb*. Colin and Pete were scout leaders and hoped to meet up with some of their Croatian counterparts in *Zagreb*. The boys went off to make phone calls while I put together a pot of stew from assorted cans for the four of us. While we were eating, a chap arrived at our door, his name was Tomitsa. He was from a local scout movement. Pete and Colin had found their contact.

We were off to the city, to have another go at finding the elusive Mario. This time we struck lucky, the warehouse was closed but a phone call brought him to meet us. He gave us a tour of his storage buildings which were close to the railway and told us that his organisation helped the poor people of *Zagreb* as well as refugees. A very strong anti-abortionist, his pet cause was a clinic for pregnant women. He stressed just how grateful he was for the great amount of goods that our charity had sent.

We went along with Mario to arrange the collection of a lorry load of supplies from a warehouse. It was in the same compound where our first convoy had arrived in December 1992. It was also where the Pope had arrived to conduct a Mass just one week before our visit this time. In his car Mario was carrying a large stack of posters advertising and commemorating the Pope's visit, he gave us a large bundle of them for our friends back home.

On leaving our large vehicle at Mario's house, he drove us into the city to play at being tourists. We arranged that he would pick us up near the cathedral in three hours. We wandered around looking in the shops and browsing the street markets. There seemed to be no shortage of essentials but the prices were high.

Every few steps begging children would be tugging at our sleeves, no doubt thinking that we were wealthy tourists.

The cathedral was on a hill on the outskirts of the city, Mario found us there and took us for a pizza supper. He was disappointed that we had to leave the next morning and asked that we spared some time to look in on his pet anti-natal clinic before we left. He said that he would send someone at 9am. to

170

lead us there. Our camping site was in the railway goods yard, it was very quiet with no trains running during the night.

A charming young lady arrived to lead us to the baby clinic. She was another Nada and was quite amused that we had her name on our van. Convoy of Hope in Croatian was '*Convoj Nada*'. At the clinic the doctor who was to show us around was either busy or had not turned up. With many apologies, Nada took us instead to a children's theatre, where she and a friend treated us to coffee. They presented us with a set of colourful posters advertising plays based on Croatian fairy tales. Nada thought that our local schools would like them as a thank you for goods sent to *Zagreb*.

We left then heading for *Ljubjana*, making a little detour to *Lake Bled*, a popular holiday resort before the war. Into Austria where once again we strayed off the main route to picnic close by a beautiful lake. We strolled through a very pretty holiday village with picture book chalets, the balconies dripping with trailing plants and bright flowers. The place was alive with small birds feeding from heads of maize which were hung beneath the eaves of the chalets.

Moving on to *Salzburg*, we spent the night sandwiched between a couple of lorries. Next day our wheels seemed to fly as we travelled toward the home stretch. We arrived in Bournemouth on Saturday 24th September.

NOVEMBER 1994

Six vehicles of the Convoy of Hope boarded the ferry Sally Star on November 1st. With us were four other Old Stagers, Tony, Rob and Lut, Shirley with Kelly as her co-driver and Chris from Weymouth, his horsebox now long gone and he was driving a transit. New on this trip were Danny and Eric from Reading, with Lisa in a seven and a half-ton lorry. On the outskirts of *Brussels* we made a stop to pick up Miriam, Tony's passenger for this trip.

We were to meet up with our nephew at the service station at *Hockenheim*, to pass on Christmas parcels from his family in the U.K. A note left at the sweet and tobacco kiosk told us that he had waited as arranged until after 10.10, we arrived just ten minutes later and had just missed him. We would have to take the gifts for a very long ride and deliver them on the return journey.

Chris had his transit choc-a-bloc with packed goods. As we prepared to turn in he mentioned that he would have to sleep in the driving seat. With no extra passengers this time we offered him our spare bed, which he readily accepted. As we arrived at the German\Austrian border the next day, there was a long queue of trucks waiting. November 1st was a Bank Holiday on the continent, All Souls Day. All lorries would have been off the roads, now they would be trying to make up for lost hours. Our lorry would be in for a very long wait. A few words over the C.B. and our truck followed us through the car lanes and got away with it.

At *Graz* a detour to bypass road works led us by way of unfamiliar roads to the *Gralla* services. We all got together for supper in the restaurant before turning in. The following morning was spent in the tedious job of dealing with borders and

172

the documentation before taking the road to *Zagreb*. On the route to *Rijeka* we were so familiar with the mountain road that we were playing the locals at their own games. The difference being that when we overtook tankers on blind corners, we were depending on our mates ahead to warn us of oncoming traffic.

As we reached the coast, Chris left us to go on to *Rijeka* to search for a family who had appealed for help, this had been via a contact in *Ljubjana*. The rest of us went on to the *Ad Turres* to spend the night. Chris caught up with us there after a successful trip. He had also met someone, who on hearing that we were intending to make it to *Gospic*, had asked if Chris could bring back a supply of potatoes!

In the morning a decision was made to unload some of the heavier goods before travelling up the steep climb to *Gospic*. In our trailer were brand new blankets donated by R.A.F. Manston, they were for Josep's refugee group who had only one blanket to each bed when we first met them. We also had a great deal of children's shoes, some of them were left to be useful to growing families.

The other vehicles went off to various camps and hostels in the area. Most of us who had been to *Crikvenica* had personal contacts by now; ours was at *Odmaraliste*. With the help of family and friends, we had been able to make up 34 individual food and toiletry packs for the enforced residents of the small hotel.

With a good supply of shampoo given by our local Salvation Army and one sphygomometer, a gadget for measuring blood pressure. We had been asked for this on our last visit. We had found a doctor in Reading only too pleased to donate one of the instruments.

Many of the refugees suffered from heart conditions from the stress of the situation in their beloved country. One lady in particular, Evitsa, with high blood pressure, was so happy and could not thank us enough. We received such gratitude for the kindness and generosity of those people who donated the goods that we handed over to those in need. We had arranged to meet up with our colleagues at midday, a quick lunch, then pulled out onto the coast road.

Although the day was sunny and warm, we were being

buffeted by a very strong wind known in those parts as the 'Bora'. At *Senj* we turned inland and started the climb. With each driver taking his or her time, there was no hurry and concentration was vital. At the top we were soon passing damaged buildings, now and again a village that was completely wiped out. We were passing a large field, when someone noticed that sitting forlornly in the middle of it was a Dakota C47 aircraft. We stopped to have a look at the plane, there did not seem to be anyone about, until some of us pointed our cameras over the fence. Suddenly men in uniform appeared, just as if they had been hiding in the long grass. We didn't wait to be asked questions and moved on.

In *Gospic* we presented ourselves at the police station, to ask where our goods would be most needed. We were invited into the building for refreshments and to be welcomed by the female Chief of Police. She was tall, with short skirt, long legs and a mass of long dark hair. We were asked to leave the goods in a damaged building in a rubble-strewn yard attached to the police station.

Among the boxes in our own load, were beautifully wrapped Christmas gifts from Spetisbury School in Dorset. We asked the lady Chief if she would see that the gifts were distributed at the right time to the children of the town. She gave us her word that it would be done. Shirley and Kelly were saving their load for *Pakrac*, Lisa and the boys were intended theirs for *Slavonski Brod*. Those with medical supplies were to take them to *Gospic* hospital just up the road from the police station. As we lined up ready for the off, a car pulled up beside Tony's van. The lady police chief elegantly stepped out to let us know that we would not be required to take the potatoes to *Rijeka* after all!! Was this all a secret message?

In darkness and heavy traffic we made our way down from the mountain. The journey was pretty exciting as we overtook tankers and trucks with the help of the leading vehicles. With the C.B. they could tell us when the road was clear enough to overtake. We would give those in front of us warning of local drivers hopping in between our vehicles.

Safely on the coast, we made for *Crikvenica* and the car park of the *Ad Turres*, then a nightcap with some of the crew before settling in. We made our usual visit to Nada and friends with time for socialising. We had news for Nada. Our son Tim, and Tracy the young lady who had been with us on our first visit in December 1992, were to be married the next month, two years after their meeting. Nada was delighted with the news and although that lady had very little in the way of personal possessions, she made up a gift parcel for the happy couple. Two-crocheted table mats, a small silver cross and a silver heart, for faith and love in their life together.

Meeting up with the convoy again, we travelled on to *Rijeka*. Zinka, a pharmacist friend of Tony's, had invited all of us to her home. The six vehicles caused a bit of a stir in the narrow lane outside the home of Zinka' parents. The twelve of us were invited into the lovely house for coffee and home-made bread still hot from the oven.

As we travelled over the mountains towards *Zagreb*, our camper was the last vehicle in the convoy. On rounding a tight bend we passed a damaged car slowing to a halt, scattering bits of metal along its path. We pulled out of the bend to come upon our vehicles parked along a layby. We found out that Tony's trailer had side swiped a local car. Rob and Lut went to check on the couple still sitting dazed in their car, they were not hurt just a little shaken. The police and a breakdown truck were quickly on the scene. Tony was taken off in the police car to make a statement. It was obvious that we would all be staying put for a while so I set to making sandwiches and coffee for everyone.

After making 30 convoys and travelling 102,000 miles, this had been Tony's first accident. He was brought back to us after being fined 100 marks. The damaged wheel was removed from his trailer and we were able to resume our journey. It was dull and misty as we reached the problem area of *Karlovac*. All quiet as we passed through, no traffic lights to worry about, they had all been shot out.

On the motorway to *Zagreb* we stopped in a large parking area. It had been a service station before the Serbs wrecked it and left a tangled mass of steel girders.

Tony, Miriam, Robin and Lut were going on to *Pojatno* refugee camp near the city. We would be taking on the job as lead vehicle going on to *Lipik, Pakrac* and *Slavonski Brod*. In

175

Lipik we made a short stop at the Mark Cook orphanage, just to say Hello or *Dobar Dan* to the children.

In *Pakrac* we arrived to a great welcome, the jungle drums had been working and we were expected. The young volunteers offered accommodation to those needing a bed. The rest of us headed for the hospital grounds for the night. We woke to hear the police from the lookout post at the top of the building, changing shifts. We had noticed that a great deal of work had been done inside the hospital since we last were there. Windows had been replaced and rubble had been cleared from the rooms.

Shirley, Lisa, Kelly and the lads went up to take chocolate and cigarettes to the lookout post. Then we moved into the town. The girls had loaded their goods with the volunteers' projects in mind. The young people worked with schools and in helping the elderly in their own homes, their latest idea was a youth club. Shirley had books and games, taped music, basketballs and baskets, table tennis and all manner of equipment that the youth of *Pakrac* could use for recreation. Our contribution to the supplies was a spin drier.

A visit then to Anton the shoe mender. When we were there last he had asked for leather. Shirley's contacts had come up trumps and she had brought three rolls of soft leather suitable for shoe uppers. The town now had an operational shoemaker. He was so thrilled and excited with the gift that he knelt on the floor and on a sheet of paper, he drew the outline of each of our feet with measurements.

Lisa, Danny and Eric had arranged for their aid to go to an address in *Slavonski Brod*. Chris was to leave us at that point to go on to visit his friends in *Ljubjana*. We set out on the long journey, skirting the triangular area which was held by the Serbs, determined that we would not make the same mistake. While travelling toward *Nasice*, we noticed a new signpost pointing to *Slav: Brod*. It was not marked on our maps but it was going in the right direction. The road took us up a steep climb and through very pretty forest area. Onwards and upwards, the road surface was good until we reached the peak of the 'mountain', then we found ourselves on a very rough unmade track. Shingle, uncrushed rocks and rubble made very slow going.

At one point we came upon a coach, with hunting parties

standing by it. Denys called and asked if we were right for *Slavonski Brod*. One chap nodded and pointed in the direction that we were heading. After about ten miles of rocking and rolling, we were back on tarmac and on a road that we recognised. Only when we were on the outskirts of the city did we find out that Lisa's destination was the hospital school that we had visited a few months before. A school that was newly built and fully supported by local businessmen. Lisa had been misinformed somewhere along the line.

Father Ilya was there to greet us and had tea made for the seven of us. Lisa realised the situation when she saw for herself the comparative luxury of the school and its equipment. She became very upset to think that she had travelled so many miles to deliver aid to where it was obviously not needed. Over the tea and while the priest was otherwise engaged, the situation was discussed. Denys told Lisa that there were many places that would be only too happy to take the goods she had brought.

Father Ilya accepted some religious statues of Saints, altar candles, educational toys and games. He did not seem too put out when Lisa explained that the rest of her goods were destined for refugee camps. As we left, Kelly asked if we could stay in the town long enough for her to visit friends she had made on an earlier visit. We parked near the hospital to spend the night.

In the morning we set out to return to *Pakrac*, to unload Lisa's medical aid at the hospital. Not quite as easy as it sounds, in that country paperwork was all important. The administration staff needed papers to state that the goods were intended for *Pakrac* hospital. With a typewriter on board, an official-looking document was made up on our British Humanitarian Aid note paper. DELIVERY TO PAKRAC HOSPITAL. THIRTY BOXES OF MEDICAL SUPPLIES. The invoice and the goods were accepted.

School books and writing materials were left with the volunteers to be used in the schools. The food, clothing and toiletries were to be taken to *Rangi Nekova*. The camp was a very good example of the plight of many such groups of displaced persons. Children played in the dirt and rubbish beside a busy railway line. Lisa, Eric and Danny were happy unloading their goods with the help of the cheerful inmates of the camp.

Shirley, Kelly and I went to Hut Number 4, to visit Ruza, Anton and their children. They had once lived on a farm at *Doboj (Doboy)* near *Sarajevo*. Anton and his brothers owned horses and cattle. They now lived in the army huts with their families and their elderly mother, they may never be able to return to *Doboj*. Travelling with us in the camper on this trip, was a special doll, her name was Lucy. She was given into our safe keeping by a young lady from our area.

Rachel had asked that we should give Lucy to someone who would love her. Anton and Ruza had two daughters, one of them Josepa, was laid up with a badly cut foot. I felt that Lucy would have a good and loving home with Josepa. We took lots of photos of Lucy with her new Mama, to take back to Rachel.

Monty Mouse was another special toy given by Rachel's little brother, he was adopted by Josepa's sister and a large pink rabbit was taken into care by 6 year old Marina. Kelly and Shirley still had loads of sweets to give away. Anton escorted the girls to each family's room, where they gave every child a handful of candy. Lisa and her crew handed out cans of food, while in a room across from Anton's a new baby became the centre of attention, amid a pile of soft cuddly toys.

At last it was time for us to leave, we said goodbye over and over again. We moved out to cover as many miles as possible before settling in Austria for the night. On the way back through Germany, arrangements were made over the phone for our nephew to collect his Christmas gifts from the sweet shop in *Hockenheim* services.

DECEMBER 1994

The December convoy left without us. We had a very good excuse not to be travelling with them, the wedding of Tim and Tracy. A happy ending to the story that had started with the first Convoy Of Hope. We wished them luck and happiness and at the reception we made a ceremony of presenting the loving gifts from Nada, a lady who had lost everything in the cruel civil war. Chris from Weymouth, a clever cartoonist, presented the couple with a framed drawing, which had captured the spirit of the first convoy when Tim and Tracy found each other.

MARCH 1995

Once again 7 vehicles and 16 hardy souls were making the long journey to a war torn country, hoping to ease a little of the suffering. Tony with Patsy from Wales, Danny with Simon and Ben a freelance journalist. Dave from Littlehampton with Gilly, Bob from Kent with Joy. Chris from Weymouth on his own for a change, he usually took along a gigantic teddy bear as his 'seat cover'. Jim from Manchester driving a lorry, Corinne his co-driver had stepped in at the last minute. On the Sunday before leaving Corinne had heard how Jim's second driver had dropped out, he had thought that he wouldn't be joining this convoy.

We had two passengers in the camper with us. Tim. M. from Wimborne and Shirley from Sunbury. A very motley crew. The weather was pretty cold as we travelled through Germany and there were traces of snow on the fields and forests as we passed into Austria. There were spectacular views of snow capped mountains which took on a pink glow as the sun set. At the border posts of Slovenia and Croatia, the usual waiting as loads and T forms for customs were processed.

While waiting at the entry to Croatia, some of us went into the tiny bank to change marks for the Croatian kuna. When we first came to this country the currency was dinar. Then there were 10,000 to the pound. The following year it was 14,000 to the pound. Recently the currency was changed to kuna, with 8 to the pound. Not too long a wait on this occasion. On previous trips we had been known to have wasted a whole day sitting at the border, waiting for customs clearance, or health inspectors, or for an official's signature on a paper. All done and correct we made for our route to *Zagreb* and the mountainous road to the coast. Our lunch break was at one of the bistros, which was roasting whole pigs on spits. Plates of the succulent meat with crisp crackling and the wonderful fresh bread. No war or shortages in these parts.

At *Crikvenica*, our refugee friends were mostly self-supporting by this time, some had jobs. There was no desperate need for food and goods but we liked to take little gifts and our company when in the area. This time we had some wedding cake for Nada from our son and his bride and their December wedding. We had with us photos from the occasion, Nada had never seen us in our Sunday best, we were always in track suits and convoy sweaters when we visited her.

We spent a very noisy night with a strong wind whipping up the trees around us. The next morning saw us following the coast to *Karlobag* then turning inland to the climb into the mountains. From the warmth of the coast the temperature dropped considerably. Snow appeared alongside the verges although the road was clear. We made a stop at the top to admire the terrific view, also for the young (and not so young) to have a snowball fight.

We were expected at *Gospic* hospital at 1.30, lunch was prepared for us. A vegetable stew and a dish of thinly sliced pork chops for those who liked to eat meat. Fresh bread, Coke and mineral water. After lunch it was time to unload. A customs man came to look into each vehicle before we sorted out what was to be left there. The lady doctors kept an eye on what was being unloaded. We had boxes of catheters and X-ray jackets from our local hospital, they caused a lot of excitement. Baby food and toiletries were accepted.

After the work, tea was laid on with bread and cheese, the doctors sat with us, most of them spoke a little English. There were plenty of laughs over pronouncing some of our words. We moved out around 5pm. taking a different route back to *Zagreb*. More straightforward and not so mountainous. A few months before, this route would have been in enemy hands. The night was spent at a services near *Zagreb*.

We were making for *Pojatno*, a camp of corrugated huts in a large compound. Refugees from many areas lived together there. Women and children surrounded us and the vehicles as we unloaded boxes of bedding, food, shoes and clothes and a large amount of vegetable seeds. Danny caused a great deal of laughter by giving a group of children new toothbrushes, then drilling them by numbers while they cleaned their teeth around a large drain.

Some ladies standing by were watching and all the while their hands were busy making lace tablecloths. The ladies asked us for crochet cotton but none of us had any to give. We made a note to put that item on the shopping list for next time. Toys and Frisbies were given to the children, some of the younger ones had got hold of a load of bubble wrap from our trailer. They sat in a row happily popping the bubbles. Next we were to visit the camp at *Rangi Nekova*, we ourselves had gifts for Ruza and family. For Josepa a bag of goodies from Rachel of Mudeford, an iced Easter cake for the family from Jean of Somerford, a plastic storage box full of food and useful items for the family from Kelly.

Ruza was just about to make coffee for us, when we were called to leave in a hurry. A convoy of Austrian aid trucks were trying to get into the camp. Our vehicles were in their way and we had to leave. Tony was to leave us at that point, he was returning to the U.K. The rest of the crew were following us to *Lipik* and *Pakrac*.

The children's home at *Lipik* was one of the first buildings to be attacked in the war. The children had been saved by living in the cellars while the battle went on around them. Englishman Mark Cook arrived in the devastated town and when he saw the state of the orphanage, he promised that he would help to rebuild their home. This was done by a great deal of publicity, the B.B.C. and Martin Bell played a part in the raising of the £1,000,000 needed. The home did not need help from us, it was well supported, in fact they passed on goods to other establishments. The staff and children were always pleased to see us when we were in the area.

On the outskirts of *Lipik* were the remains of stables, the original home of the world famous *Lippizaner* horses. The stables were in ruins and we were told how the horses had been running terrified in the streets until they were shot. Luckily the breed is now found in many parts of the world. The U.N. were using the stable yards as a base for their vehicles.

In *Pakrac* we received a warm welcome from the Dimiri family of the Faroan Bistro in the town centre. Mother is

Serbian, Father a Moslem and their three daughters were born in Croatia. The sort of family which made a nonsense of the war and the people who suffer the most. They were a wonderful, friendly family, always delighted to see us. Their hospitality was second to none. We met up with a group of the volunteers in the bistro and enjoyed their company for the evening. Mama Dimiri invited all of us to lunch the next day, Sunday. We settled for the night in the main street.

We had arranged to unload at the hospital, there was no one to deal with the paperwork as it was Sunday. No problem, we would unload and have the papers signed on the Monday. While the men dealt with the goods, I fetched out my trusty typewriter to make out the official 'delivery note'. 527 boxes of supplies that had not been needed at *Gospic*. Then we all drove back to *Lipik* to where the volunteers had opened a branch of their organisation.

In charge of this house was B.J. or Big John. He had been with the team helping to rebuild the orphanage with Mark Cook. When the job was done B.J. stayed on with the volunteers. Into his care we passed on children's shoes and loads of vegetable seeds which had been donated by a well-known firm in the U.K.

Then we went on to keep our lunch date at the bistro. Mama Javanka fed all of the convoy members, veal cutlets and fried potato. Local children gathered around the doors, those of our crew still having toys to give away played at Santa. One little girl was given a baby doll, she promptly named it Shirley. That afternoon a football match was to take place in the park. U.N. lads who were Argentinians playing against the volunteers. The volunteers were short of a couple of players so a couple of our convoy drivers stepped in. The rest of us sat in the sunshine to watch the match and to cheer them on. The U.N. won hands down.

Shirley came with us to visit Anton the shoemaker, he was surprised and pleased to see us. From his workshop he proudly brought a pair of mules and slippers for each of us, made with the leather provided by Shirley's contacts. He had spent the winter months preparing his gifts of gratitude to us. Tim had come along for the visit, he spoke German as did Anton, they had very lengthy conversations.

Anton and Maria insisted that Denys and I spent the night in their home, we gave in and accepted. The camper was safe inside their gates with Tim and Shirley in charge. We slept in a gigantic bed with a soft feather mattress. In the morning we drove to the hospital to have our papers signed, a must for customs and excise. The rest of the convoy was to head for home. We intended to do a little sightseeing on the way back, none of us needed to rush the homeward stretch.

Travelling through the Croatian villages we had fun giving away carrier bags full of vegetable seeds to folk we saw digging in gardens or plots beside the road. We received a few puzzled looks, some thought that we wanted payment. There would be a good amount of homegrown produce later in the year.

The four of us enjoyed the trip home, straying off our normal route to take in the snow covered scenery around some of Austria's lakes. We arrived back in England on 18th March.

MAY 1995 CHERNOBYL

A charity called The Forgotten Children of Chernigov had contacted our now registered charity, British Humanitarian Aid Ltd. with a plea for help. In the city of *Chernigov* only thirty miles from *Chernobyl*, a large building had been acquired to be used as a rehabilitation centre. It would be able to take up to two hundred children suffering from the effects of the infamous nuclear disaster.

Fourteen British vehicles left Ramsgate docks on the 2nd May 1995, fully loaded with fittings, furnishings, medications and toiletries. Some were also carrying toys, video cartoons, a TV set and video.

Making the journey along with our motor home and trailer, was a 40ft. articulated truck from Hertfordshire, the drivers were Martin and his mother-in-law Sheila. Mike and Pauline, June, John and Ray, were travelling in a couple of loaded A.A. vans with tool kits at the ready in case anyone had mechanical problems. Robin and his wife Lut from Havant in their Land Rover Discovery with trailer. Chris and Ian in a car loaded to the hilt with boxes. Chris had a fair knowledge of Russian which could prove very useful. Tony B. with his wife Val in their well decorated van with matching trailer.

The rest of the vehicles were transit vans containing, Dawn and Bill, Lisa and Lee, 'Uncle George' and his wife Marion, Danny and Phillip, Simon and Dave, Chris our cartoonist from Weymouth and last but not least, Bob with Pauline in a van which towed a transporter trailer, in case of breakdown by one of the smaller vehicles.

Chuck, one of our best loved colleagues had died from cancer just a few weeks before this trip. All the vehicles on the convoy were proudly carrying stickers dedicating the convoy to Chuck. His widow Iris came to the docks to see us off. As we waited to board the ferry, news came of renewed fighting in the areas that we knew so well in Bosnia and Croatia. We all gave a thought to the many friends that we had made in those towns and villages. It was so ironic that we were not travelling to that part of the world on that particular month.

Tim M was again making this trip possible for us, with help of friends in his area he had been able to fund a large part of the fuel needed. He had booked his passage with us way back in March. Robin's Belgian wife, Lut (pro. Loot), had asked if we could find room to take her sister Miriam with us. The guest flat up in the Luton was available, we picked Miriam up on our way near *Brussels*.

By way of *Gent, Eindhoven, Hanover* and *Berlin*. We spent the first night at a service area which had been the border of East and West Germany. We settled among the lorries for a peaceful night. On a bright and sunny morning we could see the buildings which were used by the guards when this was a checkpoint. From there on the roads were very rough and uneven. As we reached the German\Polish border at 4pm. we were informed that the border post closed at 6pm. Four hours later we were still waiting. A call over the C.B. asked that all our drivers should take their passports to the office. A move then to exit Germany and enter Poland. Passports were checked, computerised and rechecked.

Robin had made identity cards for our members to wear as badges, Miriam, Tim and I filled in the details of each person and put them into their plastic covers while we waited. So many hours of daylight were wasting. Finally cleared to go, we left the motorways behind and travelled through towns and villages towards *Warsaw*.

In one town a youth walked out into the road with his head down, not looking where he was going and walked right into the camper. The large mirror on the nearside door hit him, we thought that he must be lying in the road, at best unconscious. As we stopped Denys called on the C.B. that we had hit a kid who had walked into the vehicle. Tim and Denys went out, dreading what they might find.

The lad was still on his feet, his hands on his head with blood running down his face. His mates were all standing around laughing as though it was a big joke. The convoy had come to a halt, waiting for the verdict.

We were told later that this was a trick to get unsuspecting travellers out of their vehicles, while they were checking on the 'victim' his mates would be rifling the contents of the vehicle. They hadn't accounted for our lorry-sized mirrors of for the fact that Miriam and I stayed in the camper with the doors locked.

We stayed overnight at a town called *Mysliborg* and were on the road at 8 the next morning. As we were making for the *Warsaw* ring road and entering *Potsnan*, Denys had a problem with the gears The convoy was called to a halt, the A.A. team sprang into action. After some consideration it was decided that the camper needed garage attention. Chris and Ian drove off to find a garage with a workshop, they were back in a very short time with a couple of mechanics. After sizing up the problem they decided that our vehicle should be towed into their workshop.

Martin of the artic, dropped his trailer and towed us the short distance to a Fiat garage and workshop. This was ideal as our vehicle has a Fiat engine. It was a novelty to these chaps as the Fiats in that part of the world were like toys compared to our 20ft. home on wheels. They had the camper up on the ramps so quickly that I had to jump out of the door while it was being hoisted off the floor. The engine was dismantled while we were shown into an office where we were plied with coffee. One of the A.A. crew stayed with us to report progress to the convoy which had parked up nearby.

For six hours we watched the coming and going of customers and the chaps working on the camper. We drank innumerable cups of coffee while the job was being done. The friction plate had disintegrated, Denys was shown the remains when we went to sort out the bill. There was a lot of discussion on how we were to pay, we had no local *Zloti*, the manager settled for $210 U.S. which was about £126, quite a pleasant surprise. The mechanics had worked flat out to get us on the road and they would not accept a tip, they did eventually accept a few cans of English beer! Our convoy had eaten and rested at a service station while waiting for us, we fed on the wing as we drove on to *Warsaw*.

The next day, 5th May was Miriam's birthday, we had all signed a very large card which Lut had brought with her. That morning all the crew stood outside our door and sang 'Happy Birthday to You', then it was photo call time. There was a bit of horse-play as Big Ray swept Miriam off her feet and made for our camper amid cheers. We moved out then to the Poland\Ukraine border at *Chelm*. We had been expecting to be met there by a representative from the *Chernigov* charity. There was no one waiting for us but we were three hours later than had been planned.

It took us six hours to get through the two border controls, some of our drivers chatted to an English trucker, he told of how his brother had been in *Chernobyl* at the time of the 'Big Blow'. He was at that time very ill. On the move into the Ukraine, we saw prisoners at work on repairing a bridge, with armed guards standing over them. The roads were in a terrible state with very deep potholes and covers missing from drains. The road we were on was called the Military Road, dead straight and bypassing all towns and villages. It did present a problem with no garages or filling stations.

All our drivers had been advised to take extra fuel in jerry cans but we needed to keep those for real emergencies. A local motorist was flagged down and with Chris's help was asked for the nearest filling station. Luckily we were not too far away from one just a short way off the Military Road. We had been told that fuel was scarce in the Ukraine. At the services Tony had to pay 500 marks up front before any of us were allowed to fill up. Lut stood by with a pen and notebook, she noted how many litres each vehicle took. Then we paid Tony what we owed.

By midnight we were all tired and hungry, more than ready to call it a day. On arriving at a police checkpoint with a large parking area, we received permission to park there for the night. This was somewhere between *Koval* and *Sarni*. At eight the next morning we thanked our hosts and hit the road. Tim and Miriam were great company for each other. Although Miriam spoke very good English, Tim added to her knowledge of English expressions, sayings such as 'Letting your hair down' and a 'Watched pot never boils' while we waited for our morning cuppa.

Living in such close quarters with strangers was never a problem, most of us were living in track-suits. To change or get ready for bed, our little W.C. room was privacy for ablutions or for slipping out of daytime wear. Those travelling with us in the camper, had luxuries not enjoyed by those travelling in vans and trucks. Most of those travelling in the vans carried Calor gas rings for cooking or for heating water. Anyone who knew us well, knew that we would always help out with a cup of tea or a hot drink before turning in.

Lunch was in a park beside a lake, a beautiful setting but we all noticed an absence of birds and waterfowl. While going on towards *Kiev*, one of our shock absorbers collapsed under the strain. Mike and the boys were out with the toolbox and had the job done in 20 minutes. While all this was being done a truck driver stopped. He told Tony that a blonde woman was waiting for an English convoy at a Shell filling station about five kilometres down the road. This would be the contact that we had missed at the border.

We met with Nina, who was a Ukrainian then living in Manchester. It was she who had approached our charity on behalf of the *Children of Chernigov*. We all refuelled at the Shell station. The diesel was very cheap, we were the last in line and must have drained the tanks as we were sucking up the last dregs of fuel.

On the road then with Nina in the leading van with Tony and Val. Alongside the road now and again, we saw pick-up trucks with jerry cans of fuel for sale. A couple of our vans broke down on the way to *Chernigov*, their fuel filters were clogged up with sludge from the poor quality fuel. Mike and his crew removed the filters, washed them out with petrol and got the vehicles on the road again. We reached our destination at about 8.15. The Mayor and his committee had expected us at 5!

We parked next to a large hotel and went inside to a great welcome. Before we realised what was happening we were grabbed and pulled onto a dance floor. A wedding party was in full swing, the folk were full of good cheer and vodka. We were rescued and led upstairs to a function room. A table was laid for a meal and we were told, 'Please you will sit.' We were served soup with bread, meat and fried potato. Vodka and many speeches starting with 'Dear Friends' followed the meal.

Accommodation in the hotel was free to our members, Tim and Miriam were happy to stay in the camper with us. Although it was 10pm. we were told that we would be unloading that night. The explanation was that the next day was Sunday and there would be no local help to unload the larger vehicles. Monday was V.E. Day when there would be celebrations and the same problems.

The building which was to be the rehabilitation centre was just a large empty shell, ready and waiting for the aid that we were bringing. It had a very narrow entrance from the road, with only room enough for one van at a time to unload. The local help made a human chain to carry the goods into the building. There were X-ray beds, baths, wash-basins and toilets with all the fittings. A three piece suite, carpets, curtain materials, prams and cots, disinfectants, vitamins, soap and shampoo and tons of toys and games.

There was no lighting in the building so our generator was put to good use, running spotlights from the A.A. vans did make the task a little easier. The job was completed at 4am. all 14 loads in the various rooms and we hoped that it would help in the caring of so many damaged children. We all drove back to the hotel, most taking up the offer of the free accommodation, a few like us would sleep well in the vehicles.

We slept until 9am. then we took the luxury of a full English breakfast. Some of our party went off to explore a local market, others were using the local car wash. Kids with buckets of water from the nearby river, were washing down the vans for a couple of dollars or a handful of sweets. One of the buckets contained a live fish. A very old and grizzled man came to our door, he put a crumpled 'coupon', (local money) on our doormat, he then crossed himself, mumbled a few words and went on his way. A chap hobbled by on crutches, I felt sorry for him until Denys noticed that the missing leg was strapped up behind his back.

The Mayor and local dignitaries had expected us to stay three or four days, they had some events planned for us. That afternoon we were to be taken on a picnic as guests of the Mayor of *Chernigov*, to a local beauty spot beside the river *Desna*. We were to leave the larger vehicles in a secure parking area. We, with the crews of the other trucks and the artic, were to get lifts where we could in the now empty vans. We hitched a lift with 'Uncle George'. Some 20 miles from the city, we turned off the main road into a narrow lane which in turn became a footpath. In the back of the transit we were having a rough ride.

With deep forest on both sides we were wondering where we would end up. Suddenly, over the C.B. came a woman's voice, " It looks like they are going to get rid of us." The track ended in a clearing beside the river. We were released from the van and could see a couple of wooden huts and a long trestle table loaded with food. The Mayor and the Minister of Education were there to greet us.

Although we had promised our family that we would not eat local food while in the *Chernobyl* region, how could we refuse the hospitality? All the while plagued by mosquitoes, we ate and enjoyed the food washed down with vodka and a strange tasting fruit cocktail. Fully relaxed, we enjoyed the fresh air and the company. The Mayor made a speech thanking us all for coming so far, for bringing hope and help to the children of his region. It was all translated by Nina.

We were given answers to many of our questions.

From 1979 up to 1995, 28,000 children had been affected by the radiation, which caused cancer, deformed limbs, thyroid, blindness and Downe's Syndrome. The lack of iodine in the children's systems had made the situation worse. Mothers would not accept that their babies were less than perfect at birth so treatment would be delayed. The families in the most poor areas believed that it was taboo to have a damaged child. Drugs were very expensive in this country so the children did not get the best treatment. The Soviet Union gave no help, *Chernigov* was not recognised as a problem zone by their government.

The Western world believed that *Chernobyl* was in Russia, aid and funds were being sent to *Moscow* and were not passed onto the Ukraine. We were told that the Mayor of *Chernigov* had cut through much Red Tape to build and organise the rehabilitation centre. Money was scarce for such projects. Things were much worse since the Ukraine became independent the Mafia and crooked businessmen had taken control in many areas and crime was rife.

We were told that only the direction of the wind at the time of the disaster saved *Chernigov* from great fatalities. The concrete sarcophagus which encased the reactor had split and could blow again at any time. Everyone in the area lived in fear, it would not be possible to close down the reactor as the whole area depended on it for electricity. It would be too big a task to evacuate and re-house so many people.

Tony replied to the speeches on our behalf and said that he hoped to organise another convoy to *Chernigov* in September. We then raised our glasses in salute to Chuck. Then it was time to relax, some went boating on the river, a car radio provided music for dancing. One or two of our hosts tried to teach convoy members some traditional Ukrainian dances. One of our ladies asked Nina, "Where are the loos?" Nina laughed and said, "Well there are so many wonderful trees and green bushes."

The time flew by and it was getting dark, time to say goodbyes and get back to our transport. We were in a valley with soft, sandy soil, some of the vans needed pushing out of the soft patches, others made a run at it. Most of the passengers walked out of the lane until the vehicles were on firm ground. We arrived at our parking places at around midnight.

Although we were used to catering for ourselves, each morning we were rounded up by a bossy little man who insisted that the hotel had put breakfast for us.

He would come to our door and say, "You come, you must eat!," then inside the building, we would be ordered, "Please wash hands." Breakfast was cheese with beetroot and sweet coarse bread rolls, then we received a fried egg on a saucer, coffee and fruit juice.

Later with Nina and the Mayor leading in a car, we drove in convoy to a filling station, where every vehicle was refuelled free of charge. Then we were taken on a sightseeing tour of the town, passing grim looking blocks of flats and quaint wooden houses. There were ladies sitting outside their gates selling vegetables, it seemed that it was a good year for radishes, they were on show everywhere. In most areas chickens roamed free and we passed woods of beautiful silver birches.

On the outskirts of town we came to a large parking area at the foot of a well-decorated man-made hill. Flagpoles edged a flight of steps which ended at a monument at the top. As we alighted from our vehicles, TV cameras suddenly appeared and a few of the crew were asked to say a few words on film about the hardships of our journey and the welcome we had received. Masses of scarlet tulips were thrust into our arms and we were asked to walk up the steps to the monument. At the top an Eternal Flame was burning on a memorial to 'The Unknown Soldier'. An obelisk bearing the dates 1941-1945. We were filmed going forward two at a time, and laying the flowers on the tomb.

Back in the car park we were surrounded by people and children, many of us gave away the remaining teddies and toys that decorated our windscreens. We had been expected to take part in the celebrations for Liberation Day on the 9th when there would be a grand parade through the city, our vehicles could have been in it. Some of our colleagues needed to be home at the week-end. the convoy would stay together.

The Mayor and his company escorted our vehicles to the main road to *Kiev*. They made a stop to thank us all and wished us luck on the journey home. We travelled together as far as the border, then those in a hurry pressed on while the rest of us stayed overnight. On going through the border next day, we each had to pay a 'toll', a pack of cigarettes, a car sticker or a can of drink before the guards would stand back to let us through the barrier.

In Poland we made a stop at a gnome shop, one of many along our route. A makeshift building with a large display of garden gnomes and interesting tourist souvenirs such as the heads and pelts of wild boar, garden statues and windmills, ornaments, glassware and working spinning wheels. A few dollars changed hands and souvenirs were stowed away among clothing for protection. In Belgium, Miriam phoned her husband as soon as we crossed the border. She arranged to meet him on the *Gent* ring road but an accident held us up for an hour in the *Antwerp* area. Daniel and their children were waiting at the services, but they had heard reports over the car radio so guessed that we would be delayed.

We arrived in England at 4am. on the 12th May and took Tim home to Wimborne before settling into our home patch to recover.

JULY 1995

On our return from the *Chernigov* trip, we received urgent requests from contacts in *Pakrac*, Croatia. One letter was from B.J. Big John. It told that a van, which was used by the volunteers had been badly damaged in the latest conflict. John asked if we could get hold of a replacement vehicle, such was his faith in us. The second appeal was for some plasterboards to repair the ceiling in the building which was used by the volunteer group. The third letter told of 21 elderly villagers, who had been made homeless and were being cared for by Help The Aged International. They were in desperate need of bedding and nightwear.

As usual our generous contacts came up with the goods. Through Colonel Mark Cook, who knew B.J. well, we were donated a mini-bus by scouts of Shipton-on-Stour, near Stratford-on-Avon. The scouts had worked on the bus as a project, getting it in a roadworthy condition to give it away to some charity. We travelled to the Midlands to collect the vehicle taking a tow bar with us. Danny from Reading, a convoy colleague, came with us to steer the bus while it was on tow. It was in such good condition that Danny decided to drive it back to his home.

The chap handing the keys and logbook over to us, explained all the details and showed the boxes of spares for the vehicle and clothing for refugees which were stowed under the seats. He wished us luck for the journey, We returned to Reading where the mini-bus would stay until we could get it to *Pakrac*.

With a son-in-law in the building trade the second request was not too difficult. Steve advised us to call in at his suppliers, to get what we needed and have it put onto his account. Twelve plasterboards were loaded onto our trailer. If they had been just one inch longer we would not have been able to close the doors.

The parents, teachers, pupils and staff of Spetisbury School were keen to help us once again. A large amount of bedding, pillows and blankets, night clothes and dressing gowns were waiting for us to collect on the day of the school fete. Our own family rummaged in cupboards and drawers to find spare blankets and nightwear for the elderly victims of war.

Finding the funds for the 3,000 mile trip was always the biggest headache. We ourselves took bric-a-brac, books, flower seeds and fancy items to car boot sales. The street collections were bringing in less because Bosnia was not so much in the news by that time. While we were counting the pennies and thinking that we would be dipping into our own resources to cover the expenses, a local businessman came to the rescue. He had read of our missions in the local press and gave us a handsome donation of £200.

The departure date was to be July the 11th. A very small convoy of three vehicles. With us would be Danny and his friend Karen in a transit and the mini-bus. Two young people wanting to join the volunteers in *Pakrac* had asked Danny for a lift.

Danny had suggested to them that they could drive and fuel the little bus to *Pakrac*. So Shelley and Bill found themselves a part of the Convoy Of Hope instead of hitching a lift.

Our 'lodger' for this trip was to be Emina, the youngest daughter of the Dimiri family in *Pakrac*. Danny had brought her to stay with his parents for a brief spell away from the traumas of living with a war on her doorstep. Emina's family were a small part of the tangle of nationalities involved in the civil war.

From the ferry we drove out into the Belgian countryside. The bright sunny morning gave way to mist then thunderstorms. I fed the seven of us on our famous convoy stew at *Aachen*. Emina had been excited at the thought of going home. There were a lot of things she did not like about England. First and foremost she 'hated cereals for breakfast every day.' She didn't like not being allowed to stay out after dark, at home there was no problem with youngsters walking about on their own at night and that was in a war situation!!

As we drove through Germany the bus seemed to be burning oil so a stop was made to buy some. As we travelled on, we passed a coach parked up on the hard shoulder obviously in trouble. We pulled in to see if we could assist. On discovering that the problem was a shortage of fuel Danny siphoned some from his van. The 48 passengers from the bus were on the grass verge watching the proceedings. With diesel in the tank the coach still would not start.

A young lady from the group told us that the passengers were all Romanian, they now lived in Germany and were going to their old country for a holiday. They were all very worried, if the police should discover a vehicle broken down on the autobahn because of a shortage of fuel, the driver could be fined 1,000 marks, about £400.

The coach had seen better days, the young lady told us that in the last downpour the driver had not been able to see where he was going, the wipers were not working. We could only offer to take the driver to a phone to get help; he refused because that would mean a fine for sure. As we pulled away having done all we could, the engine of the coach burst into life and everyone scrambled on board. The last we saw of them was the coach taking the next exit off the motorway.

As we neared *Regensburg*, the mini-bus ran out of petrol, lucky that we were carrying some in a can for our generator. Just before *Passau* we suffered a burst tyre, after a wheel change we entered into Austria. We and our colleagues never tired of the scenery in that beautiful country, it always looked so perfect even the farmyards were neat and tidy. The cows were immaculate, just like they had been prepared for a show. A night stop at *Graz* gave the crew a chance to have showers. By handing in the keys to their vehicles, they received the keys to the shower cubicles.

In the morning we entered Slovenia. There was a new rule. The border guard looked at our green card insurance certificate, and told Denys that he must have Slovenia on it next time. He said, " Yugoslavia no longer here." Our trailer was sealed so that we should not be able to sell our goods in their country, as if we would! It seemed a little useless when it was not possible to seal a transit van. More problems when we arrived at the Croatian border, Denys had taken young Emina into the office with him, thinking that she might be a help with the language barrier. That was not the case. Emina had heard that the mini-bus was to be donated to the volunteers, and she said so.

By taking the vehicle into the country in that way would mean that we would have to pay taxes on it. Denys got around the misunderstanding by telling the officials that the two volunteers with us would be using the bus for their one month's stay. A fax was sent to B.J. and we had to stay put until a fax came back to confirm that we and the bus were expected. Only then would the guards let us through the barriers.

Emina was very upset, she thought that she was in trouble and couldn't understand why. We talked her out of her misery and promised that she would be able to joke about it all with the volunteers later. On then to the *Zagreb* motorway, our paperwork getting us free passage at the new toll booths. Taking the *Kutina* turnoff our route took us through small villages. At first they were very pretty with masses of flowers, chickens and geese in the gardens, old folk sitting on roadside benches. Then the contrast, roads pitted by mortar shells, houses without roofs, others with large holes blown through the walls, some just piles of rubble.

We made for *Lipik* and B.J.'s house to deliver the mini-bus. We had decorated it en route with names of the convoy crew and of the Shipton-on-Stour scouts. Emina was anxious to get home to her family so we left the others and drove on to *Pakrac*. A great reunion at the Faroan Bistro, with ice cream all round for the hot and weary travellers. Before too long the rest of the crew joined us, Shelley and Bill were taken off to settle in with the volunteers. Danny and Karen were invited to Javanka's house for showers and to rest.

We sat with B.J. for a while as he told us *about Okucani* (*pro: Okuchani*) village, 20 miles south of *Lipik* and occupied by the Serbs in the early part of the war. This year during the uprising the Croats took the village back, driving the Serbs out. Families fled leaving their pets and farm animals to fend for themselves. Later it was discovered that the elderly and frail members of the families had been left behind, they would have been a hindrance in the evacuation.

Help the Aged International had taken the 21 old folk into a large building in the village to be cared for. On hearing that we had the goods as requested for them B.J. suggested that we drive there that evening. On a narrow country road we passed over a temporary bridge and were stopped at two checkpoints. Denys and B.J. had to show their driving licences for identification. As we travelled on B.J. pointed out where mass graves had been uncovered and a well where the remains of women had been discovered. All Croats murdered by the invading Serbs. Houses and property had been destroyed and explosives left in the ruins.

As we neared the refuge for the old folk, we saw an old lady sitting on a wall and nursing a cat. Probably the only friend she had in that ghost town. B.J. went into the building to let someone know that we were bringing the supplies. A couple of men came to help but they looked so frail that we gave them the lightest boxes to carry. As well as bedding and nightwear we had pasta, flour, sugar and canned foods.

While we were unloading, the police came to check us out, they thought that we might be looters. A lady invited us in to meet some of these abandoned souls, some in in bed and others sitting in chairs. The lady told them who we were and that we had come from England to help them all. They wanted to touch or hold our hands, a pitiful state to be left in by their own families that they had cared for.

Our interpreter told of one old chap of 94, he slept with a hammer clutched to his chest, guarding a small box of personal possessions kept under his bed. B.J. left a note for Maya the representative from Help the Aged, she lived in *Daruvar* and would arrive in the morning.

Back for the get-together with the volunteers, among the international group was a lad from Switzerland. Sascha told us that his father had a garage full of donated paint, which was meant for the *Pakrac* project. The problem was how to get it to Croatia. He asked if we would take a trip to his home to collect it if they paid the expenses. Well it was late and Denys had driven a lot of miles over the last few days, we said we would sleep on it. B.J. arranged that we could unload the plasterboards at his house in the morning. We slept that night beside the hospital.

Danny and Karen had been invited on a fishing trip and picnic with Fikret and the family from the bistro. We were to visit Anton and Maria. They never knew when we would turn up until we arrived on their doorstep but were always pleased to see us. Maria's first words were always, "Have you eaten?" Over beer and coffee they looked at the photos that we had taken on our last visit. At 12 we had to leave, Anton asked that we return at 2 to eat with them. We met up with B.J. and the helpers to unload the heavy plasterboards, they were to be put into an outhouse. This building did not have a roof until Danny produced two large tarpaulins, which covered the large gaps.

We were carrying a large amount of talcum powder, too much for B.J to handle, he suggested that we take it to *Lipik* hospital. The doctor there was pleased to accept the goods but needed paperwork declaring that the gift was meant for this hospital. Nama Problem, The trusty typewriter came out and the necessary documents were produced. 30 boxes of baby talcum powder each holding 25 containers, two boxes of baby milk and feeding bottles and a large bag of toys. Dr. Viktor Tica signed and gave us a certificate of thanks from the hospital. Also promotional leaflets which showed the hospital as it once was. Some contrast to the shell and bullet marked frontage before us.

On to our lunch date with Anton and Maria. Vegetable soup, sausages and pasta, washed down with ice cold water from the well in the yard. We all sat out in the garden after the meal, Anton brought out three young puppies and a kitten, which played around our feet while we lazed in the sun.

While we talked a neighbour came to join us, Anton looked at us and said, "This man's mama..." then made a sign with his finger across his throat, then "*Chetniks*." Making us understand that his mother was killed by the Serbs. At 6pm. we left to meet up with B.J. and Sascha, to talk over the possibility of us collecting the paint. We had to consider Danny and Karen. As it happened Danny had been asked to run the bistro for a couple of days, while Fikret and Javanka celebrated their twentieth wedding anniversary. They fancied spending the week-end in Hungary. Everything was falling into place. A second night behind the hospital, I remembered the nights spent there with shells flying over the top of us.

The first thing on Saturday was get a tyre for the camper. L.J. (Little John.) and a young lady called Tim, came with us to make sure we got a good deal. Tim had a very broad Irish accent, we found out later that she was Dutch! The Vulcanizer was very helpful, he didn't have a new tyre our size, so he fixed us up with a part worn tyre, which was alright for a spare and would get us out of trouble.

By way of *Zagreb, Llubjana, Kranj* and *Lienz*, we were then travelling on the old roads with wonderful scenery. Sascha navigated as he had travelled the route by coach. We drove into storms in the mountains as we headed for *Innsbruk*. Although the weather was very warm, there were still patches of snow on the distant peaks. We ate while travelling, made a couple of stops for fuel and for the men to stretch their legs. We reached the Swiss border at 11pm. No one bothered us so we went on to heading for *Bregenz* and the village of *Bommen* where Sascha's father lived. He let himself into the darkened house and we slept beside a row of garages.

We woke at 7.30, church bells were ringing. At 9 Sascha came to invite us into the house for breakfast with his family. Jorge, his father, introduced us to his partner, a very sweet lady named Barbara. The table was laid for breakfast in the dining room of the lovely house with beautiful views of the garden and the meadows beyond. In the conversation around the table we found that Jorge was a surgeon and Barbara was his assistant. He had to leave us at 10am. but asked us to join them for dinner that evening.

Barbara helped weigh and load the cans and buckets of paint into the trailer. 58 containers, total weight 800 kilograms. Three quarters of a ton in old money. After coffee in the garden to rest a while, Barbara loaned Sascha her car to take us sight seeing. We were to drop her at the hospital first. She invited us in to look around part of the hospital. Piano music met us as we entered a large hall. Jorge was about to make a recording, we sat quietly and listened as he played *Clare de la Lune* on the grand piano. It was quite beautiful.

Sascha then drove us to very pretty villages beside the lakes, he took us to where he grew up. The houses were works of art, most of them had pictures and scenes painted on the walls. We visited the stately home where Napoleon the Third once lived, it was open to the public and full of wonderful works of art.

Next, a steep climb up a mountain road took us to a

medieval castle called '*Hoheklingan*' where we sat on the battlements and ate delicious ice cream. Then we drove across the German border to *Konstanz*, where we strolled beside the lake and stood under a massive statue. Sascha told us that the statue was of *Germania*. On her upturned hands she held two figures representing the Pope and the Devil, the balance of good and evil.

On the way home Sascha made a quick check to find out when the Danzas office would be open. We needed to get our T-form, the paper needed for customs when taking goods from one country to another. It would be open at 8am. the next day. Back at the house I typed out a loading form, listing all the cans and containers of paint. Dinner was a meal of risotto and meat, during which we did most of the talking about our trips to the former Yugoslavia. Jorge was ready for an early night, as he explained that he was to operate on the liver of a Yugoslav first thing in the morning.

Up at 6.30, I filled the flasks ready for the long haul back. We were at the Danzas office when it opened at 8. Sascha attended to the paperwork, no charge for the service. We made a stop at a bank then a delicatessen for Sascha to buy cheese, which he had promised his friends in *Pakrac*. To save time going back we used the motorway, from *Innsbruk* to *Salzburg* and then to *Graz.*

On our old route then into Slovenia. No problems but a seal was put on the trailer. Going into Croatia, Sascha was charged 35 marks for bringing gifts into the country. He and Denys argued with the authorities, telling them that we were trying to help their own people. On checking the loading form, one of the customs men asked, "Is the paint new?" No, it was used. The containers were not full!!

My husband was losing his patience. At 2.30am. and after a long day driving, he was not in the mood for stupid questions. One young lady in the office had tried to find out what fee we had paid at the Swiss border. Apparently, by holding a lighted match at the back of the T Form computerised marks show. She had no luck, so her colleague had a go, the already singed paper caught fire. Denys demanded to know the woman's name, he said he was going to write to her Government and to the British

Ambassador. He and Sascha stormed out of the office.

Sascha handed the paperwork to the official at the gate only to be shouted at for setting fire to the T Form. As our friend explained that the woman in the office was responsible, he told Sascha, "Bring her here." She then had to face the music again, it was not her day.

We parked up at the *Zagreb* motorway services for a few hours sleep. At 6am. four English trucks parked up next to us. Denys went over to chat to the drivers and found out that they were police and firemen from Sheffield, visiting as many refugee camps as they could find, Denys gave them directions to a few that we knew. Moving out at 8 we made for *Kutina* where the seal was to be removed from the trailer. Back at *Pakrac*, a lot of excitement over the amount of paint. B. J. signed the loading forms as having received the goods.

Our mileage to and from Switzerland was 1,191 miles. Sascha settled up with us and assured us that it would have cost a lot more if he'd had to hire a van to do the job.

At the bistro, Danny and Karen had enjoyed their weekend, Danny had been serving English coffee to the locals. We were expected to lunch at Fikret and Javanka's, they wanted to know all about our trip. Then as we decided to make our way homeward that evening. we went to say good-bye to Anton and Maria. They could see that we were tired, they offered us the use of their bedroom for a few hours before leaving. The room was cool and in spite of the work being done on the roof, we slept until 4.30. After a cold drink and fond farewells, we left to meet up with our travelling companions. While saying goodbye at the bistro, one of the volunteers, Colin, begged a lift back to the U.K. He collected his kit and our two vehicles headed for Austria. Extra expenses had made us a little short on marks for fuel. Colin had 60 marks which we exchanged for our sterling.

We arrived home on July 20th to find that our generous businessman had opened a charity shop on our behalf.

UKRAINE SEPTEMBER 1995

Our September trip was to be Croatia, this was changed almost overnight owing to circumstances. Two vans planning to join us backed out when the war situation changed in the former Yugoslavia. We felt that we would prefer not to travel alone without backup support. With private funding from a couple of sources we decided to join the convoy of seven vehicles destined for the Ukraine.

Leaving on the 16th September, were Tony and Val, Robin and Lut, Bob with a flat bed trailer, Jim and Derek, Ben and Sharon from Reading, Chris from Weymouth all in transit vans, Peter and Dave in a seven and half ton truck, and Tim M. with us. Each vehicle carried jerry cans to fill with fuel before we left Poland. Fuel in the Ukraine was sub standard and not easy to obtain in the large quantities that would be needed by our convoy.

At the Ukraine border we had only a short wait for documentation. We met up with some British lorry drivers, they told us that they had been waiting over 24 hours for their clearance. The weather had become very cold as we travelled on the 350 mile Military Road. Long, straight and badly in need of repair. Our vehicle really suffered on this stretch of the journey, Denys skilfully avoided the potholes and raised drains. With very little oncoming traffic there was plenty of room for dodging the worst of the hazards.

Our night stop was at the picnic area beside the lake, where we had rested in May. Having made good progress we were a day ahead of schedule, our drivers spent some time in checking their vehicles and making minor repairs. Two stray dogs were roaming around the vans, one was due to have pups. They were lapping up the attention and the scraps of food given by the crew. Some of the lads went off for a walk, saying that they were going 'bear hunting'. We went for a stroll around the lake and saw a lizard and a pair of woodpeckers. There seemed to be very little wild life for such a large, wild and beautiful area, miles from any habitation.

As we enjoyed the peaceful atmosphere, the U.K. trucks we had seen at the border came in to join us. On their way to *Kiev*, they stopped long enough to have a coffee and a chat before leaving to make their deliveries. The 'bear hunters' returned after having found some lumberjacks who had been generous with their vodka.

After a relaxing afternoon, we all turned in early. The air had become very cold and we felt sorry for those having to sleep in the vans. We had plenty of our own blankets so were able to lend some out to our colleagues.

There was frost on the grass and a very red sunrise as we prepared to move out. It was Lut's birthday, a gigantic card, with a cartoon drawn by Chris was presented. We had started out on the 200 miles to *Chernigov*, when our problems started. The camper slowed down to walking pace. Diesel put into our tanks from the jerry cans had blocked the fuel filter. Our mechanics sorted out the problem by cleaning the filter and washing it out with petrol. After a few more miles the same thing happened again. Then as we pulled into the side of the road to avoid a drain, the camper hit a pothole, Denys slowed to a stop, as he did so the trailer hit the same hole and the tow bar snapped off.

Ben and Sharon took our trailer on tow, as we were heading towards *Moscow* the filter clogged again. While we travelled at half power, the truck stayed with us until we could pull in to sort the problem out again. We had been expected in *Chernigov* at 5pm. Although we had started out early that morning, the problems had delayed us. A meal was ready and waiting in the hotel, with after dinner speeches along with plenty of vodka. Rooms were available for those looking forward to warm beds. We three and Tony were the only ones opting to sleep in our vehicles. We could keep an ear and an eye open for anyone prowling around the vans during the night.

In the morning our guide-cum-interpreter was Ivan, a teacher. He led us first to a school for the blind and partially sighted. We were given a tour of the classrooms and met some of the children. Ivan told us that the equipment they had for testing the eyes was very outdated but the best that could be had in this country. Three very pretty girls with serious eye defects, sang some traditional songs for us.

Next we were taken to a school for deaf and hard of hearing pupils. They entertained us with a musical play, the children with their eyes constantly on their teacher and following her every movement. Then we were off to a state run kindergarten for children of four to seven years old. They put on a show for us dressed in their National Costume. Two of them had greeted us at the door with the traditional offering of bread and salt. At the end of the show, the children came forward and placed red cardboard hearts on strings around our necks, like 'Jim'll fix-it badges'.

The next call was to an orphanage at *Preluki*, for babies up to 5 years old. We took toys and teddies into the children. The men were soon on their knees playing with cars and trucks with the little boys, or drinking 'pretend tea' with the small girls. Sharon, Lut, Val and I enjoyed the cuddles and affection given by some of the little ones, while Tony entertained a group of fascinated youngsters with his doggy puppet. One of the carers told us not to be surprised if some little tot should ask of us, "Are you my Mummy... or Daddy?"

The second children's home was for kids of 6 to 16. This as far as we were concerned, was what had made the trip worth while. 260 youngsters in the complex of buildings. We arrived amid a very noisy and excited group of kids, they all wanted to help unload our goods. With two vehicles at a time and two long chains of boisterous helpers the storeroom was soon filled with hundredweight sacks of porridge oats, bedding, clothes and shoes, mattresses, toys and games, pasta and rice, milk powder, sugar and children's medicines. Soon the storeroom was full and overflowed into the passageway.

With Ivan in tow we were shown around the buildings, school rooms and bedrooms. We noticed particularly that the staff talked to the children in such a caring and friendly way. We were told that five out of every six children in this home were suffering from some radiation-based illness. Also that sixty per cent were bed-wetters so the bedding and mattresses we had brought would be very useful.

In the assembly hall a concert was put on for our benefit. Ivan stood at the side of the stage and told us what each song or sketch was about. It tore at the heartstrings to hear a little lad from an orphanage singing of taking flowers to his mother and another singing of 'riding on Daddy's shoulders.' Some of the 'orphans' were children of alcoholics and criminals, taken from their parents by the state. They are never returned to their homes but kept in the institutions until the age of 16.

As we walked around the estate, many of us found small hands creeping into our own. As the children overcame their shyness, names were exchanged, we managed to get our tongues around some of them. Names such as Sergai, Nicholai, Natasha and Victorya. I am sure that most of us lost little bits of our hearts among the children of the Ukraine.

While walking around the extensive grounds, we admired some statues. One was of a family, two children and a mother, or maybe she was a carer.

Another statue was of a life size bear which gave us all a giggle. On our previous trip to the Ukraine in May, the convoy was driving along a road lined by deep forest. Sheila who was travelling in an artic truck suddenly exclaimed over the C.B.
"Oh look, there's a bear!" Tony spent the rest of that trip with his eyes peeled, desperate to see a bear.

What he didn't know was that on one of our stops, Denys had asked Sheila to call out and say that she had seen a bear. Tony was one of the greatest 'wind up merchants' on the convoys. This time it was Tony who'd been had. Sheila was such a lady that Tony wouldn't have suspected a trick. The joke went on for months, most of the convoy members were gradually let in on the 'bear truth', Tony suspected nothing and still watched out for a bear.

It was still going on until on this trip, he mentioned to one of the teachers that he would really like to see a bear before leaving the country. The lady looked puzzled and told our friend, "But there are no bears in the Ukraine!" He looked around at all of us, trying to keep straight faces, then the penny dropped.

In one of the offices was a huge painting of a stern looking, bearded man wearing a traditional fur hat. He was *Chevchenko*, a famous writer or hero. Tim mentioned that he would like to read some of *Chevchenko's* works and hoped to find some of his books before leaving *Chernigov*. To Tim's great embarrassment he was presented with the picture as a gift. From then on we were all careful of what we admired.

When the work was all done we were shown some of the attractions of the city. Ivan and a young lady, Natasha gave us a guided tour of the museum which was once a palace. In a small room, not normally seen by the public, we were shown beautiful relics made from pure silver encrusted with precious stones, ancient books and icons. A visit to the Cathedral of the Transfiguration, where inside a service was being held to celebrate the feast day of St. Theodossi. Dimly lit by candles and a choir was chanting, ladies were standing inside the doors, with shawls over their heads. Outside the doors, beggars lined up hoping for a hand out from anyone who might feel generous.

We stayed just a few minutes, then took a walk along the ramparts of the city, where huge canons, centuries old, stood in a row overlooking the road that we had used to drive into *Chernigov*.

Then came a visit to the Vodka Distillery, from the spirit in the vats to the bottling plant, the packing sheds and trucks being loaded with cases of the national drink. This was followed by lunch in the boardroom, with speeches and samples of their product. On the table were three bottles of Champagne, Sharon decided to open one of them. There was an almighty explosion and before anyone realised what had happened, Sharon and the area around her were covered in broken glass.

The ceiling had been made up of glass panels, the cork came from the bottle with such force that it shattered one of the panels. Sharon's hands were cut and the dishes of food had to be replaced. Amid apologies from our colleagues, our hosts were very kind about the incident. Two more birthdays were celebrated in *Chernigov*, both Val and Chris became one year older.

On the day we were leaving, a 'Mr. Fix it' was found with the equipment to weld our tow-bar onto the camper. Denys was about to discard a couple of empty, leaky jerry cans from the trailer, when they were retrieved and accepted as payment for the welding job done on the tow-bar. Now that Derek and Jim's van was empty, they were having problems with the shock absorbers not functioning, no replacements could be found in the *Chernigov* area, so the vehicle was winched onto the flat-bed trailer until such time we could find somewhere to have it repaired.

After many farewells and, "See you soon," we set off in convoy with a carload of dignitaries in the lead. They escorted us to the city boundary and waved us on our way.

We were through the Ukraine/Polish border in record time with the help of a letter from the Authorities in *Chernigov*. Once in Poland, the A.A. men looked for a suitable garage to get new shockers for the transit. At our overnight stop at *Chelm* a garage was found and mechanics who could do the job in the morning. While we were parking the vehicles, a security guard came to see what we were doing. Our drivers told him that one car was 'kaput', he said we could sleep in safety, adding that he would keep watch all night.

The A.A. chaps went shopping for the parts needed first thing in the morning, while we waited a young lady came to invite members of the convoy to take coffee in the office of the building. The van parts had been found and we were on our way by 11am. with the transit fixed and travelling under its own power.

Problems arose in Germany. We were caught up in a traffic jam. Road works somewhere ahead held us locked in a hold up, in seven hours we managed to travel 8 miles. In the camper we were better off than most. I was able to make hot drinks and sandwiches at the frequent stops and passed refreshments over to our colleagues. The men took advantage of the pauses to get out, stretch their legs and chat to other drivers.

We were amused at the dashes by some drivers and their passengers making for the bushes. The scene which tickled us most of all was the sight of a small girl making her way across the grass verge in front of us. She suddenly stopped and returned to the car to be given a toilet roll for the business. The rest of the journey home was plain sailing, no more mishaps.

The businessman who had given us a generous donation in July, opened a small charity shop in Bournemouth during

October. This was to help support us in our efforts to keep the supply convoys running. We supplied a large amount of donated items, which we would normally have sold at car boot sales. The shoppers coming in to buy, generated more goods as they turned out attics and cupboards. We had quite a high profile in our community with the local press covering our exploits. We were able to show proof that our goods indeed reached the hands of desperate people.

NOVEMBER 1995

All was well, in the first month the shop raised enough to fund us on the next convoy which was in November. We started out with 10 other vehicles. Everything was fine until in the mountain passes of Austria our engine developed a distinct rumble which worsened as we reached the Slovenian border. With being unable to obtain breakdown recovery once we left Austria, Denys contacted the A.A. from the service area in *Graz.*

One of the transits took our trailer in tow and the convoy carried on to the Slovenian border. Also with them went our lady passenger Iris. We all thought that the fault would take only a day or so to sort out. The breakdown truck arrived and the camper was winched onto it. There was about two inches to spare behind our rear wheels with four feet of camper suspended over the open road.

Once in the garage the problem was found to be the gearbox. It was removed on the Thursday evening, dismantled and the parts were sent for on the Friday morning. We had permission to stay in the vehicle so we lived on the ramps in the garage.

Spending our time playing cards, going for walks, reading, relaxing and having our meals while business went on around us. In the evening we had the 'pleasure' of a local band practising in the building opposite, they did pack up at 10pm.

We were not locked inside the main building, the ramps were under cover but with access to the main gates. Saturday and Sunday were spent with the company of an American radio station, 'Radio Blue Danube' kept us informed of the weather situation. In Austria it was pretty bad, many roads were blocked with snow. We gave a thought about the convoy as their first destination was *Gospic*, seven thousand feet above sea level.

Denys did try to hire a car from a local firm, thinking that

211

we just might be able to meet up with our colleagues and let them know of our situation. The firm were horrified to think that we wanted to take one of their cars into a conflict zone. They would not hear of it, nothing we could do but sit the weekend out.

Monday morning we were up early and watching for signs that our gearbox was being sorted out. We had a definite language problem, no one at the garage spoke more than two words of English. Late morning we saw a delivery van enter the yard, the suspense was too much. Denys took a wander over to the workshop where he saw a mechanic working on our gearbox, progress.

We went for more walks, I was getting plenty of exercise getting up and down from the camper perched on the ramps. More cards and more coffee, we had plenty of provisions to keep us going. About 5.30 that afternoon we heard the sound of a trolley coming our way, we crossed our fingers and waited. There were a couple of bumps and the camper shook, the gear box was going in. Eventually one of the mechanics climbed into the cab and started the engine, it seemed okay.

More by signs that with words, they told us to sleep there that night and they would test-drive the vehicle in the morning. One more night spent on our ramps. Tuesday morning we waited in the office while our home was road tested. The chaps came back and gave us the thumbs up sign. Then the bill, 17,000 Austrian schillings, £1,000 sterling. Paying the bill with Euro cheques was quite a game. Five cheques were made out and paid into three banks, we left the garage at midday.

All weekend we had talked over that we should make for home when the job was done. Once out on the open road, I said that I felt tempted to go on to *Pakrac*. Denys was in the same frame of mind. After coming so far it would be a shame not to go on and visit some of the friends we had made there.

Over the weekend we had been listening out for anyone from the convoy on the C.B.. There was a chance that we might see them somewhere on the road to *Zagreb*. We heard their voices first, then saw the vehicles on the other side of a motorway. There were lots of cheerful calls, they were pleased to see us on the move and still in the area. Some of them were going on to Switzerland to pick up goods for a camp in *Maribor*, our trailer was going with them. Crossing the borders now was no problem as we were not carrying goods, we were tourists.

We did not see snow until well into Croatia. Arriving in *Pakrac*, we met up with B.J. of the volunteers, he told us of a new refugee camp and invited us to go with him to check it out in the morning. We set out at 10am. to what had been a compound for U.N. vehicles on the Croatian \ Bosnian border. With snow and slush it was a veritable sea of mud. About 600 refugees had been brought in recently, among them were Serbs, Croats, Moslems and gypsy families. They were to be joined shortly by 200 more.

The gypsies had been segregated and were housed in a row of brick sheds along one side of the area. The U.N. had brought in 40 shipping crates, each container was a home for eight refugees. The remaining women, children and old men were sheltered from the bitter cold under a canvas marquee. A representative from U.N.H.C.R. United Nations High Commissioner of Refugees, was in charge of the welfare of the camp. Three ladies from the local Red Cross had an office in one of the containers. Over coffee, the electric kettle run from a generator, we were told of the many problems facing them. Blankets they had in plenty but if they were soiled they had to be burned. They could not wash blankets in buckets. Sheets would help, pillows and pillow cases were needed. A hot meal was supplied for every one each day. Breakfast was a problem, local bread was available but the refugees ate it without spread. We were asked if we could bring jam, peanut butter, marmalade etc.

As 200 plus children would swamp the local schools, voluntary teachers would be holding classes in a newly set up activity centre. Without our trailer we did not have much to give, just a parcel of pens, pencils and erasers advertising that great team of aerobatic fliers, 'The Red Arrows.'

Portable toilets, a large generator and water tankers were provided by the U.N. In the gigantic marquee protecting the refugees from the bitter weather to come, we gained permission to take photographs. Family groups posed for us, quite happy to have their picture taken. Outside, washing was hanging from every available place. What would it be like in the depth of winter?

There were many such camps but we decided that we would make this one, *Pushkara*, our project for 1996. With good reason to get home and start working on it, we told B. J. that we would leave first thing in the morning. He asked a favour, would we take a lady back to the U.K. with us? She had joined the volunteers 10 days before and had been unwell for most of that time. With Daphne and her luggage on board we made for home, feeling that it had not been a wasted journey. Daphne's husband was on the docks to meet her as we arrived at Ramsgate.

One week after returning home we found out from Tony that our medical packages had been delivered to *Gospic* hospital, the clothes, blankets and toys to the orphanage at Skrad and the food taken to *Rangi Nekova* camp. We were just sorry that we could not deliver it ourselves.

December 1995

For the last two winters I had been suffering from bronchial problems and chest infections. Living as we did in fields was not helping so we put our names forward for a 'Housing 21' retirement flat. We were offered one in the Westbourne area and moved in just before leaving for the Christmas run to camps and orphanages on the 19th December.

Our December newsletter began :-

Dear friends, we were to help Father Christmas this year. He contacted us in a right old state, and said, " I understand that you know the area which was Yugoslavia, pretty well." To which Denys replied, " We should do, after having visiting that country more than twenty times." At that Santa asked if we could possibly help him out, explaining that as there were so many children not in their own homes, it had made his job very difficult. It took up a lot of his time on Christmas Eve trying to sort them out.

He suggested that we started out a week earlier than he did as our camper would not travel as fast as his magic sleigh. We could take presents for the children in the refugee camps, this would mean less disappointed faces on Christmas morning.

Well, as we were always up for a challenge, we took on the job. There would be no time to collect gifts from Santa's work shop at the North Pole so we would have to rely on friends and contacts in the South of England. Spetisbury School, friends from Hamworthy and Bournemouth. Uncle George and contacts from Essex all helped to fill our trailer with beautifully wrapped gifts and useful goods.

Danny was eager to help, he rallied his friends into filling his van with presents, crackers and gifts, games and soft toys. He brought along his mate Jonathan to help him with the driving.

Tony filled his van and trailer with presents that would have made Santa really proud of us. Travelling with Tony was one of Santa's own little helpers, Patsy from North Wales.

There had been some concern about the weather we might encounter on the continent at that time of year. The lowest temperature on our way was just below freezing with small amounts of snow in Austria and Slovenia. Our first port of call was at the orphanage in *Lipik*. Goran the Director greeted us and immediately invited us all to lunch. Friday was a no meat day, vegetable stew was ladled into each dish from a large bowl. While we ate Goran told us that some of the children had gone away to stay with relatives and friends for the holiday. We left a large pile of presents to be distributed by staff when our young friends returned.

From *Lipik* it was just a short journey to *Pushkara*, the refugee camp that Denys and I had visited with B.J. one month before. At that time there had been 600 displaced persons from the *Banja Luka* district. Some of them had since been moved on to Canada and the States to start new lives. Their territories had changed since the peace agreements had been signed.

Tanya, a young lady from Texas, was our contact for the camp and had sent Denys and me a letter requesting items such as jam for the daily bread ration. We had obtained the very best, the brand of preserves that were on sale in Harrods. Chris from Weymouth had not been able to join us on this trip, he supplied a quantity of chocolate spread and peanut butter.

We had gifts for the activity centre and schoolroom, a dartboard and a half dozen sets of darts, packs of playing cards, footballs, table tennis bats and balls, and tennis balls, books and pencils, knitting and sewing materials. Keith, who had opened the charity shop, had donated a parachute to be used in games for the younger children.

All this with Christmas parcels and shoeboxes were stacked up in the wooden container huts. Tanya and her helpers would see to it that the gifts were distributed fairly.

Pakrac next and we had a wonderful meeting with Anton and Maria, they had a thriving little business with Anton's shoe making and repairing skills. We just had a couple of personal gifts for them. Then we went into town to spend a little time with Javanka and her family in the bistro. We had gifts of make up and perfume for the girls.

Then it was off to the *Zagreb* motorway services to spend the night, after a convoy stew and a game of travel Trivial Pursuit. Going on the next day to *Karlovac*. Beyond this the little patches of snow gave way to a landscape of white, then in the mountains rain and fog made the going slow. The holiday season meant that there were fewer heavy lorries on the road to hold us up. The outside temperature jumped up and down, from 55 degrees to freezing and back again.

In the village of *Skrad* we turned into a very narrow lane and down a steep incline to our second orphanage, or as they prefer 'Children's Home'. We were welcomed into the building with coffee and the local spirit. As in *Lipik* some of the children had gone to spend a holiday with relatives or friends, some of those left behind wandered in to talk to us. The home is a Catholic institution run by nuns.

Lunch was put out for us, we tucked into soup with bread, then fried potato with rissoles, a pudding with thick custard and sweet black tea. After the refreshment the work of unloading, rice, shampoo, talcum powder and plenty of gifts for the children staying for Christmas and for the others when they returned.

On our leaving, the wet steep drive proved to be a problem to our front wheel drive camper, the tyres spun and slipped on the wet surface. We made it out to the road after the other vehicles gave us room to take a run at it. On then through fog which thickened as we climbed, until on the long steep run to the Adriatic Highway, the skies brightened and the air became warmer. Our first drop was at the hostel that had been adopted by Chuck and Iris on the first convoy that we had been on together, December 1992. Sadly with Chuck no longer with us, it was up to us to deliver in his name. Also we carried two large parcels of chocolate from John and June, regular visitors to the camp. They could not make the Christmas run this year.

The refugees in the hostel were from the old city of *Vukovar*, like our own friends of *Odmaraliste*. There were so many groups living along this particular stretch of coastline, with no homes, no future and no hope. A very lively and cheerful crowd took us into the dining room and in minutes we

217

were sitting around a huge platter of chips surrounded by one dozen fried eggs. By the time we finished the meal, it was dark and raining, a decision was made to socialise that evening and unload in the morning.

Eventually we slept in the driveway, Tony and Patsy were our neighbours in their van. Danny and Jon had been given a room in the hostel. We surfaced around 8am. with breakfast provided in the hostel. Fresh bread with jam and cheese spread, with very sweet black tea. We ate watched by three or four interested seagulls, they sat on the rails of the balcony. Now and again one would soar past the large picture windows overlooking the calm blue sea. We wondered how much it might have cost five years before to be hotel guests and to sit where we were and having our meal.

Later, using the reception area, we unloaded and sorted the gifts into separate piles for boys, girls, men and ladies. Some were labelled 'for a family'. With the help of the ladies, the presents were given out room by room. There was quite a pantomime as Tony and the director, neither able to speak each other's language, sorted out names and ages of the children to receive the various parcels. Some of the smaller tots were given extra toys with their parcels. The older children received colouring books and crayons from Danny and Jon, there was so much excitement with everyone having fun.

Lunch was provided for us, we 'enjoyed' squid, deep-fried with potato, which had been mashed and mixed with some sort of green vegetable. The residents fetched their meals from the kitchen and took them to their rooms, leaving us alone in the lovely dining room.

Tony was to leave us at that point, he would be spending Christmas day with friends in *Rijeka*. Some of the gifts he was carrying would be delivered to a clinic for the very poor. Patsy came on board with us to make the rest of the trip. With the transit van following we made our way to the far side of *Crikvenica* to Nada and her friends, We all crowded into their little room for coffee as we explained that we had Christmas gifts for the children. Down to the vehicles where Danny and Jon sorted the packages into piles for boy or girl. The adult parcels had all gone.

218

We piled the parcels up on the patio as the weather was so nice, sunny and warm. Nada sorted them into family piles then handed them over to the parents to pass on to their children. Nada became very emotional and told us that these would be the only gifts the children would have for Christmas. Some of our famous jam was delivered to the kitchen along with enough talcum and shampoo for each family. There was some sad news, Evitsa, the lady for whom we had delivered a sphygomometer for her blood pressure, had died two weeks before our visit.

Just one more call to make and that was to Josep's group at the annex to the *Ad Turres* hotel. The children there were older but we managed to find suitable gifts for them, The director Zelko wrote the names, sex and ages for us to match the gift to the child. We called into the reception of the *Ad Turres* hotel to call our families to wish all at home a Happy Christmas. Then returned to Chuck and Iris's hostel to spend another night in the driveway.

We enjoyed a hectic Christmas morning, playing games with the children teaching them Pass the Parcel. Using some old copies of our local newspaper and miles of sticky tape. Danny and Jon were in charge showing the kids what to do. It all started out well but soon turned into a riot. Every one cheating with paper and toys littering the floor. It all finished when the kids piled on top of our colleagues.

Time then to leave, there were many goodbyes before we broke away to hit the road. On to the road to *Zagreb* and a stop at *Rangi Nekova*. Rachel from Christchurch had made up a special parcel for Josepa, daughter of a family from near *Sarajevo*. There were not so many gifts left but with Danny and Jon opening up some of the shoeboxes of presents they were able to give a little something to each child in the camp.

We returned to the U.K. feeling that we had fulfilled our task to the best of our ability. About 2000 children had received a little of the Spirit of Christmas. We delivered the goods provided by the good hearts of folks at home.

MARCH 1996

Eight vehicles started out from Ramsgate on March 2nd, taking the Sally Ferry to *Dunkirk*. On the docks we split the convoy. Five vans headed for the Ukraine, Tony from Canterbury, Rob and Lut from Havant, Bob from Essex, and two vehicles driven by Sharon and Peter from Reading.

Our camper and trailer led the mini convoy to Croatia, Malcolm and Mervyn with a large transit van and Chris from Portisham towing a trailer, bringing up the rear.

Taking a new route we headed for *Lille* and *Mons*, arriving at *Aachen* around 5pm local time, one hour ahead of the U.K. Refuelled and had a quick meal at the services then made for *Hockenheim* for our night stop. Chris had asked in advance for the comfort of the spare bed in the camper as he expected the nights to be very cold, that night it was minus six.

Our cab heater was not working very well, Malcolm and Mervyn had a spare thermostat in their van. This was fitted to the camper before leaving *Hockenheim* at 9.30am. We snacked as we travelled. Being a Sunday there were no heavy lorries on the Autobahns making travel for us a lot easier, but the services were choc-a-bloc, we used a picnic area for our lunch stop.

The dull start to the day soon turned to snow, which thickened as we approached Austria. No problems on the main roads as they were kept clear by snow ploughs and gritting lorries. Our heater was working well. On arriving at the toll tunnels we were amazed that the free passes for goods vehicles carrying aid were no longer available. The transits were charged 38 marks each. We had always had to pay for our camper so it made no difference to us, (We have a camper, so we must be on holiday!!!) Malc and Merv left us to spend the night with friends, while we and Chris stayed at *Gralla Services*. A clear cold night, minus eight degrees.

In the morning we found that our water system was frozen solid, we had to heat water in a pan for washing. The boys met up with us at 9am. then we headed for the Slovenian border. Exit Austria was easy but entry Slovenia took a lot longer and we were charged 60 marks per vehicle to enter the country and drive 30 miles to the Croatian border. We entered Croatia at mid-day. The men went to present the paper work, they were shocked to hear they could be arrested and put into prison. It seems that the convoy that went out in August last year had missed being cleared by customs when they made a delivery to *Gospic* Hospital. To make things worse a lot of the aid had been sold by one of the doctors.

Denys protested that we were not on that convoy in August, but it made no difference. The customs needed proof of where we were taking the aid this time. A fax was sent to the camp at *Sisak*. We waited for the confirmation that we were expected.

3.15 when we were allowed to go, after paying 260 kuna (about £35), with orders to report to the customs in *Sisak* at 8am. the following morning.

Heading towards *Zagreb*, then taking the motorway to the *Sisak* turn off, we followed the directions given over the phone by Tanya, our contact at the refugee camp. Asking for directions in *Sisak* it seemed that we were on the right track. Tanya had said that we would be able to see yellow painted houses a good distance before getting to the camp. It was dark by then so that was not a lot of help. As we were driving down a long track we were overtaken by a local car. The occupants were calling out and beckoning us to follow them. On reaching a turning the car flashed the right indicators and sped on ahead. The right turning led us into the camp that we were looking for.

Tanya came to meet us and told us that most of the people in this camp were displaced Croatians, many of them from *Vukovar*. The camp was made up of small neat prefabricated bungalows, built about one year before by the Japanese. Each home had two bedrooms, kitchen and bathroom. Most of them had a car parked outside and some even had satellite T.V. dishes. It was quite a weird set up, different from other camps that we had seen. Then we were told by our hosts that part of the camp was home to the Moslems, who did not get help from the State as the Croatians did. Tanya and her friend were living in one of the small homes and offered accommodation to our convoy friends, sleeping space on the floor only.

Up early on a freezing morning with a very red sunrise, Tanya and a local lad were ready to lead us into *Sisak* to the customs shed near the railway. The customs officials, a man and a woman, asked to see inside the vans and examined the goods we had brought. Some boxes were opened and sell by dates were checked. They obviously were not happy with some of the baby food dated Jan. 1996, and some cans of chick peas dated 1993. They discussed the matter between themselves but finally told us that we were clear to unload at the camp. They took away our loading lists to be photocopied. They would be returned to us at the camp later.

A good deal of the boxes on our trailer were from Daphne and her friends from Billericay Baptist Church. Daphne had spent some time with Tanya and her co-worker Abigail in Croatia in 1995. She understood the need for help in camps such as the one at *Sisak* and at *Okucani* which had closed down at the end of the year. She had sent a camera for Abigail to take snaps of the goods as the parcels were being delivered.

Later as we chatted to Tanya she told us that a woman of 37 had died of a heart attack the morning we had arrived. She left two sons, one of the boys was 17 and his father lived in Sweden. The younger boy was 7 and his father was Bosnian. The two boys did not want to be separated and it was causing problems. The boys had an Aunt in *Banja Luka*, who was sister of the dead woman. She too had a heart problem and it was feared that the news of her sister's death would be too much for her.

At last our paperwork arrived and we started the long process of saying goodbyes. Abigail begged a lift from us, she was staying in *Okucani* for a few days. Not far from the camp, Malcolm and Mervyn had a problem, the back axle of their van seized up. Denys dropped our trailer and tried to tow the transit. It would not move. The boys told us that they had friends in *Slavonski Brod* and was sure that they could get help from them. Perhaps to get a mechanic out to fix the van, or as a last resort they could fly home.

All they needed from us was a lift into *Slavonski Brod*.

Abigail wrote a note in Croat to say 'Car is kaput, gone to get help' and put it in the windscreen. With Malcolm, Mervyn and Abigail on board we set out first for *Okucani* to drop Abigail at her 'digs', then took the motorway to *Slavonski Brod*.

In the early days of the convoys that would not have been possible as the Serbs had control of that stretch of road. Then it would have taken us 4 hours to do the journey which these days took us 50 minutes. Chris's small trailer, now empty, had been bouncing dangerously on the rough roads. It was now safely tucked inside our box trailer. The only goods left to deliver were the clothing and shoes in Chris's van, destined for the clinic in *Rijeka*. We still had a couple of boxes of medical items for *Pakrac* hospital.

In *Slavonski Brod* we all helped to carry Malc and Merv's kit into the bistro owned by their friend Ivan. Ivan arrived and while we drank coffee, we were all treated to the warm welcome we had come to expect from the local people. Before leaving our friends we arranged that they would phone us the next evening when we expected to be in *Crikvenica*. They would contact us at the *Ad Turres* hotel and leave a message. If they needed a lift home it would be no problem.

Just three of us then, we decided to stop overnight on the motorway services and go on to *Pakrac* the next morning. As we were about to leave at 9am. a British lorry came in and parked near us. Denys and Chris chatted to the driver who was on his way to *Budapeste*. Taking a road we had not used before, we made for *Lipik* and *Pakrac*. The road was badly potholed and seemed unused but it led in the right direction. First to the rebuilt hospital, where we met with Doctor Dragitsa. She was pleased to accept the catheters, syringes and needles sent from our local hospital at home.

Dragitsa invited us to her own flat where we were shown her paintings, many of them done during the dark days of the war. Some of them were really beautiful, some hard to understand. There were portraits and landscapes and others with some deep hidden meanings. There were portraits of *Sai Baba*, an Indian Holy Man of whom Dragitsa is a devotee as are some of our convoy colleagues. I was admiring one small study of a vase of flowers, it was for sale. I bought it for a souvenir and it

223

hangs on a wall of our small home, with many other mementos of our travels.

A couple of quick visits to friends in the town, then we went on to *Lipik*. Spending a little time at the demolished church, took photos of the ruins and of the church bells which had been mounted on a frame work of telegraph poles. On again to take the mountain roads to *Crikvenica*, we came into fog, snow and ice as we climbed. We had estimated that we would reach the *Ad Turres* by 9pm. It was ten minutes past nine as we pulled into the car park. There was no message from Malc and Merv. We got together over a nightcap before settling in, the temperature was plus six.

The next day we played at being tourists. First we went into the town to look for a wedding present for Kelly, a young lady from our area, who had been with us on a few of our trips. Later we made a social call on Nada, her daughter Ivana was finishing school at 19 and told us that she would like to visit England for a short holiday. We got to talking it over and decided that it could be arranged. She could come back with us after one of our visits and we would return her on the next convoy.

A visit to Zinka had been arranged, with lunch at her parent's home. Zinka's Papa was Serbian and very ill with cancer, Mama was Bosnian, a large and jovial lady. She could speak no English but she understood more than she let on, as we all talked her expressions spoke volumes. Zinka was working in the afternoon so we went into town to look around the shops. We were expected back for supper. As we tucked into chicken with vegetables served from a large bowl, Mama proudly announced that it was *Engleska* (English) stew.

The next morning, Saturday, Zinka had arranged for us to visit an old people's home and a centre for rape victims.

In the first we met two women who were caring for 87 old folk, most of them bedridden. The unpaid angels of mercy washed, fed, and changed the dressings without any other help. We were taken into the women's wards. The first lady we met had fallen and broken both legs. She complained to Zinka that her legs and feet were hurting, Zinka explained that she was suffering from bedsores and asked if we could get creams or sprays for this complaint.

The next patient was blind and needed company. We stayed, held her hand and talked to her for a while with Zinka interpreting. It seemed that none of the patients had visitors. In the men's wards the smell was so bad that we did not stay too long. Some of the old chaps were just staring into space. The next place Zinka took us was to a centre, which cared for victims of rape. On other occasions we had heard of, but not seen for ourselves, the camps where women were taken and raped by the invaders. Horror stories were told of how the babies had to be removed from the mothers as soon as they were born, before the deranged women strangled their offspring.

In the building we met some young mothers who had decided to keep their babies. The centre was run by nuns who were caring for a group of very young mums with their cute babes. We promised that we would bring disposable nappies on our next visit to *Rijeka*. It was time that we made tracks for home, with Chris following and a clear run, we crossed the continent in two long hops, good weather and no problems.

On our return the local paper carried a story of a nurse who was retiring from her profession. She was to make the most of her life of leisure by gathering parcels for the women of the former Yugoslavia and needed a lift to take the gifts to Bosnia. Her husband Clive and their five sons were giving Pam their full support. There was a contact number. After reading the article, I hovered over the phone a couple of times during that evening, not sure if I should make the contact. When I did call, Pam told me that a couple of callers had put forward our names to her. She was delighted when we invited her to join us on our next expedition in May.

MAY 1996

Tony was concentrating on taking aid convoys to the Ukraine. Denys became the organiser of convoys to Bosnia and a Director of our Registered Charity, British Humanitarian Aid. Four vehicles from the Yorkshire area were wanting company and help in coping with documentation on their journey to *Mostar*. We ourselves were heading for *Sisak* camp.

Tim M. was once again, joining us in the camper and became acquainted with Pam on the journey to Kent. We met up with our friends from 'Up North' at Ramsgate docks. The channel crossing gave us all time to get to know new faces. Steve and Chris, Ian and Frank, Andrew and Dave, Nick and Ray all from around the Huddersfield area.

The journey across Europe was quite uneventful, driving through Germany was made easy with the absence of lorries on the roads as it was Sunday. Heavy vehicles were not allowed on the Autobahns on a Sunday. In Austria the mountains were shrouded in mist but at that time of year there was plenty of daylight to admire the views. At *Gralla* services, some of the crew had welcome showers before turning in.

At the Slovenian border the usual hassle to get through the customs, each vehicle having to pay 50 marks before they would allow us into their country. In Croatia there were new rules. No canned meat or fish. Our canned goods were hidden behind all of Pam's 250 shoeboxes so Denys thought it was safe to say that we were not carrying the banned items. We had with us letters of request from the camp at *Sisak* which should have made it easier to get through the customs but that wasn't so. Faxes had to be exchanged from our destination and from the organisation in *Mostar*, before we were free to enter the country.

At a service station on the *Zagreb* motorway we were to part company with the Yorkshire boys. They were to go down to

226

the coast, we were to make for *Sisak* and the refugee camp. The boys had a date with a nun on the Bosnian border, we would meet up again in a day or two.

We set out taking the motorway east to the *Sisak* turn off, snacking on sandwiches and coffee from the flasks as we travelled. No trouble finding the camp this time. We were met by Tanya who soon had the unloading organised. Tim and Pam handed out the shoeboxes, each one had been lovingly wrapped by Pam's 'team'. The children crowded around us excitedly, every one eager to claim one of the gift parcels. Tanya made sure that the boxes of food were safely stowed in the storeroom to be distributed fairly late on. With Pam's permission, gift boxes were kept back for the friends we would meet later.

Our load for the camp consisted of a large amount of canned food, toiletries and shoes. Wool, sheets and teddies, school items, paper, pens and colouring pencils, English early learning books, pillows, four dozen spools of crochet cotton, first aid supplies.

Vegetable and grass seed which had been specially requested. A TV set from Daphne and her friends from Billericay. Also well received were some English newspapers and magazines for Tanya and her New Zealand friend Abigail. The two girls were in charge of the welfare of 500 refugees.

On leaving the camp we made for the mountains and the coast. Pam had heard of the local hog roasts at the roadside cafes. We had planned to stop at one of them for our evening meal but we had left it too late. Perhaps we would make it on the return journey.

Since the winter the roads had deteriorated from the snow and ice, giving us a really rough ride. Making the steep descent to the coast we arrived at the *Ad Turres* hotel car park around 10pm. The Yorkshire boys were there patronising a nearby bar. After getting a quick meal, we joined our colleagues for a nightcap. Ian took over the entertainment with his guitar. The locals, (some of them from the Croatian football team) sang along with him. The party was in full swing at 11pm. when the police came in and put out all the lights of the bar. The hint was taken, the party was over.

The Yorkshire convoy left next morning going on to

Medugorje to spend a night before going into *Mostar*. Our next stop was to Nada and her family, they had asked for a small cooker which could be used in their room. Up to this point we had only been able to bring goods which had been donated and so far no cooker had been given. With funds in hand on account of the charity shop supporting us we were able to buy a small Belling cooker, complete with two rings and a grill\oven. Their reaction and the joy on their faces could not have been greater if we had presented them with the keys to a three bedroom, detached home of their own.

Also given were three of the parcels, presents from Pam for the family, a fourth was for Ilya who had lost his wife Evitsa around Christmas time. On earlier visits we had discussed bringing Ivana to England for a holiday, as she was leaving school in June. We finalised the plan and arranged to bring her out in July. At 19 and with a good knowledge of English, she would not be too much of a problem.

Next we made a flying visit to Zinka, taking her two hospital hoists and slings for lifting helpless patients in and out of beds and baths. They were to help the two ladies coping with 87 elderly patients in a nursing home. Other supplies for Zinka were disposable nappies for the rape centre.

It was late afternoon when we started out on the Adriatic Highway en route for *Zadar*. We hoped to make it to our layby near the freshwater spring, which ran into the sea. It was after 10pm. when we pulled in to the parking area, put up the shutters and drew the curtains to settle for the night.

Up bright and early, in the daylight we saw that a Shrine had been built beside the water since our last visit. Denys and Tim filled our water containers with the cold fresh water bubbling out from the spring. On the coast it was summertime and quite a contrast to the weather on the continent. Breakfast, then we hit the road for the *Meslenica* bridge. Pam was amazed at the remains of the structure hanging high above us as we ventured slowly over the pontoon affair.

On then around *Zadar* and towards *Split,* we made a lunch break at *Makarska*. Lovely views with fishing boats and sailing ships riding at anchor. We pressed on then to *Metkovic* and the Bosnian border. The passports were checked and the now empty trailer was examined. We were through, on to *Medugorje*, only twelve miles from the besieged and blitzed town of *Mostar*.

In the main street there was no sign of our convoy. A couple of calls on the C.B. had brought no answer. As tourists we strolled around the souvenir shops, walked around the patio which surrounded the white church and treated ourselves to coffee in a Bistro. Rain drove us to shelter in the camper, when we heard Ray's voice on the C.B. They were on their way back. At a get together on their return they told us that they had made their drop at an organisation called *'Dragan Susac Pamila'*, a connection with the Red Cross. They had accommodation at a bed and breakfast house, where a meal was waiting for them.

Ray came to chat with us later and said that the boys would be leaving in the morning. Some of them had to be at work on the Monday. As we had missed going into *Mostar*, a chap named Sean would guide us into the city first thing in the morning. We were to be ready at 8.45.

We slept parked up in a side road, and were up in plenty of time. Sean arrived in a bright yellow Toyota and led us over mountain roads, to the long steep stretch, which had become known as 'Sniper Alley'. On entering the town Sean pulled in and came to tell us that we could go just about anywhere in safety, he had to leave us there as he was returning to New Zealand that day.

We drove down streets that were completely demolished, took photos of the remains of buildings and famous bridges. In other parts of town, life was still going on. Small groups of locals stared as we drove by, our camper and trailer caught a lot of attention. We parked up to have lunch at mid-day, right next to a couple of IFOR trucks taking on fresh water in gigantic containers. Pam rewrote the names of some of our aid destinations, which the rain had washed from our trailer. Then we made tracks for *Medugorje*.

While we were souvenir hunting earlier we had noticed a tour guide office called 'The Paddy Shop', we just had to find out why. A couple of Irish ladies came to chat, they had seen our colleagues' vans in town. They had a couple of carrier bags of just about new children's clothes, and asked us to give them to refugees.

About 1pm. we set off for *Split*. We had heard that the inland roads had been opened since the Serbs had been ousted from the territory so we decided to give it a try. Heading for *Knin* we were travelling quite well, until a split road with no signs, found us trapped in a village precinct. The owners of a couple of parked cars moved their vehicles to let us out. Locals were hanging out of windows watching the manoeuvring.

On again, some of the roads very good others quite bad in places. As we climbed into the mountains and the *Plitvice National Park*, beautiful landscapes, but many damaged villages. We spent the night on a layby in the mountains. Next morning we drove on hoping to refuel and take on some fresh water. A local garage had plenty of fuel but no water. The owner explained, "It's because of the war." Our route brought us out at the south side of *Karlovac*, which was badly damaged. From *Karlovac* we took the motorway to *Zagreb*.

We were to deliver a parcel to a family in *Babina Greda* about twenty five miles past *Slavonski Brod*. We asked for directions to the address on the parcel. Two chaps from a coffee bar jumped into their car and led us to the house. The parcel was from our son and his wife, (Tim and Tracy). They had contact with this family through their church. English speaking Anton, aged 16 had phoned members of our family wanting to say thank you to Tim and Tracy for a previous parcel. The family Breskic, Mum, Dad, Anton, Sister Marijana and Grandma were refugees from Bosnia, all living in a house belonging to a man in the village.

Anton wanted us to go with him to see his village, this meant a trip across the river *Drava* on an antiquated one man ferry into Serb occupied Bosnia.

We dropped our trailer before setting out. Anton explained our presence to the border guards who checked our passports and made a search of our vehicle. We drove on and off the boat with the back end of the camper grounding badly. We were not allowed to visit Anton's family's house as it was occupied by a Serb family. We did manage to visit an Aunt and some of his relations. We sat outside one house drinking coffee and bitten to death by vicious mosquitoes. Very hot and dark as we returned to the ferry. We parked up outside Anton's home lulled to sleep by a chorus of bullfrogs and crickets.

Next morning we were expected to breakfast in the restaurant where Anton's mother worked a couple of hours each day. In blazing sunshine we sat outside under parasols and ate hamburgers. A procession of carriages came by, a local wedding of an influential family. The traditional carriages were pulled by beautifully groomed and decorated horses. The occupants were dressed in national costume. One young driver wearing a top hat, looked so proud as he posed for Denys's video camera. We counted at least 24 carriages of wedding guests, The last in the line contained the orchestra, guitar, violin, mandolin and cello. The musicians doffed their hats as they passed by us.

Soon it was time to say our goodbyes. Another group of very warm-hearted people to remember. We hitched up the trailer, gave the clothes from *Medugorje* to some of the neighbours and dollies to a couple of small girls, then left the village. As we drove out to the motorway, we saw two parachutists drop from a plane which circled above a field where a marquee had been set up for the wedding reception.

On the motorway and nearing *Slavonski Brod*, we decided to look up another lady called Nada. She had kept in contact since we first delivered aid to the Anton Mehanovic centre over two years before. We found the town centre but could not find the flats where Nada lived. As we drove down yet another road Denys spotted a lady on a bike. She was peddling like mad and waving, trying to catch up with us. Not Nada but one of her workmates, Meira. She phoned around and soon we were having coffee with the ladies we knew at the centre, including Nada.

On the wall of the hall were framed photographs of us and colleagues of the many trips made to the organisation. The boss arrived and we had a chat as best we could. The conversation was very hit and miss with the language barrier. His son Tomi was contacted and it was arranged that we should all meet at the cafe near the monastery and close to the river.

The Green Park cafe was owned by a local man who had spent some of his youth in London and had very fond memories of that area. Tomi arrived on his bike and greeted us warmly. Over coffee Tomi and Tim had a very deep conversation about the problems and the politics of the situation in the country.

Nada worked part-time in the library and bookshop of the monastery church. She left at 5pm. to be on duty as a service was about to commence. We all went into the church, the singing was beautiful and touched the soul. Although we could not understand the language, we could feel the sentiments. Later that evening we met with Nada and her niece at a bistro in the town, it would have been pleasant but for the determined mosquitoes. Nada told us that before the war the river areas were sprayed but now there was no money for jobs like these.

We left the city at 9pm. and spent the night at a service area on the *Zagreb* motorway before going on to *Lipik*. An hour spent with the children at Mark Cook's orphanage before going on to *Pakrac*. A social call on Anton and Maria where we found them entertaining a cousin from Australia and their son from Germany with his family. That evening as we all sat out on the veranda, we heard stories of what happened when the war was on their doorstep.

Anton's son told of how in 1991, they were warned that the Serbs were coming into the town, he stayed to pack family belongings. Without lights on his car, as he reached the crossroads on the outskirts of the town, a tank careered across in front of him. The tank hit the front of his car, turning it around until he was facing the opposite way. The occupants of the tank hadn't noticed him and he continued on his way to safety.

The cousin told his story of how in the Second World War, he escaped from Yugoslavia by walking over the mountain ranges to Austria. From there he made his way to Australia, settled and married there. He became a builder and now builds the most luxurious homes imaginable. He showed us photos of his own house with swimming pool and beautiful gardens.

The house where Anton and Maria now lived, belonged to the son. In the war years it was not exactly a safe haven. Two houses away, in the same street, were the shattered remains of someone's property. In the days of occupation by the enemy, the house where we were sitting and talking, was used as a look-out post by the local police. While the beer and slivovic was flowing, we told the stories of how we strayed into Serbian held territory, not once, but twice. There were gasps of amazement and as this was translated to Anton, he said that we deserved medals for bravery.

With all our aid delivered and friendships renewed, we made for home. We hoped that our passengers felt that they knew a little more of the plight of such warm and wonderful people in a country torn apart and unable to solve its problems.

JULY 1996

Three vehicles displaying the heart logo boarded the Sally Ferry at Ramsgate on the 2nd. July. Danny and John from Reading had brought along their mate Andy. John and June from the Birmingham area had brought along a passenger, Sandy. Our passenger for the trip was Pat, our own sister-in-law.

We were taking a different route this time, *Lille, Mons* and *Charleroi*. On nearing *Liege*, Danny's van developed a knocking noise under the bonnet. Fearing that it was a big end, the men decided that it would be best for them to return to the U.K. Very sad all round. Our two remaining vehicles travelled on to *Aachen* where we had an hour break. Then on to *Hockenheim* for the night.

Wednesday was taken care of by travelling through the second half of Germany and into Austria, stopping twelve miles short of the Slovenian border. The weather had been cold and wet all the way since leaving home.

The next morning was bright and sunny as the men coped with the customs and border officials. At the Croatian border we met up with a convoy from Edinburgh Direct Aid, one of their drivers was from our Bournemouth area. They told us of how they had lost one of their lorries in an accident in Germany two days before. The crew of the truck were now in hospital but not too badly injured. Their convoy was returning refugees and their personal effects from the U.K. where they had been living for the past four years.

On the *Zagreb* to *Belgrade* motorway we took the turning off for *Lipik*. Part of John and June's load was a water pump for the *Lipik* fire truck. It was desperately needed and requested on a previous trip. The crew of a Birmingham fire station had heard of the need and donated the pump. At the orphanage, Goran the director of the home, phoned the local fire station. Two firemen arrived to receive the much-needed appliance. A shoebox of goodies was left for each child in the home, these were donated by the members of John and June's Church.

In *Pakrac*, after a meal of convoy stew and local bread in the grounds of the hospital, we went into town. We met up with Englishman B.J. and Sascha from Switzerland. They were making good headway with repairing homes and properties in the war damaged town. B.J. told us that the paint we had fetched from Switzerland had already been put to good use. Arrangements were made to deliver medical items at the hospital.

On then to *Slavonski Brod* and the *Antun Mihanovic* Centre. As we arrived we could see a queue of people waiting at the door. We thought that the Bush Telegraph had been working but we were wrong. They were not waiting for us. They were waiting for their weekly rations and the staff on duty were not known by us. A phone call soon brought the ladies who usually dealt with the unloading. We apologised for the small amount that we had brought this time, explaining that one car was 'kaput' and had returned to England. They were pleased and grateful for what we had brought.

The ladies had brought with them, from their own homes, carrier bags containing food. It was laid out on a table and we were invited to join them for lunch. The wine was a cordial of elderflowers, very refreshing. Some one had sent for Tomi and after a couple of hours with the cheery bunch, we had to take our leave, promising to return in September. Tomi told us that his birthday was in September and asked us to come and help him celebrate.

Taking a road east and then north we drove though very pretty villages and found ourselves in *Osijek*, quite a large Cathedral town, apparently undamaged by the war. We headed back toward *Zagreb* on our old route and stopped overnight at a bus station near *Varazdin*.

Next morning as we headed for *Zagreb*, Pat and Sandy asked for a break where they could take photographs of storks' nests. We had passed many of these strange structures of twigs and leaves, usually on chimneys, or deserted buildings or even on telegraph poles at the side of the roads. In a village with a

235

large car park, we could see a nest way up on a tower. Denys and John pulled in for the ladies to get their pictures. The stork is the emblem of *Slavonski Brod* city. It is considered good luck if a pair should nest in a town or village.

Our journey took us over the mountains to *Crikvenica*. In the *Ad Turres Hotel* a fax from Danny was waiting for us. It said that he and his crew had arrived in the U.K. safely.

It was a relief, as if they had broken down completely in France, they would have been waiting a week for our return. John and June were to visit one hostel on the coast, while we visited *Odmaraliste*. Our main reason for this visit was to bring Ivana back with us for a holiday in England.

For the past three years we had been taking essential goods to the group living in former holiday accommodation. Recently they had become self-supporting. Some had found jobs and the cost of living had become easier. Our visits this year had been as friends, just bringing the odd item when needed. At first the idea of Ivana coming to England had started as a joke, gradually it had become a possibility. Now it was to happen.

With Ivana and her luggage on board, we set off with medical items for Zinka and her old folks nursing home. Shoes and clothing for the clinic which dealt with the very poor. Zinka was not at home when we called but her parents received our load which was stored in their garage. Some of the goods had been sent by Chris who had been unable to deliver them himself at this time.

Ivana and Zinka's Mama had a lengthy conversation in their own language while we drank coffee. We were a little apprehensive as Papa was a Serb, but no one came out of the meeting upset or angry. After the refreshment we backtracked to *Crikvenica* to meet up with John and co, for the start of the long journey home. On the coast the temperature had been 87 degrees. As we travelled across Austria it was 40 degrees.

On reaching the U.K. we called into passport control, Ivana had all the right documentation for entering England. She was taken into an office and she looked very worried as we were told to stay outside. She came back to us a little later with an official who told us that we must not allow her to be exploited for publicity, she must not work or attend any school during her stay.

On the road home, things were fine until we heard on the radio that there was a problem on the A31 at Cadnam, a road traffic accident involving a fuel tanker. By listening to the B.B.C. and the C.B. we found that traffic jams were blocking all the routes home. Rather than sit for hours in the traffic we decided to have a pub lunch in Timsbury, near Romsey, introducing Ivana to a Ploughman's lunch. We managed to get home in the late afternoon, taking Ivana to her temporary home with Tim and Tracy.

Ivana made the most of her stay in England. Being deprived of shopping trips in her own country, she could never get her fill of clothes and shoe shops. She really wore me out on our jaunts into Bournemouth. At times I would find myself a seat on a bench in the busy shopping precinct, while she made the most of trying on garments and footwear. She had a certain amount of cash that her mother had saved from her wages for the trip to 'foreign parts'. We ourselves were only able to give her a small weekly allowance.

Unknown to us, one of Ivana's non-refugee friends had arranged to come to England by air for one month. Tracy's mother offered Maiya a room for her stay, so the girls had company of their own kind. They were taken out by one or another of our family to visit local beauty spots and places of historical interest. We held picnics and family barbeques. Ivana became very homesick after about six weeks and ran up a large phone bill. We paid her expenses from our funds. Maiya returned to *Zagreb* at the end of August, Ivana was more than ready to go home by the time we were to make the next mission to Croatia.

SEPTEMBER 1996

Two days before we were due to leave on the next mercy mission, we had a phone call from Tomi in *Slavonski Brod*. He was asking if we could get a wheelchair for a man who had lost a leg in the conflict. Denys made a few phone calls and by the time we reached the docks at Ramsgate, we had been given three wheelchairs.

Five vehicles had arranged to travel with us on the September trip. Two had to back out from lack of funds and one for mechanical problems. We were left with one seven and a half ton truck and one converted ambulance. In our camper we were carrying two passengers, Ivana returning from her two month holiday and Sean, a young lad from Emsworth. He had collected toys and funds for the Convoy of Hope and desperately wanted to make the journey to see the gifts reaching the camps.

All went well on the first day although we left on a much later ferry than on previous trips. With our later time table we made our first night stop at *Nuremburg*. We were to have left early the next morning but the other drivers had forgotten to change to continental time and slept late. It was Sunday with no heavy traffic on the roads so we were able to make up the time. Our two young passengers dozed, played cards or read, finding the motorways pretty boring. We entered Austria and drove on the old roads and through many tunnels. Two stretches of motorway had tollbooths, On exiting the booth of the second we had a problem.

The fee had been paid and as we collected the receipt, the barrier lifted and Denys pressed the clutch pedal down, it came away under his foot. At busy times of the day there would be about a dozen tollbooths open to the traffic. At that time of night there was only one and we were blocking it. Terry moved some of the barriers from the next entry and drove the lorry through.

He intended to tow us up the incline and clear the way for vehicles behind us.

The toll booth attendant panicked, thinking that the lorry was going through without paying, (as if he would). With toolboxes at the ready, the men weighed up the situation. They discovered that the pedal had broken away from its fulcrum and required a welder to fix it. At eleven o'clock on a Sunday night and miles from anywhere that was out of the question. Denys suggested that if everyone got their shoulders behind the camper to get it moving, it might move sufficiently for him to drop it into first gear. Then he would be able to drive to *Gralla* services, changing gear without using the clutch. (Denys gave me all these technical details).

The next morning, Ken took Denys and the broken clutch into a place recommended by an attendant at the filling station. The rest of us waited, an hour later they were back with the job done, the pedal was fitted and tested, all seemed okay. We headed for the Slovenian border at 11am. By 4.30 we crossed the Croatian border. Ivana was a great help by vouching for us, verifying that we had been helping her people for the past four years.

We made for the *Zagreb* motorway, with a stop at the *Plitvice* services for a meal and a break. Terry and Lizzie in the truck were to leave us there, to head for *Split* via the inland route to *Knin*. This route went through the *Plitvice National Park*, it had been closed to most traffic until recently. The Serbian forces had been in control of the countryside and the beautiful *Plitvice* lakes. As Ivana was keen to get home to her family, we decided to go over the mountains to make *Crikvenica* our first call. Ken and John pulled into the *Ad Turres* car park for the night as we drove on to the far side of town to deliver Ivana and her luggage.

A great welcome home and there was a lot to tell and talk about. We were made to promise that we would be back for breakfast in the morning. At the hotel car park we found that Ken had pitched his tent on a patch of grass. During the night there was torrential rain, we thought about Ken, but it didn't keep us awake. In the morning we found Ken and John drying their belongings as they had left a skylight open in the ambulance, also the tent was hanging out to dry in the morning sunshine.

We went to breakfast at the *Odmaraliste*, as usual we had asked for a very small meal. Our tastes were not quite the same as those of our hosts and we did not like to waste their food. Coffee and fresh bread with spreads and cheese had been set out. They are very proud of their hospitality. After loads of hugs and thanks for taking care of Ivana, we left to rejoin our colleagues. A quick visit to deliver a parcel from June and John of Birmingham to their refugee friends in a nearby hostel, then we were on our way.

Ken had been with us on one of our frequent visits to *Dracevac*, a village near *Zadar*. A handful of people were still trying to survive among the ruins of their homes and at times we had taken supplies of food and clothing to them. On the spur of the moment we decided that we should go to see how things were there.

It was a lovely sunny evening for our coastal trip. After making a couple of coffee stops we arrived in the village by early afternoon, we were surprised to see a lot of work going on. A group of people were rebuilding and repairing their properties. Denys went to speak with some who were plastering over mortar shell damage to their house. We were welcomed with a glass of fruit juice and were told that they had set up a Community Centre. About two hundred people had returned to the village from the refugee camps. They would be grateful for any aid that we could bring them. Their spokesman was a young man who previously emigrated to Australia and was now back on holiday with his father. His dad told us that in the 1930's, he had been an altar boy in the now ruined church.

Denys asked if someone in authority could write to us requesting aid for *Dracevac* then we would do our best to help. They said that they would do this and would we bring a British flag to fly signifying their gratitude for our visits over the past four years. We took a few photos of Sean beside the burned out tank as a souvenir of his visit. This tank had tried to defend the village against the invaders but was hit in the fuel tank by a Serb shell. After leaving a few boxes of aid from Ken's van we made our way back.

At the destroyed bridge at *Meslenica* we stopped for our

convoy stew. We ate outdoors at the head of the destroyed bridge, overlooking the chasm and next to a building with pictures of the bridge. The words under the picture told that the bridge was built in 1969 and destroyed in 1991. Whilst we ate, vehicles arrived bringing tourists to view the ruins of the bridge. One couple, an American lady and her Croatian husband came to talk to us. Also a Canadian couple and a German couple were interested in our Humanitarian work.

A beautiful evening as we drove back to *Crikvenica* where Sean tried to phone home, the line was unobtainable, we would try again in the morning.

The next morning before leaving we made a phone call to *Slavonski Brod* to let them know we were on our way. Sean managed to phone home this time. Denys tried to phone *Rijeka*, but there was no reply. We had some medical supplies to deliver for Pam the retired nurse we took out on the May convoy. Zinka, the pharmacist was not at home when we arrived so we left the medical aid with her parents.

On the return trip over the mountains we made a detour to avoid a low narrow arch cut into the rock where we would be forced to use the wrong side of the road, on a sharp right hand bend, and a long drop to the sea on our left. The arch was OK for cars and small vans, the camper was too high and rather wide. We stopped at a wayside cafe for a local hog roast. Then on our way to the motorway and *Slavonski Brod* for our main delivery. It was late at night when we arrived at the block of flats where the refugees were housed. We parked in front of the buildings and were greeted by our contacts. They would see us in the morning to arrange the unloading.

At 8am. the vehicles were driven to the unloading area where the customs officials were waiting. They were puzzled, as from their paperwork they were expecting three vehicles. Denys explained that one truck had gone on to *Split*, this created a problem as all three vehicles were on the same T form and technically we had lost a lorry load of aid. Denys managed to talk his way out of the situation and promised that it would not happen again. The officers left us then to deliver the goods.

As we were unloading, the man who needed the wheelchair arrived on crutches. Denys lined up the three chairs and asked our disabled friend to choose which one he preferred. The other two were stored in the centre for future use. Our group of ladies helped to unload the goods along with Sean's box of toys. Unfortunately he was not feeling well and spent the day in the camper. While Sean slept Tomi took us on a tour of an ancient fort which was being excavated and restored. Then we walked along the riverbank to the Green Park cafe for coffee.

Tomi lived in a road not far from the river. He invited us to his home to meet his wife and their two delightful children. His parents were also visiting and we were invited to join them all in the family meal. They thought that it was hilarious when we called father Antun as we had thought that he was the Antun Mihanovic after which the centre was named. They put us right by telling us that Antun Mihanovic was a writer and died over 100 years before. The centre was named from the street where it was situated. Father's name was Meroslav, Mero for short.

Taking our leave then, we made for *Lipik* and the orphanage. On our last visit Goran had told us that some of the children were to be adopted as families were returning to their homes. With money and goods in short supply, children's clothes would be needed by adoptive parents. We had packed clothing of various age groups into small suitcases, which could be useful to a child leaving the home. We had four boxes of sticks of English seaside rock, a gift from our sister-in-law Pat.

Goran told us that B.J. had been waiting for us to arrive, he was wanting a lift back home with all his personal effects. He was going home after three years of working with Mark Cook and with the volunteers.

Pakrac hospital had by now been refurbished and was almost a full working establishment. The medical supplies were earmarked for this hospital. On contacting Doctor Dragica she informed us that the aid we had would be more useful at *Lipik* hospital. *Pakrac* had no inpatients up to then. She went ahead of us in her car and when we arrived she introduced us to the lady doctor in charge of the medical stores, she was delighted to receive the goods. As we were leaving we met up with a young girl being wheeled around the grounds in her chair, she gave us such a lovely smile, I gave her a teddy bear from the collection on our dashboard.

At the bistro in *Pakrac*, B.J. at last caught up with us. He knew that we were due to arrive this month but we had been delayed. We mentioned that we had a letter to be delivered to the Officer commanding the Royal Engineers serving near *Banja Luka*. B.J. suggested that we talked to Tanya or to Abigail. They worked for the United Nations office in *Vienna*, with U.N.O.V. plates on their car, and a special pass to cross the lines. Abigail advised us not to cross the border at *Banja Luka* ourselves, it was under Serbian control at times and we could have problems. The girls had business in *Banja Luka* themselves in a day or so and offered to deliver the letter for us.

A parcel we had not yet delivered, had been made up by Helen, one of our neighbours. This was a collection of canned foods and useful items for a needy person.

I asked B.J. if he could suggest a suitable recipient for the gift. Getting into the camper he gave directions to a village called *Gorni Caglic*, about three miles from *Pakrac*. He led us to a little shack in the garden of what had been a house, now demolished. There we met an elderly lady named Javanka, she lived in the one room hovel and collected walnuts from the forests to make enough money to live on. The nuts were drying on blankets, which covered the floor.

B.J. explained to her that the gift parcel came all the way from England, she was so pleased, she scooped up some of the walnuts from the floor and gave them to me in a bag. B.J. checked to see that she had a can opener, she did but it didn't work. We gave her ours from the camper.

With B.J. and his luggage on board we set out on Sunday morning for home. Denys was having trouble with the fifth gear jumping out, it was getting worse and we travelled back with just four gears, even so we were home in 48 hours. I don't think that Sean had really enjoyed his adventure, he had spent most of the travelling time sleeping, at least he would be able to tell his friends that he had been on an aid convoy.

A few short weeks after our return we received a letter from Tanya with a request for help, The letter said:-

"Dear Duke and Mary, I hope you made it safely to England and that B.J. was good company for you. We will certainly miss his company in Pakrac. Faroan's is simply not the same without him. He is really dedicated just as you are with convoy after convoy. Humanitarian Aid is especially appreciated now in Croatia, since Dayton was signed, it seems most of the aid stopped then. After five years of war, people need some assistance to get back on their feet again."

"In that light and since my new job does not allow me to solicit or distribute humanitarian aid, I am writing to ask you a special favour. It is on behalf of a refugee family still residing at Mala Gorica camp. This family of four was evicted by Serbs in Bosnia in August 1995 and have been in transit ever since. They ran out of what little resources they had and the humanitarian aid at the camp is simply not enough. Although they are entitled to a small monthly allowance, the Croatian government severely discriminates against the few Bosnian Moslem refugees there, they have not received any financial assistance."

"The mother broke her arm during the winter. Just as she was recovering, the father slipped in the snow and broke his arm. They have not been able to receive proper medical attention since they cannot pay. The fifteen-year-old daughter has not attended school for two years. To attend school in Croatia, she must pay five hundred dollars which the family could not afford. The family are awaiting resettlement in Sweden, although the quota for Sweden has already been filled."

"They cannot return to their home in Gradiska, Bosnia, because their house is occupied by Serbs, it is in Serb held territory. On their behalf I am wondering if it might be possible to get together a package to help them meet very basic needs through this winter. The following is a list of items urgently needed."

"Food. Canned meat, fruit and vegetables, jam, honey, oil, crackers, sugar, pasta, rice, canned cheese. (Anything else, you guys are experts at this.)"

"Clothes. 2 pairs men's boots size 41, sweaters for family. Mum, dad, boy 21, girl 15. warm long sleeved shirts, turtle necks, socks, sweatshirts, mittens\gloves, scarves, hats."

"Hygiene products. Shampoo, toothpaste, toilet paper, maxi-pads, Q tips, soap, laundry detergent, dish washing liquid, towels."

"Luxury items (not necessary but always special and

appreciated.) Chocolate, peanuts, chips, cookies, cakes, any junk food."

"I think it would be best to deliver it to me, if possible. At the camp it would be seized for sure. I frequently visit the family to take them fresh fruit, vegetables or other things that they need. Perhaps we could meet in Pakrac. Anyway whatever is best for you. If you can get donations it would be great. I so admire the work that you do. Love Tanya, Civil Rights Project, Pakrac, Croatia."

CONVOY OCTOBER 1996

We almost had to cancel this convoy. Having the gearbox in for repair, it would not be ready until 6pm. on the 28th October. Our ferry sailing was 8.40am. of the 29th.

Our convoy colleague, Chris from Portisham near Weymouth, arrived in Bournemouth to travel with us to Ramsgate. Only to discover that he had his wife's car keys in his pocket. He left his trailer with us while he dashed home with the keys. In the meantime we collected up our gear for the trip and stashed it in the van. On Chris's return we set off for Ramsgate docks.

Two vehicles from Huddersfield and destined for *Mostar*, left Hull Docks two days before hoping to meet up with us on route. Early on Tuesday morning (29th) Sue and her daughter Lisa from Herne Bay arrived to join us. Tony arrived to see us off bringing a passenger for us, Gill, a lady who had collected aid and funds for our cause.

Documentation and tickets obtained, we boarded *Sally Sky* for a very calm crossing. Over breakfast on board we got to know a little about Gill from Canterbury. We had been concerned because we had been told that she was disabled. Apart from the fact that she used a walking stick no one would have guessed that she had an artificial leg.

The first two days travelling were uneventful. Lisa and Sue had no C.B. radio so they travelled behind us and in front of Chris in case of any problems. Via France, Belgium, Germany and Austria, arriving at the services at *Graz*, a few kilometres before the Slovenian border. No sign of the vehicles from Huddersfield. We thought they may be using a different night stop. The next morning we set off to exit Austria and enter Slovenia. At this border we had to purchase travel insurance, which cost 70 marks with 50 marks for T forms (export and import of goods). Custom seals were put on the trailers these were to be removed only by customs officials at our destination. This procedure took about two hours.

Then we made our way to the Croatian border. More paper work and a fee of 60 marks for more T forms. Another three hours wait while telephone calls and faxes were exchanged with our destination address, to eliminate black market.

Our first drop was to the *Antun Mihanovic* organisation of *Slavonski Brod*. We could not unload until the morning as we had to wait for the customs officers to break the seals and be in attendance and to check the paperwork.

November 1st 'All Saints Day' is a Bank Holiday on the continent. The customs officers agreed to come out to us if we sent a car to collect them from town. While we waited the ladies at the establishment made us coffee. The customs arrived and checked that our seals were intact.

Satisfied that we were bona fide they left us to unload our goods which consisted of canned and dried food, clothing, blankets, toiletries, toys and a donated knitting machine with a large amount of wool from a lady who visited the charity shop.

Work done, we took a stroll to the river and 'Green Park Bistro'. Chris had brought a couple of souvenirs for the proprietor who had lived in London, a model of a London bus and a Tower of London plaque.

Sue, Lisa, Gill and I sat outside in the sun with our Cokes. We noticed activity on the newly repaired bridge connecting *Slavonski Brod* with *Bosanski Brod* occupied by the Serbs. A convoy of tanks with headlights blazing were coming towards us across the bridge. A little worried and fearing an invasion, I hurried into the bistro to tell our colleagues what was happening. Tomi told us not to worry, the American forces were moving out and going home. We were invited to have lunch with Meroslav, who is the head of *Antun Mihanovic* organisation. As it was a public holiday all the family were at home, the six of us were honoured guests.

Our next ports of call were to *Pakrac* and *Lipik*. On the way back we had hoped to take photos of the bombed service stations along the motorway. We were surprised to see that they had been dismantled and were now in the process of being rebuilt.

We went into *Pakrac* and parked in the main street, at the bistro we asked after Tanya, who had an office in town. Tanya was our contact at the refugee camp at *Sisak* where we had delivered aid over the past year. Although she was no longer a resident volunteer at this camp she had written to us requesting items for a desperate family. The last of our load was eight boxes of basic needs to help them survive the winter. We spent the night at the now repaired hospital. Tanya was not in *Pakrac* at that time.

After unloading our boxes at the volunteer's office we made visits to the hospitals in *Pakrac* and *Lipik*. Where our crews took photos of the once famous hot springs in the grounds of *Lipik* hospital. Serb gunfire had tried to destroy the decorative shelter of the constantly running, tapped hot spring. A lady doctor brought a half dozen empty Coke bottles to fill from the health giving water and gave them to us. She told us that the water was good for the outside of the body by bathing in it. It was good for the inside by drinking it when cold. The water was hot enough to be producing steam and we washed our hands under the running tap.

On leaving the town we made a photo stop at the now bombed out stables, once the home of the *Lippizaner* horses.

Out on the motorway heading west towards *Karlovac* and the mountain road to *Rijeka*. At the home of Zinka, our contact for this area, a chicken stew awaited us, prepared by Zinka's mama who appreciated what we were doing to help her people.

Zinka later took us to meet some refugee families who lived in the basement of a large building, each family living in one small room. One family was a young mum with two children. We were told that her husband had been killed but she would not accept the fact that he would not be coming back to her. One young lady was celebrating her twelfth birthday; we were pressed into accepting coffee and cake. Some of the young guests were disco dancing on the terrace.

On arriving back at Zinka's house a group of people helped to unload the vans. This aid would go to a clinic for refugees and the poor folk, a rape victim centre and an old peoples' nursing home. Chris stayed at Zinka's house while the rest of us went to *Crikvenica* further down the coast. Chris was to meet up with us in the morning.

After an English breakfast cooked in the camper, we drove down to the beach and shops, where Chris caught up with us. The tourists among us bought souvenirs to take home. Later we paid a visit to our own band of refugees, the friends we had made over four years before. Sue and Lisa had sweets and toys for the children.

Now we were all together we set off for Switzerland where we were to collect more aid for a return journey to *Rijeka.* Heading out towards *Ljubjana* we stopped for a convoy stew. Chris left us to find a contact and destination for the Swiss aid. We arranged to meet him on the outskirts of town in one and a half hours.

A traffic accident had created a massive tailback and we missed each other. Deciding to head towards the border, we parked on a layby hoping Chris would see us if he passed by. Unknown to us he was already ahead of us, and was waiting on the next layby. We made frequent calls on the C.B. radio. Suddenly Chris's voice informed us that he was on the other side of the motorway. He decided to backtrack to meet up with us.

The convoy back together again we drove on towards the border. Lisa had wanted to visit the duty free shop. But on approaching the Austrian border the customs men pulled Chris's van in to be searched. Everything seemed to be in order and after half an hour he rejoined us in Austria. We travelled for another hour and made a night stop. On the road by 9.30 next morning, heading towards *Salzburg* and the *Munich* ring road where we said goodbye to Lisa and Sue as they made for home, needing to return the hired van. With Chris leading the way we took route 96 towards *Brigenz,* crossing the border with no problems. Freezing cold and thick fog as we skirted *Lake Konstanz* heading for *Zurich,* our night stop. Anna-Marie, a very sweet lady, was a long time friend of Chris and his wife Caroline. She had invited us to call in for a meal as we passed close to where she lived. We spent a very pleasant evening in her company before parking up in her church car park for the night.

The next morning we continued our journey to our collecting point, *Langenthal,* near *Basle.* We travelled on the old roads as a permit was required to drive on the motorway. (extra

249

cost). Kathleen and her husband Louie welcomed us like long lost friends, although it was the first time we had met. She asked if we had been told about a load of canned fruit ready for us to collect on our way in. We hadn't.

After a lunch of soup and home made bread, we retraced our tracks about two or three miles. The man at the warehouse was formerly from Canterbury. He and Gill had a chat while we loaded one ton of canned apricots. It was only after we had loaded them that we found out that they were out of date by three years. It would be impossible for us to get them through any border customs. A discussion at Kathleen's over dinner brought a solution. Some would go to the Salvation Army and the rest to a home for vagrants in Switzerland.

Kathleen and her friends had collected a cellar full of bags and boxes of aid originally destined for *Chernobyl* in the Ukraine. No convoy available to take it there. The goods just about filled Chris's van and trailer, not enough to justify the cost of taking a second vehicle. Chris was happy to take the load to *Rijeka* while we made our way home. We arrived in the U.K. on Thursday night 7th, November.

On our return we received a letter from Tanya saying, :- "You came and went so quickly, I was nicely surprised when I walked into the volunteers' office and found the mountain of 'aid' that you had brought for the family I had written you about. The shoes were perfect, the woollies and canned vegetables are just in time for the winter freeze. I was really worried about getting vitamins into the kids."

"Thank you once again for your help. The assistance you give is more than just 'aid'. It brings light and hope into the unfortunate recipients of your hard efforts and strong hearts. Love Tanya."

DECEMBER 1996

On December 2nd. we left Dorset on our fourth Christmas run taking gifts to the children in refugee camps in Croatia and Bosnia. We had our first problem within a couple of miles. Having just collected our groceries for our ten-day trip, a broken clutch cable meant calling out National Breakdown. Within an hour a 'Very nice man' had arrived, weighed up the situation, went shopping for a clutch cable and had the job done. At 7pm. we were on our way making for Herne Bay where we were to pick up 50 gift boxes to add to our load. Heavy traffic and rain had made the going slow, arriving on Sue's doorstep at 1am. The loading was done with as little noise as possible, not to waken the neighbours.

Colin from East Grinstead had asked if we could get him a second driver. After asking 12 people, most of whom had offered their services in the past, Colin, one of our neighbours, stepped in at the last minute. Colin and Colin were to meet on the docks the next morning.

The van from East Grinstead had arrived during the night, our neighbour suggested that we call him 'Chalky' as his surname was Chalker. Tickets and T forms sorted out we boarded the *Sally Sky* at 8.45am. on the 3rd of December. Small convoy this time. Two vehicles and four persons. Our route took us from *Dunkirk* to *Lille, Mons, Charleroi, Liege* and *Aachen*. A short break to refuel and have a snack, then on to *Hockenheim* for our first night stop.

We pressed on through Germany with a lunch stop at *Regensburg*, (all our meals cooked in the camper) then on to Austria. The weather was very cold with snow on the ground but the roads were clear. Heaters in both vehicle were not working too well. Motorways gave way to the old roads and tunnels. We arrived in *Gralla Services* at 10pm.

In the morning we found that the cold weather was affecting our diesel engine, making it difficult to start and needing a tow from the transit to get us going. 10.30 when we crossed the border into Slovenia, 4.30 as we entered Croatia. There were hundreds of lorries awaiting documentation. When our turn came the officials informed us that our papers were not in order. As each vehicle had a different destination address, we should have had two letters requesting documentation, we only had one. No problem, a few minutes with my portable typewriter came up with the second letter. Printed on our own headed note paper and signed by Denys as Director of B.H.A. He told them in the office that his secretary was travelling with him this caused some amusement. 8.30pm. when we finally entered the country.

While travelling on the country roads, Colin called on the C.B. he said that he was experiencing a screeching noise from under the bonnet of his van. We pulled into a service area. While the men had their heads under the bonnet, I made up a convoy stew, just the job for the freezing weather. The problem with the transit was that the alternator had seized up. They loosened the fan belt which cut down the noise. We carried on to the *Plitvice* services to spend the night.

Next morning Denys poured a kettle full of hot water over the fuel system of our camper and she started with no trouble at all. After a quick breakfast we set off for *Slavonski Brod*. We always seemed to have trouble finding the blocks of flats where some 150 families were settled. This time however, we first found the house of Meroslav, our contact from the *Antun Mihanovic Centre*. He jumped into his little old banger of a car and led us to the hall. Tomi and the ladies were there to greet us.

Colin's vehicle was taken off to a local mechanic to have his alternator sorted, while we unloaded our trailer in the presence of two customs officers. Before long the children started arriving. We were kept busy trying to find the right present for each child and parent. Many of the gifts were donated by our friends of Spetisbury school. Thanks to Anne and Brian most of the mums received handbags containing small gifts. One lady was the mother of ten children, we were told that the youngest was a godchild of the President. Each person receiving the gifts produced a ration card as proof of identity.

Meroslav told us that a quantity of green uniforms no longer required by a well known building society and brought out by us on the last trip, were being worn by the town's cleaners. He asked if we could bring more to be worn by a local school as their uniform. The green skirts, jackets and dresses with white and green blouses were really useful. Some of the uniforms had been taken to the Ukraine by our colleagues.

Colin arrived back with a temporary repair to his van. The faulty part had been replaced with a part from a scrapped car. The best that could be done at such short notice. We drove round to park outside the flats for the night.

Up early on a very cold morning, we were hoping to visit the market. The camper played up and needed a tow start. Finding a parking space on the already busy street we walked around the few and sparse stalls.

Not finding anything to tempt us to buy, we went on to meet with Tomi at the Green Park bistro for coffee. Meroslav turned up and presented us with a landscape picture, which had been painted by his daughter, Tomi's sister, Marianna.

We left then to take the road to *Okucani*, as we were driving through the village a truck passed us going in the opposite direction, the occupants were waving frantically. We stopped and Denys went to see what was up and was surprised to see L.J. (of the brown sauce). As we chatted a Range Rover pulled up and out tumbled half a dozen of the volunteers. They had been visiting *Pakrac* and were on their way back to *Gorni Vakuf*, near *Sarajevo*. Abigail told us that the letter to the Royal Engineers had reached its destination as we had requested on our last visit.

We said goodbye to them all and wished them and their friends a very happy Christmas. We then drove on to *Pakrac* for a flying visit to our friends there, leaving a few personal gifts and cards, Anton and Maria insisted that we take a Christmas drink with them and they parcelled up some home cured pork sausages to take with us.

We had promised young Emina of the Faroan Bistro that we would try to get her a bike. Circumstances had made it impossible on this trip but we said that we would see what we

253

could do in March. We moved on then through *Lipik, Kutina* and on the motorway to *Zagreb*. Down to *Karlovac* and the inland route to *Knin*. We were on mountain roads, driving through snow and fog. The outside sensor, which was fitted to the camper's wing mirror, showed the temperature dropping from 38 degrees to minus 16 degrees and back again. Salt and the volume of traffic had kept the roads clear of snow. Our heater was working a bit better.

Our drivers kept going until we reached the outskirts of *Knin* where we pulled into a layby for hot soup with bread bought from the market that morning. We fell into our beds around midnight. Next morning we refuelled in town and made for the border crossing at *Vinjani Donji*. About 20 miles before the border, Colin phoned his contact in *Medugorje*. At the border control, we had to wait while faxes and messages were exchanged. After a while we discovered that the contact, who was a nun, would not be coming to get us through the border until 11am. the next day.

As we were not carrying goods we were free to cross over into Bosnia. Rather than just sitting and waiting we would drive into *Medugorje* to try to find this Sister Pamela. Maybe we could change her mind about leaving Colin on the border overnight. We found a great deal of change, what had been a small village was now a full sized town.

Coaches bringing the pilgrims from many parts of the world lined the streets. Although it was after dark when we arrived, the souvenir shops were still open and busy. We made for the 'Paddy Shop' as we had met some very friendly ladies there earlier in the year. The shop (a travel agency) was closed. At a loss then we drove back to the border to cook a meal, relax and wait until morning.

After breakfast we waited, at 11am. a Sister Muriel turned up. It seemed that she hadn't known that we were there since the day before, no one had told her. The paperwork done, we set off with the nun's car leading us. We and the camper were to stay in *Medugorje* while the van went on to the east side of *Mostar*.

Colin told us later what had happened. After a stop at a police checkpoint where the van was searched, they went on to a block of war-damaged flats where families were to be given food parcels and baby goods. Colin told us that at first the distribution was quite orderly but as the word spread around the flats the situation changed. Our drivers were mobbed. In desperation Colin closed the van doors and tried to give the children chocolate, the whole operation became a shambles. The Sister gave up trying to organise the mob and left the lads to it.

The result of the disaster was that Colin still had half a van load of aid looking for a home before we could cross the border into Croatia. A lot of time, effort and money had been spent to end in disappointment. After refuelling at a local garage, we set out for a town called *Grude* to park up for the night. There was heavy rain as we talked over the situation, perhaps we could find a school or community centre to take the aid. We would not be allowed to take goods documented for Bosnia back into Croatia.

In the morning we decided to turn around and head back for *Grude*. As we did so a group of kids passed by calling out remarks in English, such as "Hello", "What is your name?" and so on. Right opposite where we had parked for the night was a large school. Colin went in to find out if anyone there spoke English and knew where there would be refugees in need. The answer was "yes" on both accounts.

Someone called for the local lady who taught English, she told us that she lived in a camp for displaced persons. We could be sure that the food, Pampers and baby items would be useful to them. I made out a delivery note on the old typewriter and got it signed and stamped. The teachers brought youngsters from the classrooms, to receive toys. Colin took photographs to take back to his East Grinstead scout group, proof that the goods had found a home. He was happy and we were relieved to see the job done.

We told the English teacher that if she wrote to us officially, requesting aid for her camp, we might be able to help.

Empty vehicles then, we headed for the border and on to *Split* where heavy traffic got between us and the transit. Denys pulled into a layby on the coast for a lunch break and we waited. After half an hour there was no sign of our colleagues. Thinking that they might have broken down, Denys unhitched the trailer in case the van needed towing. We didn't like to leave the trailer unattended so I sat inside it with a book, on guard until he or they returned. An hour later the camper returned, no transit. We decided that they must have taken the inland route while we were following the coast.

We continued north, stopping at the point where the *Meslenica* bridge once stood, in case the van had rejoined our route. With still no sign of them we carried on to *Crikvenica*, where we saw the van parked outside the *Ad Turres* hotel. We found the boys in the sports room in the basement of the hotel. They were as relieved to see us as we were to see them. They had been afraid that we had broken down.

Although it was quite late we decided to visit Nada and family, to save time in the morning. We had a couple of little gifts for her and Ivana, Boris was away in the army. We told them that we would not be back again until March and asked if there was anything they specially needed. Nada said that a sewing machine would be useful to repair the family's clothing.

Colin was planning to visit scouting friends in *Zagreb*. With Chalky on board the camper, we headed for home. Leaving the Adriatic coast on the Wednesday morning we reached *Dunkirk* docks on Thursday evening. In thick fog we parked in the waiting area, only to be told that the next ferry out of *Dunkirk* would be at 1.30 the next day. We were advised to drive to *Calais* where we boarded the Sea France which took us to Dover. We arrived in the U.K. at 2.30am. Needing a few hours sleep, we parked outside Sue's house in Herne Bay. At 8am. Sue came out to invite us in for a cup of tea while we told her of our exploits and where her Christmas boxes had been delivered.

FEBRUARY 1997

On returning from our December 1995 convoy, our friend Keith, who had opened the charity shop had taken on a manager, they were selling a lot of high price clothing, going so far as putting in security equipment. All donated goods to make funds for us were priced under three pounds, we didn't need security equipment. As more of their goods were being bought in for sale, Denys protested that this wasn't on. Gradually, we got Keith to pull out altogether. Graham, the manager, assured us that he was fully capable to run the shop with help of volunteers. Funds had got low by this time as Keith withdrew his money from the charity account.

On returning from a convoy in late 1996, we found that Graham had allowed a house clearance firm to move in on the first floor of the shop, they had offered to pay a percentage of their takings into the charity, this didn't happen. In February 1997, the bomb dropped on us. The local rates department sent us a bill for £32,000. Then, as we discovered we were overdrawn at the bank by £900, Graham left the shop throwing the keys on the counter. Then we found the unpaid bills.

Just then Tony P. came back into our lives, he had brought a large amount of donated goods into the shop to boost our funds. When he heard of our disaster, he took charge and put money into the bank to clear the debt and paid off bills, electricity etc. Then came the second blow. The shop was sold and we had 48 hours to move out. We, with Tony and his family worked to move the immense amount of clothing, bric-a-brac and toys. We made everything dirt cheap to sell as much as possible. What we could not store in various garages to sell at car boots at a later date, went to the council tip. When we thought we had cleared the shop, we went upstairs to make sure that Ken and Martin had made a good job of clearing their section. We had a shock. Rubbish and unwanted furniture had been left behind. Cups of coffee, months old littered the offices. Mounds of polystyrene packaging and stripped armchairs ready to be upholstered and bags of stale take-away food. We had to clear it all! The furniture was broken up and taken to the tip in two vans and a car and trailer.

The shop was to be turned into a pub, the builders were in while we finished the clearing, they took some tables and chairs off our hands. This episode was a nightmare for all of us. I don't know what we would have done without Tony's support. Graham was missing from home, everyone was worried as he had left a message on the shop computer which could have been taken as a suicide note. Although the rates department had sympathy with our position, they insisted the bill had to be paid. The problems went on as we found that Keith had signed a contract, using our charity name, for the security equipment, so we were liable for the rental charges. We appealed against this and refused to pay for something we did not order, need or sign for. Tony got busy and took over a shop in Bridport and turned it into a bona-fide charity shop.

After months of worry and sleepless nights, the problems did resolve themselves, but we had learned a hard lesson. Not to trust everyone who offers help.

JULY 1997

With an empty trailer we left England on Tuesday 8th July, on the first part of our latest mercy mission. We were heading for *Langenthal* near *Basle* in Switzerland. Kathleen, a good friend of the Convoy of Hope, was so successful in her appeal for the refugees of Bosnia, that her cellar was overflowing.

She told us on the phone that her husband would like the use of his cellar, could we please collect and deliver the goods.

On this occasion ours was the only vehicle able to make the journey to the former Yugoslavia. Our colleagues were leaving the U.K. the day after us, en route to the Ukraine. They were to take 100 children from the *Chernobyl* region to a holiday resort on the Black Sea. Three weeks in the sun with fresh air and good food would help to build up their poor health.

With son Tim on board, we travelled from *Ostende* to *Langenthal*, arriving at 9pm. on the Wednesday. English lady Kathleen and her Swiss husband Louie made us very welcome. We relaxed with them that evening and slept in the camper outside their house that night. In the morning it was obvious from a large pool of water under the front of the camper, that we had a problem. The water pump had been leaking. Denys was able to drive into town to a Fiat garage. After a few phone calls by the manager, a new water pump would be sent from Germany. This would take 24 hours.

The weather was blazing as we returned to the house to start weighing and packing the boxes of goods. These had to be carried up a set of steps from the cellar to the yard where our trailer was parked. The boxes were sorted, weighed and recorded. Clothing, bedding and 27 cases of sanitary towels.

After lunch with the family, we walked into town. It was very hot but a pleasant walk, following the river which led us into the main shopping centre. We visited the garage and asked the proprietor if we would be able to sleep in the vehicle that night. No problem, but we should expect the work to start very early, the Swiss start work at 6am. Next morning the pump had arrived and we got ourselves ready for the walk back to Kathleen's house to wait for the phone call to say that the job was done.

We kicked our heels, itching to be away. By mid afternoon and needing to do something we took a walk to the garage. We were just in time to see the mechanic taking the camper for a road test. Kathleen arrived to help with the translating and settling the bill. Then it was back to the house to collect Tim and the trailer.

After thanking our hosts for their hospitality and help, we made our way to *Zurich* and the German border for the night stop. The next morning we headed for *Munich* and *Salzburg* where we met an aid convoy of a coach and three vans. We left the motorway to take the old road to *Graz*, stopping on a layby for a break and some lunch.

At *Graz* we topped up our fresh water tank, had a cup of tea, then phoned Tomislav to tell him we were on our way. We decided to have ham and eggs in the restaurant where in the past our convoys would make this a supper stop. The manager and his wife came to talk with us, and told us how they missed the convoys and their custom.

On our way now to deal with the borders. First, exit Austria, no problem. Entry Slovenia we had to pay 60 marks for vehicle insurance. 1 hour and 45 minutes for paperwork to be processed. Then on to the Croatian border, paperwork was straight forward, 52 marks for documentation and 90 marks for vehicle insurance. A customs officer stopped us, suggesting that we were to sell the aid on the black market, although we had a letter of authority from the organisation for which the aid was destined.

Denys explained through an interpreter that he would not have travelled all the way from England at a cost of over 1000 marks with this aid if he wanted to sell it, He would have done so in England. The lady interpreter and the customs officer went into an office. After about twenty minutes they came out, the official asked Denys to open the trailer. He looked inside and

260

asked if all the goods were used (second hand). Denys, trying to forget the sanitary towels, said, "Yes." The lady asked Denys for the receipt for the 52 marks, then gave him back the money. The barrier was lifted to let us through. We made our way to a services on the motorway a few miles past *Zagreb* where we spent the night.

Up early Sunday morning and came off the motorway at the *Sisak* turn off, Taking the old road to *Slavonski Brod* to miss all the tolls. The road was really rough. We reached the *Antun Mihanovic* hall in the town around 1.00pm. The children saw us arrive and came to see what we had for them. Tim started to give out some of the sweets. It wasn't long before the workers came to unload. Maria, Gloria, Ruza, Tomislav and his father Meroslav. Soon we were sitting round a table drinking Coca-Cola. Always pleasure before work here!

It was about 4pm. and cooler when we started to unload. They were very pleased with boxes of sanitary towels and the large amount of bedding and children's clothes. We gave Tomislav a copy of our latest newsletter and some photos which we took last time we were there. These would be added to the collection of pictures already displayed on the wall.

We left about 7pm.and headed for *Babina Greda* with parcels for a particular family; refugees from across the river.

Their town was now held by Serbs. Anton's Grandma and his little sister Mariana, were home. Unable to speak English Mariana took us to the bistro where her mother worked. She was very pleased to see us and asked a friend to be interpreter.

The friend called Goran, explained that Anton was away on a school trip to the coast. Quite a disappointment all round. Sitting at one of the tables on the patio while drinking Coca-Cola, we were told that Anton had run up a phone bill of over 100 marks in his quest to find Tim and thank him for the parcel. Zelko, Anton's stepfather came to join the party, coffee and lots of chat as a thunder storm raged all around us. Goran told us that two days before our visit, the town had been battered by a hailstorm which had flattened crops and broke windows in the school. A wedding marquee had been in danger of collapsing under the weight of the hailstones. The canvas had to be slit as about 300 kilos of ice had collected above the guests' heads.

While we had been chatting, the manager of the bistro had made contact with Anton who was on board a boat near *Split*. We all managed a little chat with him although he did most of the talking. He was very sad that we were at his home and he was so far away. We were invited to return to *Babina Greda* for their folk festival next June when there would be feasting, singing and displays by *Lippizaner* horses. It sounded too good to miss but we were not able to make promises.

Before leaving we took their phone number so we could call Anton, to save his parents the worry of more expensive phone bills. After all the goodbyes, we headed out towards the motorway and the services where we spent the night. At 8am. we were back at *the Antun Mihanovic Centre* to say goodbye and to get our paperwork stamped. Breakfast was prepared for us, bread and cheese, fruit juice and coffee. We did our best to eat enough to please our hosts. Meroslav and his wife came to join us, bringing a freshly baked cake and two paintings, Mrs. Meroslav's own work. The wife of the man who had received the wheelchair on an earlier trip, came to bring Denys a bottle of home-made wine.

On our way from the city we drove past the monastery and the river, a safe area now since the cease-fire. We travelled across country to *Zagreb* then on to *Maribor*. We were making for *Leoban* and *St. Michaels* where we spent the night parked in a layby on a mountain road.

Next morning in heavy rain, we took a route avoiding the toll roads. Making our way back to Switzerland, arriving at Kathleen's house in the late evening.

There we picked up the remaining boxes from her cellar, which would be taken out to refugees or to the Ukraine on future trips. Then we headed for home.

SEPTEMBER 1997

Pam from Wimborne was keen to make another trip to the camps of Croatia. Her home and her life had been taken up with friends bringing loads of clothing and food, which she was packing into boxes and piling up in her hallway. She had called for our help to take the goods into our trailer.

We left Bournemouth on the 22nd and were joined at Ramsgate by Ken and Rosemarie of Folkestone. Our convoys were getting smaller owing to lack of funds and media interest in the plight of the refugees.

A 10.30 sailing on the Sally Line's *Condor Rapide* crossing the channel to *Ostende* in 90 minutes as opposed to 4 hours 15 minutes on the conventional ferry. Taking our usual route through Belgium and Germany, we left the motorways at *Salzburg*, using the old roads to avoid the expensive tolls. No problems on the two day journey and we arrived *at Gralla Services* on the second night.

For the first time ever we had very little hassle at the borders. The customs seemed content with our documentation and confirmed our destination with a phone call to the *Antun Mihanovic Centre*. A very pleasant journey through Slovenia and Croatia, via *Varazdin* and *Virovitica* taking the road toward Nasice where we turned off for *Slavonski Brod*. The two hundred families that we were helping to survive were just a small portion of the forty thousand refugees who fled from the invaders. Although technically the war was over, these families could not return to their homes which were occupied by Serbian families.

Before we could unload we needed to be cleared by customs. The rules had been changed a lot since peace was declared. In the days while the conflict was happening all around these towns and villages, we were free to go where we felt the need was greatest. In time of an uneasy peace, we must stick to the rules. Customs had to know where we were to unload and the officials needed to be there to see it carried out. No one was available to come to us on this particular day. Denys and Ken drove the vehicles to the customs offices in town to get the all-important papers stamped and the permission to unload. Meroslav went with them to confirm that he was to be in receipt of the goods.

Pam, Rosemarie and I were given coffee and entertained in the hall while we waited. The bush telegraph had been working. The refugees started to arrive; first the children asking for 'bon-bons' or chocolate then the ladies with their shopping bags, patiently waiting and hoping that there would be enough goodies for all.

When the vehicles returned it was all hands to the unloading, most of our boxes of clothing had been collected by us from Switzerland on our return from our July mission. A lady in Bournemouth had given us a decorated Christmas tree asking us to present it to a family of our choice. We passed it on to the wife of the chap with one leg. Pam was giving out toys to the younger children while we were busy filling the storeroom until it resembled a well-stocked warehouse.

When we had arrived there had been only a stack of flour sacks in one corner, the only help the refugees could expect from their own government. As they were from Bosnia, the Croatian government had no obligation to them. Tomi was away in *Zagreb*, his wife Dudi arrived to make conversing a little easier. The family are locals of *Slavonski Brod*, they did all that they could to make life easier for the unfortunate people in their area.

We were to spend the night parked outside the centre, Meroslav gave us the keys to the toilet and water facilities. We settled for an early night after arranging to meet in the morning for coffee and farewells. We woke to a chilly but bright morning. While having coffee with the distribution staff, we took group photographs. As always we were asked, "When will you come again?" We could not make promises at that point as it all depended on the funding we received.

We made our way to *Okucani* and stopped for a few minutes to pay our respects at a memorial to those who were buried in a mass grave and recently discovered. The place was marked by a crucifix and a rough shelter where a service was held each Sunday. At *Lipik* we made a short visit to the children's home. They always welcomed us as, 'Their visitors from England.' Pam had brought a gift for a young lady she had met and befriended on her previous visit. Vesna and her sister had been at the home for three years. After the usual fruit juice taken on the patio, we made our way to *Pakrac*.

Over the years our convoys had helped the townspeople to survive, now our visits were purely social calls to the friends we had made. That night was spent at a service area near *Zagreb*. The next morning we drove on to *Salzburg* where we were to part company with our travelling companions. At a picnic snack beside the *Chiemsee Lake*, we wished each other a safe journey home.

As they headed for England, we were making a detour to Switzerland to pick up more goods from Kathleen.

From *Munich* we followed signs for *Lindau*, stopping for the night on a layby a few miles before the Swiss border. The next morning bright and early we set out on the last leg of the trip to *Langenthal*. As Denys changed into top gear the clutch cable snapped. He drove on to the next town which was *Lindau*, pulled into a service station to phone for A.A. assistance. In less than an hour a breakdown truck arrived. We were towed by the truck about one mile into a garage. Then the driver returned to collect our trailer. The proprietor phoned around for a new cable. Our vehicle being a right hand drive vehicle caused a problem. The cable needed was longer than for the continental left hand drive.

Denys then phoned the A.A. in England and told them of our predicament. The chap on the other end of the line promised that a cable would be sent to our garage in 48 hours. Herr Buhl, the proprietor was very helpful, he found us a parking space behind the garage with a fresh water tap close by. We also had access to the toilet in the garage.

Having at least two days on our hands, we decided to take a walk to the shops. Herr Buhl told us that we were just a short walk from *Lindau Island*, as he put it "Only 20 minutes by feet." *Lindau* was a tourist town on the *Bodensee Lake*, all old world charm with cobbled streets, fountains decorated with statues of mermaids and dolphins. We spent the time sightseeing with a boat trip on the lake one afternoon.

The clutch cable arrived within 48 hours as promised. The job was done and we went into the office to pay the bill. We were told that there was no bill to pay, the cable had arrived with no invoice. The labour was a gift to us for our good hearts. What could we say? Leaving our address in case Herr Buhl received a bill for the cable at a later date. We were on our way within an hour.

At the Swiss border we were charged 50 marks for a windscreen sticker which authorised us to use the motorways for the current year. We reached *Langenthal* and Kathleen's house by mid afternoon. She was away but her husband and daughter were wonderful hosts. Once again we cleared their cellar of boxed clothing destined for our next mission to Bosnia or our colleagues' next mission to the Ukraine. Kathleen had left a generous donation to help our funds, also instruction for her daughter to have our fuel tank filled before we left. Thank you Kathleen, Katrina and Louis for your hospitality.

48 hours after leaving Switzerland we were back home in England on October 4th.

DECEMBER 1997

Our fifth Christmas run to the former Yugoslavia, Although we were only one vehicle again we still referred to it as a convoy. The first Christmas run we had taken on our own.

We dedicated this trip to Mervyn, a tireless aid worker. He sadly passed away while preparing for a trip to *Slavonski Brod* in Croatia. He had been helping refugees to survive in this battered town. Loaded up with aid we had collected from Switzerland on the way home from our September trip, we had topped up our load with Mervyn's aid. Collected from his widow Dawn and son Bill, at their home in Ashford, Kent.

Our booking was on the 1.15pm. ferry on the 2nd of December, which got us into *Ostende* at 6.15pm local time. We drove on towards *Aachen* where we refuelled and spent the first night.

The next morning the weather looked good, we set off early towards *Munich*. Late in the afternoon the weather changed to drizzle. Denys noticed a bit of wheel spin, the rain was freezing on the road. The freezing rain got heavier and the roads became dangerous. We pulled into what at first looked like a good place to spend the night but there was no overnight parking. We called into a MacDonald's for a burger. Then Denys decided to carry on, to find a layby or services for the night.

Driving back onto the main road was not so easy. As we approached the main highway we found ourselves on ice and snow, our wheels were turning but we were not going anywhere. Denys decided the best thing to do, was to put the snow chains on and make to where we could get off the road as soon as possible and park up for the night. On the busy road I held the torch while Denys struggled to get the chains onto our front wheels, I was shivering so much and the torchlight was wavering about so that it was a wonder that he could see what he was doing. At last the chains were on and we were able to get going.

About half a mile further along the road we found a layby, and made this our night stop. Here we discussed the situation and decided that if the weather got worse we would make our way back home in the morning.

We were up early and Denys walked out to check the road conditions. The ice and snow had gone, things looked reasonable and the traffic was light. We decided to carry on to *Salzburg* and into Austria. Although the scenery was pretty with a sprinkling of snow, the roads had been cleared.

There was no problem in making it to *Graz* for our stop over on a very frosty and starlit night. The bad weather in Germany had delayed us by one day, making our arrival on the Croatian border, the day before the Bank Holiday of December 6th, St. Nicholas Day. This meant more lorries going through the border but less staff to deal with the paperwork. It took us six and a half hours to clear the customs, amid frustrated lorry drivers trying to get home and the go-slow staff.

Eventually we got under way and headed for *Zagreb*. We decided to stay on the motorways, to pay the tolls and make up a bit of time. On the outskirts of town Denys pulled into a services to refuel and fill our main water tank. This was not always possible during the winter months as often the mains water had been turned off to prevent frozen pipes. We carried on to *Slavonski Brod* and pulled into a parking area to spend the night.

Setting out early, we drove into town and called at the home of our English-speaking friend, Tomi. He would pass on the message to the *Antun Mihanovic Centre* that we had arrived. The house was full of excitement. St. Nicholas had been, bringing Tomi's two children, Adrian and Sara, small gifts. Tomi phoned his father Meroslav, he would meet us at the centre to see to the unloading.

At the centre, the volunteer staff helped us to carry the goods into the store room. Pasta and rice, soups and canned food. We had some Christmas gifts, not enough for so many families but with jigsaws, toys and games, we could be sure that most of the children would receive a little something for Christmas. A decorated tree which had been sent by Dawn from Ashford was put up in the hall. After the festive season it would be given to one of the families.

When the trailer was completely empty, the ladies, Stepha, Gloria, Maria, and Ruza provided coffee and the local rakia. We added some cans of English beer for the party. Group photos were taken with the Union Jack flag that we had brought out in September, to show the connection between our two countries. The task completed, we spent a couple of days sightseeing and comparing the town as it was five years before in the midst of war and as it was now in peace time.

Checking on the weather conditions and the mountain roads to the coast, we decided that it was worth making the journey to visit Nada and her family. We had brought small personal gifts for them, they no longer needed help from us and had asked that we spend our energies bringing aid to those who still were in need. Nada had a job as a secretary in the law courts of *Rijeka* and was able to support her family.

The scenery over the mountains was seasonal although the roads were clear of snow. The cottages, trees and mountain slopes were like pictures on the Christmas cards still waiting to be written when we returned home. Having no further problems with weather conditions we arrived home on the 13th December. While we had been away, our charity shop had been closed down. The premises loaned to our local friend had been sold. Owing to lack of funds we were unable to make plans for further trips in the foreseeable future.

OCTOBER 1998

Although we personally did not join convoys for the next 10 months, we helped others to make the journeys. We went on collecting aid, giving advice and knowledge on how to go about preparing the paperwork for customs at the borders. We were beginning to settle into a less active life. By post and by telephone we still had contact from the many friends we had made.

In October 1998, Tony had a frantic request from Kathleen in Switzerland. Once again her cellar was overflowing with goods from her many friends. It was so easy to start stirring peoples' consciences into giving, but very difficult to stop the flow. With a large donation of cash, Bob for back up and son Tim on board, we set off to meet Bob on the A 31 near St. Leonard's Hospital. He was arriving from Horsham. We had decided this time to try asking the ferry company at Poole if they would give us a discount on the crossing to *Cherbourg*.

They had quoted us a price of £400 for the two vehicles with trailers. A good deal more than we normally paid on *Sally Ferries*. It was saving us the four hour run to Ramsgate and the fuel that went with it. Our task was to deliver half of the goods to *Rijeka* on the coast, the rest to *Antun Mihanovic Centre* in *Slavonski Brod*. Also in the instructions, we were to pick up a young lady with a few boxes of aid (we were told) from *Geneva*. As we entered Switzerland from France we had to pay a tax. This enabled us to use the motorways, so saving on travelling time. Genevieve from *Geneva*, was to travel with Bob, to be company for him on the journey.

Her goods turned out to be about half a ton, (no exaggeration). Sacks of rice, flour, boxes of canned goods and toiletries. All of which had to be carried some distance from her building, while our vehicles were parked close to a set of traffic lights on a busy crossing. Our next address was to a factory near *Langenthal*, where we were to pick up a large supply of Pampers and sanitary towels. This had been arranged beforehand.

Kathleen's house was next, she had amassed a large amount of goods in her basement. We spent a good few hours sorting and packing the goods, then weighed and carried the boxes up the steps to the van and the two trailers. The loads were distributed equally between the two vehicles each to go to its separate destination.

Genevieve spoke excellent English so there was no problem there. She spent the night at the house, while we were cosy in our own beds. The next day we travelled out towards *St. Galen* and *Margareten*, where we dealt with the papers for customs and excise. This cost us forty marks for each load. On entering Austria, another fee for using the autobahns, heading for *Salzburg* and *Graz*. As we entered Slovenia, the customs sealed the trailers. Having letters of request from both destinations made the processing easier. As we entered Croatia, there was a slight delay as the police checked Bob out against mug shots, (photos of people wanted for breach of customs regulations). He was soon cleared, Denys's face was well known and we were on our way to *Rijeka* by way of the mountain roads.

At our contact's address in *Rijeka*, we met the lady who was to receive the aid from Bob's trailer. Lillyana, took us to the custom's offices in town where the trailer was to be unsealed. We were told quite firmly that the load would have to go to the Red Cross or to *Caritas*. Only official organisations were allowed to distribute aid in that area; a new law since we were last there. Lillyana said that she would take full responsibility for contacting the Red Cross. The unloading was to take place in a small disused house, in a mountain village above *Rijeka*. The goods were manhandled through a window of the building. This was to save carrying the boxes and bags along a narrow passage way. Bob, Tim and Denys unloaded from the trailer and passed the goods through to Genevieve, Lillyana and me to stack it all in order.

The local press had got wind of our arrival. They sent a photographer and reporter to interview us. They took photos of us with the vehicles as we left to make for *Slavonski Brod*. We started out on the old road then discovered that we were on a newly finished motorway and it was taking us to *Zagreb*. Suddenly we were coming into a tollbooth with a charge of 35 kuna, £7 each vehicle.

We had spent quite a lot of money on motorway tolls during the trip so we used the old roads, which took us towards *Sisak*. It took a little longer but led us through some of the former Serb held villages. Seeing the devastation on the TV newsreels could never compare with the impact that it has in real life. We could never get used to the sight of house after house, most of them just piles of bricks. Now and again an almost untouched building with people still living there among the ruins of their neighbours' homes.

A night spent on the motorway service station, then on to *Slavonski Brod*. Meroslav and his ladies were waiting to welcome us. We had phoned ahead to warn Mero that there could be problems with the customs. The officials could make things difficult under the new rules concerning delivery of aid. While we waited, Meroslav spent a long time on the phone trying to get the permission to have our goods delivered to the centre.

He typed out letters to *Caritas* and to the Red Cross, requesting their help in getting the documents from customs. With him telling me what to write, I typed the same letters in English. Armed with all the paperwork, Meroslav drove into town to try to get permission for *Antun Mihanovic Centre* to receive the goods. He came back an hour later to say that we all needed to go in to the customs offices in the morning.

Meanwhile the ladies had been to their respective homes, they had brought back items of food to make a meal for us. While we ate there was a lot of chat and teasing with a mixture of Croat, English and a little Russian. Genevieve had looked out of her element and stayed quiet. Then she got up from her chair and said that she was going for a walk. She did seem a little out of her depth with the hilarity. It was about 2.30 when she left, by nightfall we were more than a little concerned.

When she walked back through the door at 7pm., she told us that she had been over the bridge into Serb held Bosnia. As air strikes by N.A.T.O. against the Serbs in *Kosovo* were imminent at that time, we thought that she was very lucky that she was holding a Swiss passport and not a British one. We might have had a hostage situation on our hands. Denys gave her a pep talk about the dangers of going off by herself but she just could not see what all the fuss was about.

The next morning Meroslav in his little old car led our two vehicles into the city. At the customs offices we waited in a compound. After a while an official in uniform came to check us out. He unsealed our trailers looked inside each of them, said, "Okay," stamped our papers and we were free to deliver the goods.

Back at the hall there was a party atmosphere, all hands to the work of unloading. The usual handout of sweets and sticks of seaside rock for the children. Somewhere along the way we were given a load of make-up, this we put on the table for our friends to rummage through and take what they fancied. After all the boxes were safely stored, Meroslav's son Tomi came to tell us that we were expected at a meeting at the City Hall.

It seemed that as our time of helping these people of *Slavonski Brod* was coming to an end, we were to be officially thanked by the Mayor of the city. In a very comfortable office we were seated and given coffee. Then Mr Mayor was announced as he came in to join us. Tomi as our interpreter told Mr. Bartok of the many times we had brought aid and supplies to help the refugees in this city. Tomi described the long distances and the problems we had encountered on the borders to get the convoys through. Mr. Bartok told us how much our efforts had been appreciated. Being British we tried to make light of our efforts. Denys said, "WHAT WE HAVE BROUGHT TO YOUR COUNTRY, WAS JUST A DROP IN THE OCEAN". Mr Bartok said something in his own language, it was interpreted by Tomi, as, "IT TAKES THE DROPS TO MAKE THE OCEAN". He invited us to return in June of the next year to join in the celebrations of their folk festival, as guests of the city.

June was a long time away and circumstances changed somewhat before then.

Our journey home meant going via *Geneva* to take Genevieve home. When we arrived at *Cherbourg* docks there seemed to be a misunderstanding over our return tickets. In the end we were allowed on board. At Poole we said goodbye to Bob and made for home.

A week later we received a bill from the ferry company, saying that we owed £400 for our fares. When we went to the office and explained how much we had paid and that we had been granted a discount, we were told that we had been given the discount and that we still owed the £400 for the return fare. We would not be using the Truckline again.

A couple of months later, *Kosovo* was in the news and our hearts once again went out to thousands of people chased and hounded from their homes. What could anyone do? Denys and I, in our safe little home, talked about the situation.

When I got a crazy notion in my head, I would often say to my long-suffering husband, "How about…?"

While watching the TV news one day, I started up with "How about", I think he knew what was on my mind. "How about, if Tony was to ring us and say he would be taking a convoy to *Kosovo*. Would we go?"

Only days later, sure enough, Tony phoned. "If I was to take a convoy to *Kosovo*, would you come with me?" The answer was easy but the lack of funding was holding us back. Tony offered to help with the funding, we could go.

CONVOY TO MACEDONIA
MAY 1999

Monday 17th May, we left Bournemouth with our trailer loaded with 1113 kg's of canned and dried foods, baby milk and bottles, toiletries and T shirts, sheets, blankets and two folding beds.

Going by way of the M25 we went on to the M20 to Ashford Services. Arrangements had been made for the Convoy of Hope to meet in the lorry park ready for take-off at 6.30am. on the 18th.

Other vehicles arrived during the night, most of them local to the Kent area. At 5am. in heavy rain, paperwork was to be sorted out, T forms, papers needed for customs and excise, were made out and paid for, Heart logo stickers applied to the vehicles. A new idea had been dreamed up to identify each vehicle. A sticker was placed front and rear of each. With a number and a 'C' for Convoy Member for those who had not travelled with us before, or an 'E' for Experienced Convoy Member, for those who knew the ropes. Tony was 'E1' we were 'E5'. This was easier than trying to remember names of the drivers in case of emergency.

Among the 34 vehicles were a coach, a Scania artic, half a dozen seven and half ton trucks, a brewery lorry, a school Mini bus, various transits and trailers and our motor home with trailer. A reporter and photographer from the Kent Messenger a local paper, were travelling with us, they would be reporting back on how the convoy was doing during the long journey.

At 8.15 we moved out into the rush hour traffic, to drive 15 miles to the Channel Tunnel Terminal. En route there were many cameras recording the convoy, each truck and van displaying the 'Heart' logo.

Some negotiating had achieved free passage for each of us.

Tickets and duty free vouchers were issued, then a short wait to board the train.

We met up with some old friends from previous convoys, and soon made new ones. We were loaded onto the train as freight and breakfast was provided in the drivers' diner, 35 minutes later we were in Calais. We regrouped in a lorry park where we discovered that one van had developed problems and hadn't made it to the train. The driver and his mate were offered seats in the coach. We headed for *Dunkirk* and *Lille*

While bowling along the motorway another van developed a problem. We all pulled into a service station to see what could be done. After being towed to a garage, it was found that some of the prop shaft bolts had broken. It was decided that the convoy would carry on and hopefully the van would catch us up on the way across Europe.

On through France and Belgium, most of the convoy keeping together. One or two slower or overloaded vehicles lagged behind, we were detailed to stay with them as we knew the route so well. At *Aachen*, our first refuelling and meal stop we all got together again. Most of the crew ate at the services restaurant, others, like us ate from their own food stocks.

One lady from the coach, we had already christened them The Tourists, was not happy with her situation and the company. We were asked if we would take her in with us. We had often taken strays on board before as it was well known that we had sleeping space. This time we had let it be known that we would not be returning to the U.K. with the convoy. We had personal reasons to go on to Croatia. We did say that Maureen was welcome to travel with us, as and when she felt the need, until we split from the rest. Well after dark, the driver of one of the trucks had a problem with the rear lights and pulled into a layby. Most of the vehicles were on C.B. radio so we all had contact with anyone having difficulties and could call for help when needed. We and the artic driver pulled in behind the truck to see what could be done. An hour's work on the wiring got the tail lights working.

On the road again with no sight or sound of the main convoy, Maureen got very anxious. She was a very nervous lady, not quite the type that you would expect to find travelling in conditions like these. At 1am. we came upon our vehicles already settled into spaces at *Hockenheim* services. Some of our crew were waiting to guide us into parking spaces and to get Maureen to her bed on the coach. We were very close to the autobahn but managed to sleep well.

At 7am. a meeting was held in the wooded area of the service station. Tony's pep talk for all drivers new to the continent and driving in a convoy. He said that we had a long way to go and that he would be pushing everyone to the limit. At 8.15 on a beautiful morning, we moved out into very heavy traffic. We were heading for *Koln (Cologne)*, and *Munchen (Munich), Stuttgart* and *Innsbruk*. We and the tortoises, (slower vehicles), had a half hour lunch stop at mid-day, caught up and passed the convoy having their break and refuelling at the next services.

All travelling at our own speeds, sometimes we overtook the trucks making heavy going up the long uphill drags. At the *Brenner Pass*, which took us into Italy, one of our most experienced convoy members, 'Uncle George', managed to wangle us all free passage through the toll. Very steep climbs into the mountains gave views with spectacular scenery. At one steep turn a village lay below us with a beautiful full rainbow shining above it. The most amazing thing was that we were above the rainbow! The vehicles had to work hard and the C.B. radio was quiet as drivers concentrated on unfamiliar steep twists and turns of the mountain roads, also to listen out for any driver who might have a problem with their vehicle.

As we came down into Italy, we suddenly came upon the coach slewed across the road with a burst tyre. We were travelling too fast at the time to stop, so we passed on the message to a vehicle behind who stopped to help, also to notify the convoy of what was happening. We all pulled into the next services to make this a refuelling stop for the vehicles and for ourselves.

The chap who had left his van at Ashford got a message from his Dad to say that the van was now serviceable, and Dad was driving it to try and catch up with us. We had a date with the ferry at *Ancona* by midday tomorrow. It was possible that he might just make it.

The attendant at the filling station was willing to take marks or sterling from those of us who had not changed their money to lira. We got meals, socialised and rested. We chatted to some Italian drivers who were interested in us and our crowd. It was discovered that the bus had one burst tyre and the other three were bald. It was sent off to be fitted with a new set, the 'tourists' were to be farmed out to other vehicles for the night.

Maureen was back with us complete with baggage! At 10.30pm. we were moving out to get a couple more hours of travelling. The convoy was quite strung out as we were heading for *Bologna*.

We had 7 vans with us and a lot of chat over the C.B. when a couple of them pulled into the services, taking us by surprise. We followed to find out what their problem was, it seems that they were tired and wanted to take an hour's break.

There had been no sound from Tony ('Echo one') or the others for some time until we heard Uncle George calling to tell us that they had pulled into a service station about a mile ahead. At 1am. we pulled in and settled in with our lodger, after piling her baggage, and ours, into the front seats.

At 6am. we were ready to roll, en route to *Ancona*. The traffic was heavy and very hectic. Denys and Tony put out a message to the chatterboxes, if they want to chat use channel 25 and not 30 as they were blotting out important information.

The road to the ferry port was straight and in very good condition. We made up some of the lost time. We heard that the drivers of the coach had driven on after a couple of hours rest the night before and was already at the port. We had a ten minute comfort stop at *Modena* and travelled on through warm sunshine and showers. At the peage we were once again given a free passage. Some local drivers got annoyed and tried to separate our vehicles.

From just outside the main town, we were given a police escort. At each corner or junction a police officer was on duty to point the way to this strange assortment of foreign vehicles. At the docks area, there seemed to be literally hundreds of large trucks all parked in neat rows. We all slotted in where there was space.

At 1pm. a lady representative of the ferry operators, set up an information post on the tailboard of one of our trucks. She was there to sort out our bookings. The fares were a bit more pricey than we had expected, For the van and trailer, the two of us in a double cabin was 1,400,000 drachma (£650). Denys had been one of the first at the booking office but some drivers were objecting to the amount being charged and some were confused with the cabin arrangements. They were shouting the loudest so got dealt with first. I was sitting in the camper while this was all going on and could see some of our vehicles boarding the huge 'Superfast' ferry with no sign of my driver. By the time he was in possession of our tickets, there was 15 minutes to sailing time and we were the last vehicle on. We were told that there was only the one ferry a day to *Patras* our destination.

With 24 hours to relax on the boat, we made full use of the showers, the restaurants and the bars.

In the atmosphere of a sunshine cruise, some took the opportunity to get to know our fellow travellers a little better. Maureen showed her gratitude for her bed and breakfast, by treating us to a meal on board. We thought "Well, when in Rome!" and ordered a real Spaghetti Bolognaise with a bottle of white wine.

Our cabin was number 8015. We could never find it in one go, the corridors seemed to stretch for miles. While we tried to find our room, we socialised with other folk doing the same and compared notes. More than a few convoy members had an early night as none of us had enjoyed more than 5 hours sleep each night since leaving the U.K. Most of those in loaded vans hadn't slept at all. We ourselves took a stroll around the deck before turning in. The motion of the ship was very slight, all we could feel was like the throbbing of a giant heart, not at all like crossing the Channel.

We had an inside cabin, no windows so we had no idea of time, until we went to the breakfast bar. All that was available were doughnuts and coffee. We hadn't realised that we were now two hours ahead of English time. Lunch was served from 11.30. There were two main eating areas, a restaurant with all the trimmings and a cafeteria. We chose the latter and enjoyed various meats served in a pepper sauce with French fries.

We sat with a large group and talked. Some had heard of

our earlier travels and wanted to know more about Bosnia during the war years. At 4.30 we cleared our cabin and queued for passport control. The officials just glanced at our passports and waved us through to the vehicle decks. There we had to squeeze between gigantic trucks to get to the camper, not easy for a full-blown figure like mine. We drove off the boat to regroup in the lorry park on the docks.

We drove through *Patras*, which caused havoc among the local drivers and police. On the outskirts of the town we refuelled at two separate filling stations. While we waited our turn, Denys spotted a tap with a hose at a nearby car wash. Always on the look out for a means to fill our on board tank, he dashed out to do just that. A couple of miles outside the town, we were to take a small ferryboat at *Rio*. We were packed into the small craft like sardines, some of our vehicles had to wait for the next boat but they ran frequently.

Luckily we had missed the hottest part of the day. It was a very pleasant drive with wonderful scenery, sea, mountains, flowers and a colourful sunset. We were last but two in the convoy at that point with transits in front of us, some of them making heavy going of the steep climb.

On one such steep uphill turn, there was an almighty bang from somewhere under the bonnet, steam poured into the cab from all directions. I took the microphone and called "Mayday, Mayday, Mayday, the *Dukemobile* is in in trouble."

A voice came back asking what was the problem. Denys had pulled us in and taken over the mike, he said that we had burst a water hose. The artic had been behind us and the driver said that he would tow us into the first available pull in. A towing chain was fixed between us and the truck. Mike in a transit van, who had been 'tail end Charlie', last vehicle in the convoy, stayed to report to the others what was happening.

Slowly we made our way up the steep mountain road, the artic was towing the camper and our trailer. Going downhill was worse as without the engine running Denys could not use the brakes. At times the old camper was nudging the artic, we could not have had a sturdier vehicle to pull us up the hills. By starting the engine from time to time in short bursts, Denys was able to slow us down on the gears to stop us from crashing into the monster truck. Good thing that Maureen wasn't with us at that time.

We made it to a service station, where it was found that our radiator had burst. While the mechanics among our crew talked over what would be the best solution, the rest of us made the most of the facilities in the restaurant, the bar and the toilets. With about 80 people all arriving at once the owners of the restaurant must have thought that there had been an invasion. One of our lady convoy members spoke a few words of Greek and in no time she took charge of ordering food for those who wanted to eat and helped out by serving it at the tables.

Among the men there were ideas thrown around as to what should be done about our predicament. From welding the radiator to towing us to a Fiat garage, if one could be found. For this we would need a rigid towbar. Everyone was happy to stay put for the night and review the situation in the morning.

The restaurant was serving breakfast at 7.30am. The view from the restaurant was breathtaking. We were still in the heart of the *Pindus* mountains and goats were clambering up the slopes in front of us. A girder had been 'borrowed' to make a tow bar, the plan was to take us into the nearest town where it might be possible to buy a radiator. One of the transits had a tow hook and took our trailer. At 8.15, we moved out, Tony in the lead with the artic towing us behind him. The others followed at a distance keeping the C.B. channel quiet in case of emergencies.

We were doing okay considering that it was mostly downhill with steep hairpin bends, until the tow bar came adrift from the truck and jammed itself under the camper. The whole convoy stopped where they could, spread out all the way up the mountain. A couple of our chaps wearing fluorescent jackets, helped the local drivers to pass us safely. Soon we were on the way again, until on the flat, the artic picked up speed and the tow bar broke away again.

We were only a few metres away from a garage and Denys managed to roll the camper into the forecourt. A mechanic there suggested that we might get the repair done in *Lamia*, 25 miles further on. Tony had a light, rigid tow bar in his van. It would not have been strong enough to pull us on the mountain roads but it might be strong enough now we were in flat country. Bob took Pippa, the lady who had a little knowledge of Greek, in his van to go on ahead with the radiator to see what could be done in *Lamia*.

With Tony's van only half the size of our camper and a lightweight tow bar, we moved slowly out. It all went very well, the convoy was to pull out 20 minutes after us to go on and find a large parking area near *Lamia*. We arrived in the town with no further mishaps. Contact with Bob was made and he came to lead us to a *Pirelli Garage* in a busy main street.

There seemed to be some anti-British attitude at the work shop. At first they shook their heads and didn't want to do the job. Denys gave up in disgust and turned around to pick up the radiator from where it had been leaning against a wall. It was gone. One older chap had started braising it, while his mates were dragging their feet. At 1pm. the radiator was being fitted, Denys started the engine to test it, then we saw water pouring from under the dashboard. A hose needed replacing. The mechanic got to work again, then discovered that the fans were not working. Denys made the chap understand that it would not be a problem and asked Pippa to sort out the bill, 10,000 drachma, about £20. We gave the chap four bottles of beer as a tip.

Bob called the convoy to find out where they were parked. They were at a restaurant on the road to *Larissa*. We joined them there at the 'Oasis Restaurant'. We had thought that they would have got tired of waiting for us and might have gone on. They were all pleased to see us travelling under our own power and said that they would not have gone on without us.

The fans not working was not too big a problem. One of the crew offered to fix the wiring so that the fans would be running all the time we were travelling, that would keep the engine cool. We moved out then, having lost a day we needed to make up the time. Heading for *Thessalonika* and on motorways in the heat of 100 degrees, we passed within sight of *Mount Olympus*. I was hoping that the old Greek gods were looking kindly on us.

Denys, (known as Duke on our convoys) kept an eye on the engine temperature and it was fine. At our next comfort stop for toilets and cold drinks, just about everyone came by to ask if all was well. Travelling on and around 11pm. Tony decided to go on ahead to find us a large parking area. He left us to bring on the convoy. In the distance we could see the flashes from mortar shells, we were very near to the *Macedonian* border.

We caught up with Tony at a filling station with plenty of room for all of us to park. There was no one about except a couple of friendly dogs wandering around. As we got ready to settle in Denys was not feeling well, we thought perhaps it was from standing in the sun while waiting for the radiator to be repaired.

In the morning after a cup of tea he was vomiting and blaming it on a snack pot meal that he hadn't been able to finish the night before. A paramedic and male nurse travelling with us came to the camper, they seemed very pleased to have a patient to work on. They took his temperature, blood pressure and checked his sugar level. They agreed that it could have been the meal and sunstroke combined. Nothing life threatening.

The filling station was open for business. We all filled with fuel and retrieved our trailer from the chap who had been towing it and finding it heavy going. A delay while everyone got their paperwork ready for the border.

There were long waits at the customs, each driver and passenger had to show him or herself with passport at a police check. There were anti- NATO slogans painted on the road and walls. One said 'NATO FASCISTS, RETURN FROM SERBIA IN YOUR COFFINS'.

We moved forward slowly 8 vehicles at a time. While passengers or co-drivers took the T forms to an office the drivers moved forward one at a time to have their registrations checked against the documents. Then at the exit of Greece, a changing of the guard was in progress, soldiers in National costume with escorts were changing guard with great ceremony.

A few yards further on was the entry *Macedonia* border. In two lines the convoy waited while Tony presented the papers. We were informed over the C.B that two Irish lorries had been kept here since Friday, (48 hours). After one hour we had to fill in cards of identification for visas. Another hour passed and we were told that we must go to a small office and purchase insurance to drive in *Macedonia*. This took another hour, each driver having to show all vehicle documents. The prices charged seemed to be different for each vehicle, almost as it was done by guesswork. Our vehicle was almost the cheapest, about £33, others were from £130, the big truck topped the lot at just £20.

At 3pm. a police car came to escort us to *Skopje*, about 80 miles away. The police car travelled at quite a pace and the convoy got stretched out. Some were heavily laden and slower than the rest, the C.B. helped a lot at times like this. We travelled through wonderful scenery and a terrific downpour of rain. At tollbooths we swept straight through at the annoyance of local drivers.

We came upon mountain roads but with heaters full on to absorb the heat from the engine we had no problem. Denys was feeling his old self again and we enjoyed the ride. As we approached the town the convoy closed up a little and we were all together as we were directed into a large area. It looked like a lorry park-cum-market and we were parked up really close to each other.

It wasn't long before the cooking stoves and provisions were out for a well-earned meal. Army lorries were trundling through and helicopters were flying low overhead. There seemed to be an airfield close by. Maureen and the tourists were fed on the bus. Just when everyone was getting on with their meal it suddenly poured with rain, there was quite a scramble to get everything under cover.

Word got round that we were staying there for the night. A chap from U.N.H.C.R. (United Nations High Commission for Refugees) would arrive in the morning, when it was likely that we would unload. Maureen came and asked if she could sleep in our vehicle. I moved our belongings and made room for our guest. We turned in early, parked close by was a refrigeration truck, with the motor running all night, this disturbed us from time to time.

Up at 6am., English breakfast of eggs and bacon for three of us. Denys went out to socialise, I got on with my diary, nodding at Maureen's chatter when needed. We heard news that the Macedonians were trying to push the refugees into *Albania*. Denys and some of the drivers were talking to British soldiers, one said that they came from West Moors. This was where we

284

used to live, when we lived in fields in the camper. All the drivers were told to drive their vehicles onto a weighbridge. No explanation as to why. We were charged 50.marks for the parking of each vehicle and 30 marks for the weighbridge. Then we were directed back to our parking spots to wait while it was discussed where we would take our loads. We were quite used to the waiting game on these convoys. The younger members tended to get impatient.

At 3.30 we were told that we would be unloading at a central warehouse. Just about that time the van that had broken down in France turned up. What a story they had to tell. They had appealed to Radio One, asking if anyone could help get them on their way to joining an aid convoy. The radio station arranged for a transporter to pick them up. Repairs to their sick vehicle were carried out en-route.

With a representative from U.N.H.C.R. to lead us we drove to a large compound, no sign of a warehouse. At the gate a guard asked for vehicle documents or International Drivers' Licences to be held by them while we used this U.N. lorry park. By this time we were not surprised at anything. A meeting was held and plans were changed, the vehicles were to be split into four sections. We, with the Sheppard Neame brewery lorry and one smaller van were to be taken to a 'Save the Children' warehouse.

With a car to lead us, our mini convoy was taken about twelve miles out of town to a small village called *Glumovo*. We drove down a narrow lane and to a building much like a double garage with sliding doors, a group of helpers came to unload the goods. The little van and the lorry were unloaded first. I was not needed so took charge of the camera work, taking pictures of the goods as they were stacked.

A crowd of kids had come to see if there were any handouts. We gave them Red Arrows pens, the lorry drivers Chris and Terry had some sweets for them. We were then led back to the compound. On the way we passed some of our convoy going in the opposite direction, complete with bus and 'tourists'. We found out later that they were going to a refugee camp and were expecting to stay overnight.

I cooked a convoy stew and invited the four drivers who had been with us to 'Save the Children' to share the meal. Some

285

of the others came back and it seemed that we were pulling out in the morning.

In the compound with us was a Russian convoy, They had six trucks, an accommodation vehicle and their own fuel tanker. At 7am. Maureen came to visit, she had been with part of the convoy delivering aid to a village in the mountains. They had returned at 2am. People were moving about eating breakfast, the men were shaving by using wing mirrors of the vans. Biding time, until at 9 a representative from *Doctors of the World* organisation came to lead us to a refugee camp.

This is what most of the convoy members had come for. It was suggested that the larger vehicles should be left in the compound, the occupants were to travel where they could in the now empty transit vans. We took eight in the camper with us. Heading towards the *Kosovo* border, we were led through the town. In open country, we passed our colleagues returning from their drop zone. A call on the radio told them where we were going, they made a quick turn around to join us.

For 40 miles we drove through mountain scenery, then in a village we turned into a rough track. Passing some very modern looking villas, we suddenly saw the camp ahead of us. A fenced in enclosure with neat rows of tents, washing was hanging on the wire fencing. Crowds of men, women and children swarmed to greet us. We parked and made sure the vehicles were secure before taking cameras to get evidence of what the folks at home were seeing on TV newsreels.

We had plenty of scope for photos and video, as they all clamoured to have their pictures taken. The adults were very friendly and the children polite and patient as the sweets and chocolate were handed out. The refugees were segregated from the village by the fences, but kids being kids, there were gaps under the wire for minor breakouts.

Everyone found a group to talk with, babies to fuss over and the school aged children had a chance to practice their class room English. I had a baby put into my arms, the mother told me that the baby was three months old and her name was Alinda. The people were remarkably clean and tidy and there was a great absence of litter. The camp didn't look too bad on a warm and sunny day but I tried to imagine what it might be like in winter or in a downpour of rain.

Two larger tents were being used as schoolrooms, in one of these we saw children drawing pictures, many had drawn tanks and exploding bombs.

Most of the boys had perfected the Churchill V sign, we were shown it at every turn with 'Thank you NATO' (they pronounce it NATTO) from many of the youngsters. When we finally broke away, we met with an American lady doctor. She treated us to coffee and doughnuts at a small cafe almost opposite the camp.

She had come out to work voluntarily at *Sanakos* camp for one month with an organisation called *Doctors of the World*. She told us that she would go home, pack in her job and come back for as long as she was needed. She told us that there were 6,000 refugees in the camp at present and 20,000 more were expected any day. Many of those we had spoken to still had relatives in *Pristina*.

When we had arrived at the camp, it had been arranged that our U.N.H.C.R. representative would be ready to lead us back to *Skopje* at 1pm. It was near 2pm. when the vehicles started rolling out. We were still minus one passenger, a couple of lads went off to find him. As he wasn't wearing the blue team T-shirt, it was like looking for the proverbial needle. He was located and we were under way. Luckily for us, the main convoy had been held up by a funeral procession. The walking mourners were blocking the narrow lane.

In the lorry park, most of our drivers took a rest as we were expecting to leave for the start of the long journey home. At 7pm. we moved out of the compound. Our convoy moved out slowly, dodging the heavy trucks coming in to park for the night. At the exit from *Macedonia* border, the drivers received a handshake of thanks from the officials and we were on our way. In a glorious sunset we came to the entry Greece border, Tony showed a list of all our passport and registration numbers. A police officer checked each number plate as we passed through.

In the darkness the lights of the convoy were quite a sight as we wound up and down the mountains. We had a Mayday call from the Victoria hire van, noises from the engine turned out to be a broken exhaust. Not a major problem, one that could be dealt with at our night stop. Brookside Garden Centre burst a tyre, a couple of vans pulled in to help with changing it.

The next day, Tony the artic driver was to leave us, he was going on to Italy to pick up a load for the U.K. which was how he was able to bring such a large vehicle on such a trek. We had good reason to be glad that he had been with us. Uncle George and some of the faster vans were going on ahead. As many drivers took their annual holidays to join the convoys, they needed to be back in good time. Our engine temperature went into the red.

Denys pulled into a convenient layby to let it cool, in no time we had company. Two vans pulled in with the crews ready to help sort out any problem. After 10 minutes break we started out again, to meet up with the gang at the Oasis Restaurant.

We relaxed a while on the veranda of the restaurant, enjoying the sea breezes. On the menu was Greek style chicken and deep-fried potatoes. With the steep climbs ahead of us, our trailer was put onto the low loader being towed by Bob. Then we tackled the *Pindus* mountains. The camper coped well as the air was much cooler. Bob was struggling a little with the weight of the trailer but we managed to stay together. Passing olive groves and flocks of sheep watched over by shepherds, was like looking at scenes from a biblical film. We reached the services in the mountains where we'd spent the night of our incident. Just enough time to refuel, fill water bottles and buy ice-cream. We also surprised the owner by returning the borrowed girder.

On reaching the coast we had plenty of time to spare as we were booked onto the 5pm. ferry the next day,(Thursday). On a layby close to the sea we had time to relax, to talk over the journey and the task achieved. A couple of chaps went into the sea but soon hobbled out with painful spines from sea urchins in their feet. First aid with a needle from our sewing box got the spines out. Some local men told us that we could have problems from kids throwing stones at the vehicles if we stayed there, so it was decided to move on.

We drove down to the *Rio* ferry just in time to get onto the next boat. We had a slight problem, not enough drachma. Bob came to the rescue and loaned us the 2,640 to pay for the fare. On the far side we parked up and settled to spend the night.

In the morning we were all in fine fettle, refreshed and ready to go. Some of the vehicles needed fuel and found a Texaco filling station near *Patras*. At the main docks we parked in two neat lines along the quay, one or two local cars joined us thinking that we were the queue for the ferry. The time was passed by getting our tickets and boarding passes, passports stamped by the port police, taking a look around the duty free shop and visiting the cafe for a cold drink. The weather was very hot and humid and then it rained. We watched our boat come into the dock at 3pm. Then Tony called us all on the C.B. telling us that he had received a phone call from Tony Blair's secretary saying, "Well done Convoy of Hope." I could not say if it was true, but Tony does like a joke.

At 4.30 things started to move, then it all stopped. The word went around that the purser on board had got upset, because our vehicles were all booked on as mini-buses. And it was obvious to him that the seven and a half ton trucks were not. A bit of delay and we were on board, we were not last on this time. Our camper was directed on to a deck which was for campers and caravans only. If we had known about this on the outward journey we could have saved ourselves the price of a cabin. Caravan owners were allowed to sleep in their vans and hook up to the ship's electricity. There were toilets and showers for their use.

Up on the stern patio, we watched the bustle of the loading and then the ramps lifting. Inside, Maureen found us and insisted that we join her for a meal. In the restaurant, the young medic joined us at a table for four. We chose Black Angus steaks. Just as we were about to enjoy the meal, a call over the tannoy asked if there was a doctor on board. At the second call, our young friend Paul went to see if there was anything he could do. He came back to postpone his meal, there was no doctor available so he was needed to check out the chef who had a suspected heart attack.

When Paul had done all he could, he came back for his meal. He told us that if we were to see a helicopter hovering over the ship in the morning, it would be taking the chef to hospital. Showers and a good night's sleep had done wonders for all of us. We met up next morning to socialise in the lounge.

Taking a stroll around the ship, we discovered a swimming pool and sunbathing area on the top deck. We enjoyed kebabs with salad on the patio and a cup of Lipton's tea. How typically English. We docked at 3pm. and retrieved our trailer from Bob.

We were to say goodbye to our companions of the past two weeks. Outside the docks, the convoy would be taking the motorway to the *Brenner Pass*, We would be turning onto the coast road, going north to *Trieste* and *Rijeka* in Croatia. For the first mile or so after the parting of the ways, there were lots of goodbyes and good luck messages flying over the airwaves until we were on our own.

Travelling on a very scenic route from *Ancona* to *Rimini*, *Venice* and *Trieste*, most of it was within sight of the sea. Now free from a timetable and endless waiting, we travelled on to stop overnight near *Venice*. One place I would really love to see and we passed by it in the dark! The next day we were heading for *Trieste*. Our route took us through the town, early morning and the traffic was very busy. Still hugging the coast we made for the Croatian border. No problems on entering the country but we were asked if we had a licence for the C.B. radio. To *Rijeka* and over the mountains to *Zagreb*.

Coming off the motorway to *Kutina, Lipik* and to *Pakrac* where we made a short visit to Anton and Maria, left them with a promise to stay longer in a week or so. In the town we stopped to say hello to the family at the Faroan Bistro, there was no one about and the bar was closed. We moved on taking the motorway to *Slavonski Brod* the temperature was around 100 degrees, 38°C but it was quite comfortable while travelling.

Over the six years we had been bringing goods to Croatia, we had made good friends and contacts in the country. Last October we had made our last official drop to the *Antun Mihanovic* centre. Then we were informed by the authorities that all aid must go through the Red Cross in future.

Meroslav Goll was the director of the organisation, his son Tomislav, who spoke very good English was usually our interpreter on our visits. Through Tomi we had a meeting with the Mayor of *Slavonski Brod*, who thanked us for our efforts and our help to his town at a very difficult time. He said that he would like to have some official connection with our home town to show appreciation to our community for the goods received over the years.

At that time he had invited us to return in June, when a folk festival was to be held so while we were in *Macedonia*, we had thought to take up the invitation. At Tomi's home we sat in his back yard, moving our chairs and chasing the shade while talking over the situation as it was. The opinion in this part of the country was that NATO was doing a good job and that the bombing should continue until Milosovic surrendered.

We had arrived on the 31st May, the festival started on the 6th June the day our insurance and breakdown cover expired. We decided to stay on for three more days before making for home. We left then, hoping to catch up with more friends, telling Tomi that we would meet with his father at the centre in the morning. We drove on to *Babina Greda*, 30 miles further along the motorway towards *Belgrade*. Near to our turning for *Babina Greda*, some army trucks passed us at great speed and we heard some loud explosions in the distance.

We were stopped by police who asked to see our passports and vehicle documents. A few years earlier we would not have been able to travel this far along the motorway. It had been under Serb control. The police let us continue on our way. In the village we stopped at the bistro and asked for Anto, he was at *Kostrina* and would be home the following day.

His Mum got him on a mobile phone and we spoke to him, he was so excited that we had come back and he wanted us to stay put until he came home.

We explained that we had an appointment in *Slavonski Brod* the next morning but promised to be back in *Babina Greda* at 6pm. A wonderful sight as we left to follow the motorway, a pair of storks were soaring above the village, probably on the look out for a good nesting site. At Meroslav's home, his wife Baritsa came to welcome us. We must have looked very hot and travel weary as she offered us the use of their shower; very welcome and refreshing. A meal of chicken and chips was waiting for us as we emerged from the bathroom.

Later Denys spoke to Tomi on the phone. He had arranged for us to visit a school for traumatised children, we had brought along a box of toys and educational materials for them. Next morning at the refugee centre, we were welcomed with open arms by the ladies who distributed the goods we brought and had become good friends to us. There were 350 refugee families living in the area close to the centre. Tomislav was working at the radio station so we went on to the school without an interpreter, hoping that we would be understood.

The head teacher welcomed us into her office with juice and coffee, after which we met some of the children in their classrooms and the gymnasium. Poor little souls, they looked bewildered and couldn't make us out. One or two held our hands tightly. The age group was from 7 to 17 years and were from disturbed or one parent families impoverished by the war because of destroyed factories or unemployment. We were made to understand that the school hoped to have a workshop where the children could learn to make objects. These could be sold in markets to help support themselves now and in the future. They needed ideas and materials to get started. We couldn't make any promises but we would try.

We took a stroll around the town as first time tourists, a lot of work had been done since our early visits when the Serbs were shelling the buildings facing the *River Sava*. When we returned, Tomi came to us with a dictaphone. He said that he would like to interview us for local radio. I was very nervous but our friend made it very informal and easy. A 15-minute chat to be edited with translation, to go out on air at 5pm. that evening.

Keeping to our promise we set out for *Babina Greda* that afternoon, At the bistro we met a couple who seemed to know that we were expected. They invited us to their table and paid for our Coca-Cola. Anto arrived, a full-grown man now and full of enthusiasm and waiting to take us to a secret place. The last time this happened he took us across the river to his home village, occupied by the Serbs.

He, and Zelko his stepfather, came aboard the camper and directed Denys to *Vinkovci* and on to *Vukovar*. The city which was destroyed and captured by the Serbian Forces in the early days of the war, many of the refugee families scattered all over Croatia were from *Vukovar*. Women and children, the sick, the injured and the elderly were all shipped out on trucks and buses. Many of the men were not seen alive again

We had seen the devastation of *Mostar* but nothing could match the destruction of this once beautiful city close by the River Danube. A couple of years back we were given some drawings showing the ruins of the most well known features of *Vukovar*. It had always been our ambition to see *Vukovar* for ourselves but then we had been warned that it would not be safe. Zelko knew the city very well, he sold chickens and eggs to a hotel beside the river. With him as our guide we had no problems, we took photos and video film, no one took any special notice of us. I picked a rose from a bush under the ruins of the water tower and pressed it for remembrance.

On our way back through the town a group of people were staring at something in the road. A snake. A man was trying to kick it under the wheels of our camper as we passed by but it was too quick and escaped into the gutter.

It was dark when we left the city, with a full moon rising and almost red. Anto talked non stop all the way back. Dropping them off at the bistro we made our way back to *Slavonski Brod*. We both had a number of mosquito bites but the experience was well worth it.

We woke early hearing planes overhead, very unusual down here. We thought it might be N.A.T.O. planes returning from the raids.

Tomislav had told us that we were to meet the Mayor that afternoon, he would like to take us out to lunch. With time to kill we walked into town and along the river bank. The air was heavy and we felt a few drops of rain, there was a cool breeze by the river and it was very pleasant. We enjoyed being tourists, it started to rain in earnest so we made our way back to the camper.

Meroslav arrived in his ancient Renault car, he drove us to City Hall. Mr. Bartok welcomed us and with a press photographer taking photographs, thanked us and presented us with gifts from the city and its people. A ceremonial vase with engraved pictures of the monastery, two bottles of local wine and some books about Croatia and *Slavonski Brod* with its ancient fortress.

We had gifts for the Mayor from our own Town Hall. Two ties with the Bournemouth Coat-of-Arms, tie-tacks and scarves all sporting the Bournemouth Crest. Also in the gift package was a porcelain pot with a view of Bournemouth on the lid, given by an official from the Town Hall. Our own contribution to the Mayor of *Slavonski Brod* was a book of scenes of the New Forest area.

After the exchange of gifts we were taken in the Mayoral car to a top rank restaurant. It was decorated in the style of a traditional *Slavonian* farmhouse. The meal was interesting. Salami and local cheese with fresh bread for starter. Then Mr. Bartok rose from the table, excused himself and explained that he had to attend the funeral of the Chief of the Fire Service. We sat, talked and waited until the Mayor's return to resume our meal. Very tender and moist pork with mushrooms and roasted potatoes for the main course. The Mayor's driver Stephan enjoyed the meal with us. He had interests in common with Denys, flying, gliding and aircraft. A very relaxed and enjoyable occasion.

After the meal we were driven to the Monastery for a conducted tour. Until about three years before we had often brought gifts and essentials to nuns in this building. We believed it to be a convent until we were told that it was in fact a Franciscan Monastery. The nuns were refugees from across the river.

Father Domacoj Simonovic gave us a tour of the libraries. We were shown precious volumes from the very earliest years, some hand written in beautiful script. On the floor were some large carved angels, some of the treasures of the church. They had recently been brought back from where they had spent the worst of the war years for safekeeping. The priest told us that this was one of the oldest churches in the city. The carvings would have been irreplaceable.

The small monastery church of the Holy Trinity was beautiful, decorated with woodcarvings in the Baroque style. Fresh flowers scented the air. We didn't let on that we had been there many times before and that Convoy of Hope members had attended services on earlier visits.

The next morning we were taken to *Slavonski Brod's* fortress, which had been built in the 14th century to protect the city from the Turks. Italian forces had occupied it in the 17th century and allowed it to fall into ruin. Since the recent peace agreement, many unemployed citizens were working together to rebuilt the old fort. One block which had been the barracks was now a school for higher education.

In this building, young people from 16 years onwards, stood respectfully, as we entered the classroom. After exchanging 'Good mornings' and *'Dobar Dans'*, we left them to continue their studies. On the top floor of the building we were shown into a well-equipped gymnasium, which enabled the youngsters to keep fit in the winter months.

With our V.I.P. tour over, we made ourselves ready to leave *Slavonski Brod* and our friends. Tomislav had been working at the radio station all day but he had said that he would say goodbye to us over the radio airwaves at 5pm. Sure enough as we pulled into a shady patch by the roadside, we heard his voice coming from our speakers. In English he said, "Goodbye to our good friends from England, have a good and safe journey, I dedicate the next record to you, it is 'Take me home country roads'." An emotional moment.

Making our way back to *Pakrac*, we drove to the home of Anton and Maria. The language barrier was always a problem and most of the conversation was done with signs and gestures but they did love our visits. Their big double bed was always prepared for us when we arrived. We played the taped interview with Tomi for them to hear, they learned more about us then, than they had known before.

Their lovely hospitality and a night in 'that bed', before we had to say goodbye with promises to come back when we could. In the town, we made a stop to visit at the Faroan Bistro. We were very surprised to see the windows were blacked out by plastic sheets. Since *Pakrac* had become a busy town the bistro had always been a popular meeting place. Javanka and Fikret were a lovely couple with three lively daughters. Their home in *Lipik* had been destroyed early in the war and they had set up home in the small flat above their business. A group of worldwide volunteers had made it their eating and meeting place and we had spent many sociable hours over a cold Coke or beer with them.

As we turned to leave, we saw Javanka walking towards us,

she had been shopping. Hurriedly getting us inside the building she told us a shocking story of how because she was from a Serbian family, their business had been blacked by the town. She was so upset as she told us, "We have no business, no customers, no money, life is more difficult now than when there was war." As we asked about the girls, she told us that Emira the eldest, was now married and living in *Daruvar*. Edina was living in England as an au pair, she had an English boyfriend, and Emina the youngest was in secondary school.

Javanka she said that she would never forget that we had brought her daughters their first make-up and blankets for their beds after their home had been destroyed. As she showed us out she said that she hoped that our friendship with her family had not harmed our respect in the town.

A very sad ending to an otherwise wonderful trip. We could not think of any way that we could ease the situation but I think our bond with *Pakrac* had become a little more fragile. We had known for the past few years that shoemaker Anton had not been pleased at our friendship with the owners of the Faroan Bistro although he never once said anything to prove that fact.

Our homeward journey took us through Austria, Germany, Belgium and France. On the Eurolink train our return tickets were still valid. In England the weather got wetter as we neared home. Around 10pm., when we reached Ringwood we knew that it would be too wet to unload our belongings when we reached home so we spent the night in Ringwood lorry park.

A round trip of 4,500 miles, a cost of £2,000 and 10 countries visited.

CONVOY OF HOPE TO KOSOVO
SEPTEMBER 1999

Four ladies of a certain age group contacted us, as they had set their minds on helping the desperate people of *Kosovo*. One of them, Jenny, had been talking to a cousin of Denys's and she was advised to get in touch with him. They knew we had made mercy missions to war zones and disaster areas and he would be able to help.

The contact was made and we had two or three meetings. We told the girls of some of the things they needed to know, also some of the problems they might encounter. The knowledge we gave them still did not prepare them for the experience.

With TV and press coverage, we left Christchurch at 1.30pm. on the 6th of September, Our new friends, Jennie, Jackie, Brenda and Maureen travelled in their camper van. Support for the two lads, Darren, and Lee (Jennie's son), driving a seven and half ton truck, loaded with goods and gifts they had spent weeks collecting, sorting and packing.

Travelling with us in our motor home, were Holly, Anna and Rob hoping to get enough material for a documentary film for national television some time in the future. With them came about half a ton of camera equipment.

We made for Dover arriving in plenty of time to sort out the paperwork, ('T' forms etc. for customs and excise) We were to be on the 5am. Sea France ferry. A convoy of 17 vehicles.

Our tickets cost £50.50, that was for the camper and trailer and five persons (special price for aid vehicles). We made space to sleep our passengers, but this was soon filled with cameras, tripods, and battery chargers. The camera crew opted to sleep outside on the docks, after cadging pillows for their hard beds.

At 3.30 we were moved into the boarding area. The lorry was booked on as freight, which created a problem as Jackie in

297

the camper was carrying the funds for both vehicles. Later we saw the camper chasing the lorry around to the freight area.

Some of the drivers on this trip had been with us in May, On the short trip we renewed our friendships and made ourselves known to others over breakfast. We arrived in *Calais* at 7am.

In cool and misty conditions we drove to *Lille, Mons, Liege* and *Aachen*. Lunch stop about 2pm. at the German border. The girls were well ahead of us in the convoy. We were near the tail end with Bob who was towing a trailer loaded with a caravan which was to be left in *Kosovo*. On to *Koln (Cologne)* and *Koblenz*, then to our night stop at *Hockenheim*. From *Calais* to *Hockenheim* 401 miles.

Our convoy leader Tony soon took the Christchurch ladies under his care, especially when he discovered that they were to be the main topic of the documentary being filmed. The smaller vehicles were to park in a quiet spot in a wooded area out of bounds to ordinary traffic, away from the lorries in the main parking area. In our earlier days the German police had arranged for our convoys to use this area.

Leaving the next day at 9am. to *Heilbron, Stuttgart* and *Munchen (Munich)* heading for *Innsbrook* and the Austrian border. Holly and company had wanted to film the ladies away from the others in a picnic area, but we got caught up in traffic jams. Crossing the border into Italy was straight forward, all the trucks managed to get a free passage on the motorway across the *Brenner Pass*, the two campers and a Land Rover had to pay 16 marks.

A break at a service station brought to light that there was friction between one of the ladies and the camera crew, which made the filming a little difficult. Holly and company got their heads together at times planning the best way to cover the situations. They interviewed me as we travelled on a quiet, but bumpy road, talking about previous trips to Bosnia and Croatia.

As we left the *Brenner Pass* the Harlequin lorry had a problem, the pressure would not build up enough to release the brakes. There was plenty of advice from the mechanically minded, but eventually a mechanic was sent for by the tollbooth attendant, the rest of us pressed on as we had a lot of time to make up.

The girls had a problem when their gas bottle cupboard came open on a busy motorway, they pulled over to sort it out. We were very surprised when they caught up with us; they were overtaking and driving like professionals until they reached their place in the convoy.

We with Bob had lagged behind a little and heard Gwen's voice calling for help. Gwen, with her sister, was driving a seven and half ton truck. They had gone through the lorry lane instead of the car lane at the peage as they were told to do. Gwen was sounding a little upset and nervous because the main convoy had gone on without her. Picking her up on the C.B. Denys called to say that we were nearby and waited for her to catch up and join our mini convoy.

Calling Harlequin from time to time, we received no reply. At 10.30 that night we heard 'Echo One', call us all into a service station, it was so busy that some of the vehicles had to go on to the next services. Whilst I was preparing a late meal, we heard Gwen tearing a strip off some of the lads for abandoning her. We turned in about 12.30, guessing that we had travelled around 500 miles that day.

In the morning Tony had put out the news that Harlequin drivers, Graham and Roy had gone on to the next services and were ready to roll at 9am. The camera crew came to tell us that they would be travelling in other vehicles, they needed to talk to some of our companions on the convoy.

Refuelled and out on the road we were now heading for *Ancona* 300 miles away. We were joined en route by the four vehicles who had gone on to the next services the night before. In heavy traffic with lorries looming on every side we made good progress.

Harlequin met us from their night stop, we all drove on until 2pm. when we stopped for lunch. I invited Holly, Anna and Rob to join us. They were too busy.

Tony got annoyed with some of the drivers who had blocked the parking area. He ordered the convoy out on the road 15 minutes earlier than planned because local drivers were finding it difficult to manoeuvre. Later we discovered that the camera crew had almost been left behind with their equipment. Luckily a couple of our vehicles were still refuelling and managed to pick them up at the last minute. We were travelling on the A14 to *Peskara* and *Bari*, one straight long route. With traffic jams and road works the convoy got spread out at times. We and Bob stayed together with Harlequin and Gwen somewhere behind us. We did have radio contact from time to time.

Another vehicle had a problem, one that we called 'Milk Float',(not the electrical type!) We, with Bob, pulled in to assist, the throttle cable had broken, not much we could do. Graham towed the vehicle to the next services where Tony and the others were waiting, they hoped to find a mechanic to do the job. It was 8pm. a decision was made to call it a day and park up for the night. A large truck parked up near us had Humanitarian Aid logo on the side and written all over the cab. We found out that it was Edinburgh Direct Aid outfit on their way to *Kosovo* like us.

We settled in at 11.45pm. At 12.30 Graham was knocking on our door, he wanted to borrow the generator to provide light so they could try and fix the broken cable on the 'Milk Float'. At 5.30am. Holly came for some camera equipment. We were told that a mechanic would be arriving at 8am. to fix the cable. By 9 we were all refuelled and ready to roll with no sign of the mechanic. Out on the motorway, the temporary job on the Milk Float seemed to be holding. Then an 'Iveco' motor parts van came chasing the convoy. We then realised that it was the mechanic we had been waiting for.

Keiron with the Milk Float and Graham with his truck for support, pulled off the motorway with the mechanic to get the job done. The rest of us plodded on through miles and miles of vineyards and olive groves, the fruit just about ready for harvesting. About 200 miles to *Bari* with glimpses of the sea from time to time. We got the news that the Milk Float had been fixed and was on the way to meet up with us.

Pulling into a services area for early lunch we decided to wait for our friends in the two vehicles. As usual the cameras were out and about.

Soon we learned to eat, chat, shop and refuel with a camera or microphone only inches from our noses. Some of our convoy mates had mobile phones which were very handy when some vehicles were out of range of the C.B. radio. On this occasion we had a call from a late member of the Convoy of Hope who was on his way some distance behind.

Paul and his wife Gill had been with us on the May trip, Known as 'Jester Minute' Paul was a Magician and children's entertainer. They had set out a day behind us and had made up the time to get the same ferry from *Bari*. The Milk Float and Harlequin caught up with us as we reached the town, where we followed the signs to 'PORTO'. Our ferry was to leave at 8pm.

Plenty of time to deal with the tickets and passport control you would have thought! After taking the long walk to the shipping office we queued for our tickets as we English are known to do. I had passports for Holly, Anna and Rob. Some of our colleagues ahead of us had received their tickets and made their way back to the docks.

When it came to our turn, there was confusion, no more tickets would be issued, we must all return to the office at 4pm. The temperature was up in the nineties, one or two younger and fitter of our group volunteered to go back to the dockside and inform the others that they must return at four. We sat outside the office and caught the sea breezes.

At a few minutes to four we all marched into the offices, our reference numbers were noted. Some of those who had paid earlier had to pay more, others were given a refund. Our tickets were for camper, trailer and three people, the two of us and Holly £450. Anna and Rob had to be booked on as foot passengers at £39 each.

Boarding started at 5pm. we had been parked facing the wrong way round to get onto the ferry. Huge trucks were pouring in and getting in our way, jostling each other to get on board first. Denys kept edging in until we were through, almost the last on. The youngsters arrived back from their shopping trip just in time. Holly had swapped her ticket with Anna so that she could get on board first to film us driving up the ramp.

With only one sailing a day, the ferry was well used. A disco party was going on at the stern end patio, our younger members soon congregated there.

Denys and I changed our currency, had a meal in the cafeteria and got in a few hours sleep as we were to dock at 6am.

On the car deck ready to move out into Greece, Holly was

still running around with her camera filming the various convoy vehicles. I was sure that she would end up squashed between the huge trucks as they didn't want anyone to get in their way. Early morning and it was still dark as we drove out into *Igumanitsa* and prepared to take to the mountains. The Christchurch camper was now behind convoy leader Tony's van.

Only two vehicles were behind us, Bob towing the caravan and Harlequin bringing up the rear. Graham in the Harlequin lorry was fine on the flat roads but struggled on hills and mountains. Wonderful scenery in a red sunrise as we drove on to *Joanina*, where we made a breakfast stop in a car park next to a football ground. We were not far from a shopping area where some of the crews went along to buy fresh bread and milk.

After an hour break we all felt rested enough to tackle the *Pindus* mountains. At times climbing over 6,000 feet and into cloud. On one down hill stretch, Gwen had a Mayday situation. She shouted that she had no brakes, Harlequin called her with advice. He told her to use her gears to slow down, and to just dab her brake pedal from time to time. Following his instructions she managed to pull safely into a layby. The brake drums were very hot which had caused brake fade. A stop then at a viewpoint to let the wheels cool and for general advice on the use of low gears on long downhill stretches. Holly climbed a steep bank to get shots of the convoy as a whole, as we started to pull out she scrambled down and grazed her bare legs pretty badly. She was more concerned for the camera which had been damaged. Luckily she had a spare camera but there was a shortage of film for it.

Rob carried out first aid on Holly's legs as we travelled on more level roads. At a comfort stop, Holly persuaded the Land Rover driver to take her and Rob into the nearest town to buy more film. The rest of us went on to the next service station to refuel and have a lunch break. There Gwen and Graham in their respective vehicles joined us.

Heading north to *Larissa* then on to *Thessalonika*, on open roads we could see *Mount Olympus* in the distance. On the long straight roads we travelled at a good pace making for the Greek\Macedonian border. Just before the border was to be our night stop, a service area where Rob, Holly and the Land Rover driver were waiting for us after an unsuccessful shopping trip.

Sunday morning, Holly came to collect some of her equipment. The shop and fuel pumps were open, diesel was very cheap. £20 filled our tank and petrol for the generator which was used to charge up the camera batteries. At home it would have cost nearer £50. At 9am. we drove the short distance to exit Greece. There Lee and Darren in the Christchurch truck could not find their T form. Without it they would not be able to cross into Macedonia. A search in their camper van did not help and panic began to set in. The message had reached everyone via the C.B. Our vehicles had started moving forward, then one of the truck drivers found that he had the missing T form with his papers.

No problem getting through the various checks going out of Greece. At the Macedonian border Holly took her camera to film some of the slogans. She was stopped by an official who told her that it was forbidden to use cameras at the border crossing. Documents and visas all checked, we had been worried that our green card insurance would not be valid as it did not mention Macedonia but it passed. The Christchurch camper was charged £70 because it was not carrying aid. As our papers showed that we were carrying five persons, we rounded up Holly, Rob and Anna. Once we were through the checkpoints they were free to travel with whom they pleased. We met KFOR convoys as we travelled towards *Skopje*, Holly took pictures using Duke's camera, then decided that we should speed on ahead to film the convoy as a unit. We pulled in just before the entrance to a tunnel.

Holly positioned herself on a ledge at the mouth of the tunnel and filmed the vehicles as they passed by. We were to pull out behind the last in the line but unfortunately a local truck got in the way. We waited at the far end of the tunnel for the girls to jump into our back door. It had been a long way to run and they arrived hot and tired.

We were well on schedule for our meeting with Kevin of the 'International Medical Corps' so we were treated to an early night stop at a service area with a shop and restaurant. The camera crew had wanted to get shots of everyone relaxing as a group. Up to this point, with late arrivals at night stops, most of

303

the group had concentrated on getting settled in for the night. On this particular evening, with time to spare, we let it be known that a convoy stew would be dished up from the 'Dukemobile', an invitation to anyone wishing to partake of a hot meal with us.

Cans of stewed steak and cans of vegetables, packets of soup mix poured into two large cooking pots.

Jennie and the girls cooked pasta and sauce, someone else provided nuts and snacks. A bowl of salad and a plate of cakes made a meal fit for kings. I had also made a vegetarian version of the stew flavoured with mushroom soup. There were around 40 persons on the convoy and I don't think anyone went without.

Tables and chairs, deck chairs and cool boxes, bottles of wine and a party atmosphere gave Holly the shots she was after. We sat until well after dark, enjoying the company and a spectacular sunset. After the clearing up, Holly sat with me in the camper and relaxed. She was a different person from the dynamic camera girl chasing the right shots. She was a little unhappy with friction building up in the small camper, between the friends. She realised that there must be tension in the travelling and that these things happened in the best of families.

Monday, one week from leaving Christchurch, we entered *Kosovo*. Leaving at 7am. we headed for *Skopje*, capital of *Macedonia*. As far as we got on our last trip out here when we dropped aid for 6,000 refugees. Not too much documentation on leaving Macedonia. At the *Kosovo* border we were met by Kevin of the International Medical Corps. In May he had been one of our convoy members. He came back out to be a volunteer worker. He led us through the KFOR check points. There were military vehicles lining the road and helicopters hovering above us.

Instructions from Kevin, were that we were not to stop for any reason until we reached our destination. As we travelled he gave out some information over the C.B. radio about the situation. In the towns and villages we passed through, there had been fierce fighting, houses destroyed or damaged. On the hills and in fields were the graves of K.L.A. fighters. Rebuilding and repairs of buildings were being carried out.

On the approach to one town we were told to close ranks and drive straight through, it was mainly Serbian. Sandbagged army posts and tanks were on view in the town centre. Holly was travelling in the Christchurch camper and we were surprised to see her hanging out of the back door. Not satisfied with the view from there she climbed onto the roof while we were still travelling.

Through the towns and in the countryside we were getting cheers, waves, V signs and cars flashing their headlights. When we were driving slowly, youngsters would come out into the road to slap their flattened hands against those of our drivers. We could understand a little of what liberating armies must have experienced during W W II.

We were led down a rough track and into a compound where the International Medical Corps had their offices. Kevin told us the plan for the day. First we would go to a hospital in *Gjislane* to unload the medical and hospital supplies. Then we would be taken to two villages in the mountains, one Albanian and one Serbian. If we were fair to both sides of this conflict then there should be no problems.

A curfew at 10pm. meant that we had to be off the road by then. We were told what to do if grenades started exploding i.e. get under some protection, and not to walk on the grass for fear of mines. Many crops had been left to rot in the fields because the area had been mined.

Returning to the vehicles we moved out of the narrow lane, Kevin leading in his Land Rover and Tony some way behind us. As we approached the main road a group of American soldiers barred our way, one of them was pointing a machine gun directly at my husband's head. Another guy came to the window and asked if one of our group was filming. It was not allowed. Well we could hardly lie, could we?

They demanded that the person who had been filming must be brought to them. They threatened to keep us there and stop the others at the border if the camera people didn't come back. Denys called for Holly on the C.B. and explained the situation. Eventually Holly and Rob came running back to where we were parked, then we were waved on by the soldiers. We couldn't help worrying about what was to happen to our friends. We hung back at the road junction but heavy traffic forced us to follow the convoy.

One of the official vehicles passed us on the way back to ease the situation and called that they would wait for Rob and Holly. It was not far to the hospital where the medical aid was unloaded including an operating table and two industrial generators. They had been requested, We had only a couple of boxes of medical aid and some spectacles.

Holly and Rob turned up none the worse for their experience. They had been taken to the office of a female intelligence officer who told them that they had been seen filming in a sensitive area. She told them that they must be more aware of the dangers and to be on the look out for bogus aid organisations. The thing that they had dreaded most was that they might have their films confiscated, that did not happen.

A doctor at the hospital told us how N.A.T.O. bombing had damaged the hospital buildings. Then he gave a short speech of thanks for our help. The film makers replenished their cameras to record the scene.

For our main drop we took to the mountains. On reaching the first village, *Ljabian*, which was Serbian, it was suggested that the Harlequin lorry and the Christchurch truck and camper should unload in this village. They were asked if they had any reservations about their goods being given to Serb families. They said they would be happy to do so. The rest of us were led up the mountain to the Albanian village, *Nova Verde* which had been cut off from supplies by Serbian settlements. They had not received any help at all from any organisation.

As our vehicles pulled into the village they were surrounded by local families. Suddenly we had a call over the C.B. from Harlequin, they were having a problem with the Serbian villagers. They were upset about the amount of goods allocated to them. The Medical Corps vehicle dashed away to sort out the problem. It was pointed out to those in charge that the goods were more than enough for the size of the village.

Jennie, Jackie, Brenda and Maureen told us later that they were so pleased to see the goods that they had collected and packed given to the needy families. They saw young babies put into the prams and pushchairs from their lorry, the mums receiving Pampers and baby goods. This had made the long journey worth while for them.

In the meantime our vehicles were being unloaded. There was quite a distance from the trucks and trailers to where the goods were to be stored. A human chain was formed, some of our women were stationed inside the building to read the English labels. Stacking the boxes of bedding, shoes, clothing, children's books and toys, school equipment and toiletries. Food was stacked in a separate room. It was hot and hard work. The locals did the lifting, our ladies pointed to the places where the boxes were to be stacked.

In the kitchen of the building, we met a lovely little lady who, we were told, had cooked a meal for all of us. In a dining area we were served mashed potatoes and a piece of meat, a strange colour and round in shape. One of our hosts told us that it was goat meat but the word went around that it might have been dog. Earlier in the day, a local lady had presented Tony with an iced cake with a heart decoration. This was cut and everyone received a small piece of it.

Our trailer and one other vehicle were still to be unloaded and it was dark by this time. Our goods were unloaded with the help from the headlights of a couple of the vans. Rob was using a miners' type lamp, strapped to his forehead to enable him to read the labels on the boxes.

We were a little embarrassed by some boxes we were carrying; they were full of small candle holders given by a well meaning source. As it happened we were told that most of the village had been without electric for some months, the houses depended on candles for lighting.

The Body Shop had donated a large quantity of shampoo, liquid soap and 50 large green goody bags filled with all kinds of Body Shop products. There was great excitement over them. Boxes of canned and dried goods, spaghetti and pasta, cutlery and pots and pans, two sewing machines, baby milk and bottles with teats, household cleaners and disinfectants.

The three Sherwell lorries, driven by firemen from Devon, were to be unloaded at another destination in the morning. A few boxes of goods from the other vehicles meant for the hospital, were put into our trailer to be delivered the next day. By the time this was all finished it was getting late. There was a curfew and with the military protection we were led to a derelict village further up the mountain. There we were to spend the night at a KFOR post, under the protection of the U.S. army. We were parked up in very close contact with the other vehicles. Holly and co came to collect sleeping bags to spend the night in one of the now empty trucks.

6am. and early dawn as we made our way down the mountain, watching a wonderful sunrise and fantastic scenery. Mist on the mountains gradually melted away as the sun gained warmth. Kevin led us into the parking area of the International Rescue Headquarters. There we were given a couple of hours to freshen up, have breakfast, do a little shopping for fresh bread, or in our case to charge up camera batteries.

Later we were to take the boxes of medical aid that had been put into our trailer, to the hospital at *Gjislane*. Teresa from one of the transits had personally made up about a dozen baby boxes. She would like to deliver them to the hospital maternity ward so we set out together. A very friendly black American soldier met us at the entrance of the hospital and directed us. First to the general store room for the medical items, then to the maternity unit.

Inside the double doors, mattresses had to be moved. Soldiers guarding the unit, slept inside the doors. Our new friend 'Smith', told us that he and his wife were adopting a baby from this hospital. He told us that there were 27 babies, abandoned by their mothers who had been rape victims. Inside the ward we met 'Smith's' new daughter, one year old and named Serena.

A lady doctor took us to see some of the little mites. She told us that the babies had to be 6 months old before they could be put up for adoption. Plans had been made for five of these children to be sent to Scotland for adoption.

In other rooms we saw rows of tiny babes, some of them two to a cot and wrapped up like tiny mummies. Each one had a large number, hand written on its 'swaddling clothes'. Number 17 was crying and was put into my arms, I am not ashamed to say that tears were streaming down my cheeks. Emotions were very near to the surface at times like those. We wished 'Smith' and his wife very good luck for the future with little Serena. He was normally stationed in Germany and his wife was coming from there in a week or so to sign the adoption papers.

Getting back to the convoy we heard that the Sherwell lorries had gone to unload at a battle-scarred village not far away. The camera crew had gone with them. They were back at 1pm. and we were all ready to pull out. We said goodbye to Kevin, leaving four large bottles of brown sauce to pass on to L.J. He had been in England until about two weeks before leaving on this convoy, we had received a phone message from him. He said that he had heard that we were on our way to *Kosovo* and was sending a desperate plea for BROWN SAUCE. Kevin knew L.J. and told us that he was working in the west of the area. He would pass on our gifts.

We were the last to move out, Holly was dashing around filming everyone leaving. We had got used to leaving our back door open for her to jump inside at the last minute. As we drove through the town, old and young alike were cheering and waving. Heading for the Macedonian border we met up with military convoys. At the border post we were waved straight through with no formalities. The vehicles were bowling along quite nicely when we came to a sudden stop. C17, one of the Devon trucks reported that he had been involved in an accident.

Each vehicle had a number, with 'C' for convoy member or 'E' for experienced convoy driver. Ours was E5. We were behind the incident. Holly dived out to record the scene and ended up as interpreter for a German speaking policeman. She came back to say that a car travelling towards us had careered across to our side of the road, hitting one of our trucks and glancing off the second before ending up in a field. None of our crews were hurt, two people in the car were taken to a hospital.

On the two lane road the traffic soon built up. One way was blocked and local vehicles started using a dirt track on the inside of our lane. Our vehicles ahead of the accident had gone on to a parking area to wait.

Suddenly a chap in a British uniform appeared at Denys's window. He asked what the problem was. We told him that one of our vehicles had been hit by a local car. He then said that if our truck needed repairs his company's workshop was nearby.

Things started moving after a while, a policeman blew his whistle at us to move on. We left the drivers of the trucks to accept or decline the offer of help. Travelling through a veritable

309

crush of traffic, we caught up with the main convoy. They were in a service station opposite the one where we had spent the night before entering *Kosovo*. We were all prepared to stay the night and wait for reports on the trucks. Anna was with them.

Rob was with us trying to sort out all the camera equipment. As he hadn't eaten many meals with us, I offered omelettes. He accepted for himself and a lad from one of the Land Rovers. While I cooked the meal, a message came over the C.B. that the trucks had been repaired and were on their way to us. As they arrived we had expected another hour or so delay while the drivers had a meal. In fact they had been treated to a three-course meal and given shower facilities at the army base.

All rested and fed, we moved on at 9pm. to drive a few more hours nearer to Greece. Holly caught up with some sleep as we drove through the night. Being empty, the trucks and vans were able to travel that much faster. We were hard put to keep them in sight. As the drivers became tired the chat on the C.B. quietened and at times we felt very alone. Then a glimpse of lights as we rounded a bend, reminded us that we were still all on the same road.

We caught up with them at the services close to the border, we refuelled to save time in the morning. A few hours sleep then crossed the border and headed towards *Athens*. Our lunch stop was at a restaurant near a massive rock formation, named *'Ayres Rock'* by our crews. Over a year later we were told by a Kosovan family that the rock was thought to be a meteorite. It had come from outer space and that monks lived in caves in the rock.

Jennie came to ask if she could travel with us for the afternoon. I think that she needed to catch up on some sleep. By then we were travelling over mountain passes, one of these, *Katara Pass* was 1690 metres above sea level. A snow plough station was situated at the highest point. Local traffic gave us some scary moments by overtaking and 'hedge hopping' our vehicles on tight bends or when tankers were coming towards us. Tony or Bob ahead of us would call us through to overtake when the road ahead was clear.

Some drivers had decided to press on to catch an earlier ferry. Rob had been travelling in one of these vehicles and now transferred his gear back into our camper to stay with us. Sometime later he realised that his passport was still in the Land Rover, the C.B. came into use again. The driver of the Rover was contacted, he waited at a service station where we were to stay the night.

The one a day ferry left at midnight, the advance party would be in time to catch it that night. The rest of us settled into making a relaxing evening, to have a meal and take our time to be on the next day's sailing. Next morning we socialised over coffee outside the cafe and under grapevines in a holiday atmosphere. As we drove to the docks later in the day, only half the original convoy parked on the quayside. No trouble getting the tickets sorted as we had return fares. A thunderstorm rolled around us as we waited.

As darkness fell, we had a bit of excitement. Two men tried to get into one of our trucks. Helen was inside dozing, she called for help over the C.B. and some of our men went to sort the intruders out but they had run off. Later the same men were spotted stowing away in the tool compartment under a Dutch lorry parked a short distance from us. A dockyard policeman hauled them out but he said that they would probably try it again.

At 11.15 we boarded the ferry. We managed to get a cabin with a window, such luxury, we got a good night's sleep. Doughnut and coffee breakfast, then the queuing for passport control. What a crush, the boat was full of Moslem families. The men with long beards and black gowns and the women with masses of gold jewellery, in gowns and headdresses with veils to cover their faces. The officials barely looked at our British passports.

Disembarking at the port of *Bari* at 9am. worse time of the day, with the rush hour traffic. Our convoy soon got split up by local vehicles and red lights. Our Christchurch camper lost sight of the vehicle in front and missed a turning. Bob was behind them with four other vehicles and we were at the rear. Over the C.B. Bob reassured Jenny and co that we were not lost, just on a different road. On leaving the boat, Holly, with Roger and Keiron were going into town to buy film for the one serviceable camera. Tony and his part of the convoy were to wait for them

311

on the outskirts of *Bari*. They would be following the A14 motorway to *Peskara* and *Ancona*. Our little group found their way on to the motorway but not sure if Tony was ahead or behind us.

The C.B. did not pick up any of their voices. After an hour or so travelling on the motorway, we discovered by a call on a mobile phone that they were behind us. We pulled into a services and waited for them. Also in the traffic confusion the Christchurch truck went off route. Lee and Darren had got themselves onto the A14 and pulled in a short while after Tony's group. We were all together again.

Pressing on through Italy to the *Brenner Pass*, where we produced a letter which proved that we were entitled to free passage. Into Austria then Germany, the convoy was now separating at times. We made our night stop a few miles before *Hockenheim*. Next morning we went on to catch up with those who had stopped at Hockenheim services. Bob met us with the news that Tony, our convoy leader, had gone on to Switzerland. There was a lot of disappointment that he didn't stay long enough to say goodbye to everyone.

Making for *Calais* and hoping to be on the ferry that evening, Jennie and Rob were with us, Holly and Anna travelling with Roger and Keiron. We made it in time to catch the 7.15 ferry but Lee and Darren going on as freight, would be on a later boat. It was arranged that we would take Jennie and the camera crew with all their gear to Christchurch. Rob was champing at the bit as he needed to get the camera equipment to Bristol before morning.

At Jennie's we stayed long enough for a cuppa and to watch the video recorded by Eddie, Jennie's husband, of the TV news, when we had left in a blaze of glory. It all seemed like months ago. We left then to return to our home in Westbourne, not able to face unloading our personal belongings at that time of night, we slept in the camper.

A couple of days later we started on a newsletter for all the interested parties, finishing with:- "Thanks to all who made this trip possible with generous donations. To the Body Shop for the goods which give people the dignity of being clean and smelling sweet, which most of us take for granted."

In the year of 2000, I applied to the Guinness Book of Records to have the first convoy of 105 vehicles recognised as a World Record. The fact that it happened 8 years before made it difficult to find witnesses. I wrote many letters trying to get verification of the size and number of the convoy and received very few replies. One that we did receive was from Paul and Jackie who we met one day in the mountains, when they were on their way to *Sarajevo*. They went on to open and fund *The Holy Ground Mission* in a village near *Sarajevo*. Their time is spent in raising funds to support the homeless and hungry.

In January 2001 the letter from Guinness accepting my claim arrived in the post.

We are still waiting for the epic film of the trip to Kosovo to appear on our TV screens. The last we heard from the film crew was that they had 35 hours of film to cut and edit.

In this year of 2002 the old camper is still going strong, it has over 300,000 miles on the clock. We ourselves feel that we have given all we can to Humanitarian Aid, for the time being. Both of us are in our seventies. This is not to say that IF the call came to help some good cause, IF the opportunity and funding were available, well, perhaps... WHO KNOWS ?